Wellington

W. H. Fitchett

Table of Contents

Prologue – The Soldier in Literature

This volume is an attempt to rescue from undeserved oblivion a cluster of soldierly autobiographies; and to give to the general reader some pictures of famous battles, not as described by the historian or analysed by the philosopher, but as seen by the eyes of men who fought in them. History treats the men who do the actual fighting in war very ill. It commonly forgets all about them. If it occasionally sheds a few drops of careless ink upon them, it is without either comprehension or sympathy. From the orthodox historian's point of view, the private soldier is a mere unconsidered pawn in the passionless chess of some cold-brained strategist. As a matter of fact a battle is an event which pulsates with the fiercest human passions — passions bred of terror and of daring; of the anguish of wounds and of the rapture of victory; of the fear and awe of human souls over whom there suddenly sweeps the mystery of death.

But under conventional literary treatment all this evaporates. To the historian a battle is as completely drained of human emotion as a chemical formula. It is evaporated into a haze of cold and cloudy generalities.

But this is certainly to miss what is, for the human imagination, the most characteristic feature of a great fight. A battle offers the spectacle of, say, a hundred thousand men lifted up suddenly and simultaneously into a mood of intense passion — heroic or diabolical — eager to kill and willing to be killed; a mood in which death and wounds count for nothing and victory for everything. This is the feature of war which stirs the common imagination of the race; which makes gentle women weep, and wise philosophers stare, and the average hot-blooded human male turn half-frenzied with excitement. What does each separate human atom feel, when caught in that whirling tornado of passion and of peril? Who shall make visible to us the actual faces in the fighting-line; or make audible the words — stern order, broken prayer, blasphemous jest — spoken amid the tumult? Who shall give us, in a word, an adequate picture of the soldier's life in actual war-time, with its hardships, its excitements, its escapes, its exultation and despair?

If the soldier attempts to tell the tale himself he commonly fails. In ninety-nine cases out of a hundred he belongs to the inarticulate classes. He lacks the gift of description. He can do a great deed, but cannot describe it when it is done. If knowledge were linked in them to an adequate gift of literary expression, soldiers would be the great literary artists of the race. For who else lives through so wide and so wild a range of experience and emotion? When, as in the case of Napier, a soldier emerges with a distinct touch of literary genius, the result is an immortal book. But usually the soldier has to be content with making history; he leaves to others the tamer business of writing it, and generally himself suffers the injustice of being forgotten in the process. Literature is congested with books which describe the soldier from the outside; which tell the tale of his hardships and heroisms, his follies and vices, as they are seen by the remote and uncomprehending spectator. What the world needs is the tale of the bayonet and of "Brown Bess," written by the hand which has actually used those weapons.

Now, the narratives which these pages offer afresh to the world are of exactly this character. They are pages of battle-literature written by the hands of soldiers. They are not attempts at history, but exercises in autobiography. So they are actual human documents, with the salt of truth, of sincerity, and of reality in every syllable. The faded leaves of these memoirs are still stained with the red wine of battle. In their words — to the imaginative and sympathetic hearer, at all events — there are still audible the shouts of charging men, the roll of musketry volleys, the wild cheer of the stormers at Ciudad Rodrigo or Badajos, the earth-shaking thunder of Waterloo. Passages from four of such autobiographies are woven into the pages of this book: Captain Kincaid's *Adventures in the Rifle Brigade in the Peninsula, &c.*; Sergeant Anton's *Recollections of Service in the 42nd*; the tale of *Rifleman Harris* in the old 95th; and Mercer's experiences in command of a battery at Waterloo. All these books are old; three, at least, are out of print, and form the rare prizes to be picked up by the fortunate collector in second-hand bookshops. Anton's book was published in 1841, Kincaid's in 1830, and is endorsed "very scarce." Captain Curling edited *Rifleman Harris* in 1848. Mercer's *Journal of the Waterloo Campaign* was written in 1830, and published as late as 1870. But it consists of two volumes, in which the story of the great battle is only an episode, and it has never reached any wide circle of readers. Yet Mercer's account of Waterloo is the best personal narrative of the great fight in English literature.

All these books are thus of rare interest and value. They belong to the era of "Brown Bess," of the Peninsula, and of Waterloo. Each writer represents a distinct type of soldiership. Kincaid was a captain in one of the most famous regiments in British history — the Rifles in Craufurd's Light Division. Harris was a private in another battalion of the same regiment. Mercer commanded battery G — fondly described by its Captain as "the finest troop in the service" — at Waterloo. Anton was a Scottish soldier in that not least famous of Scottish regiments — the 42nd, or Royal Highlanders. They all took part in that chain of memorable victories, which stretches from Roliça to Waterloo, and they were all — though in widely different — ways fighting men of the highest quality. Kincaid led a forlorn hope at Ciudad Rodrigo. Harris was one of the unconquerable, much-enduring rear-guard in Moore's retreat to Corunna. Anton shared in the wild fighting of the 42nd at Toulouse. Mercer fought his battery at Waterloo until, out of 200 fine horses in his troop, 140 lay dead or dying; while of the men not enough survived to man four guns; and these, as the great battle came to its end, fell, smoke-blackened and exhausted, in slumber beside their blood-splashed guns. Each writer, too, had, in an amusing degree, an intense pride in the particular body to which he belonged. The army with him counted for little, the regiment was everything.

Kincaid says, with entire frankness, if anybody who had not the good fortune to belong to the "Rifles" expects to be named in his book, he was "most confoundedly mistaken." "Neither," he adds, "will I mention any regiment but my own, if I can possibly avoid it. For there is none other that I like so much, and none else so much deserves it. For we were the light regiment of the Light Division, and fired the first and last shot in almost every battle, siege, and skirmish, in which the army was engaged during the war." Kincaid admits that the 43rd and 52nd — the other regiments that formed the immortal Light Division — deserved to be remembered, too; but the most flattering compliment he can pay them is to say, "wherever we were, they were." "Whenever it came to a pinch," he adds, "we had only to look behind to see a line" — consisting of these two regiments — "in which we might place a degree of confidence almost equal to our hopes in heaven. There never was such a corps of riflemen with such supporters!"

Harris, again, cherishes the comforting persuasion that his particular battalion could outmarch, outshoot, outlaugh, outdare — perhaps even outdrink — any other in the British army. "We were," he says, "always at the front in an advance, and at the rear in a retreat." He praises the army as a whole, but it is only for the sake of erecting a pedestal on which some new monument to the glory of the "Rifles" can be placed. He recalls the memory of the British army as it approached Salamanca. "The men," he says, "seemed invincible. Nothing, I thought, could have beaten them." Yet the cream of it all was the "Rifles"! Harris's working creed, in brief, consists of three articles: (1) that the finest army in the world was that which Wellington led; (2) that the finest regiment in that army was the 95th; and (3) that the best battalion in the regiment was that his major commanded! "We had some of as desperate fellows in the Rifles as had ever toiled under the burning sun of an enemy's country in any age. There never were such a set of devil-may-care fellows so completely up to their business as the 95th. They were in the mess before the others began, and were the last to leave off. It was their business to be so...There was, perhaps, as intelligent and talented a set of men amongst us as ever carried a weapon in any country. They seemed at times to need but a glance at what was going on to know all about its 'why and wherefore.'"

Sergeant Anton, again, has all a good Scotchman's austere pride in the superiority of a Scotch regiment over any other that ever carried muskets. He has nothing but an imperfectly disguised pity for those unfortunate people who have the bad taste to be born south of the Tweed. Any Scotch regiment, he visibly holds, is necessarily better than any possible regiment not brought up on porridge. And if amongst the Scottish regiments there was any quite equal to the Royal Highlanders, Sergeant Anton, at least, would like to know the name of that surprising body. In the same fashion Captain Mercer, the one educated man in this cluster of soldier-scribes, plainly cherishes a hearty belief that battery G has the finest horses, the best equipment, the smartest men, and the most perfect discipline, not merely in the British army, but in any army known to history! Pride in the regiment to which the soldier happens to belong is a fine element of military strength. Under modern short-service conditions it grows faint; but amongst Wellington's veterans it had almost the fervours of a religion.

It may be added that these writers are curiously distinct, and look at war through very diverse eyes. Kincaid represents a type of officer in which the British army of all days is rich; and whose qualities explain some of the failures, and most of the triumphs of that army. He was gallant in every drop of his blood; cool, hardy, athletic, a fit leader of the fighting line. He had been reared in luxury, accustomed to feed daintily every day, to lie softly every night; he was full of the pride of his caste; yet in the actual business of fighting, Kincaid, like all officers of the type to which he belonged, could outmarch the privates in the ranks. He fared as hardly as they, shared their scanty rations, lay like them on the wet soil, endured in every way as much, and grumbled less. He was not only first in the charge, but last in the retreat, and took it all — hunger, wet, cold, perils — with smiling face, as part of the day's work. Harris, who views his officers through a private's eyes, is never weary of dwelling on their hardihood, as well as their pluck. "The gentlemen," he says, "bear it best." "It is usually found," he adds, "that those whose birth and station might reasonably have made them fastidious under hardship and toil, bear their miseries without a murmur; while those whose previous life might have better prepared them for the toil of war, are the first to cry out and complain of their hard fate."

Kincaid belongs to this fine type of officer; but he had all the limitations of his type. He knew nothing of the scientific side of his profession. He fought by the light of nature, and looked on a battle as a game of football. He was a true product of the English public schools; gay, plucky, hardy, reckless. He lived under the empire of great feelings — of patriotism, honour, &c. — but tortures would not make him use great words to describe them. A shy and proud self-disparagement is the note of Kincaid's type. They are almost more afraid of being detected in doing a fine thing than others are of being proved guilty of doing a base thing. Kincaid himself describes how Ciudad Rodrigo was carried, but omits to mention the circumstance that he volunteered for the forlorn hope, and led it. The tone of his book is that of the officers' mess, bright, off-hand, jesting at peril, making light of hardships. He tells the tale of heroic deeds — his own or others' — with the severest economy of admiring adjectives. The only adjectives, indeed, Kincaid admits are those of a comminatory sort.

Harris is a fair sample of the unconquerable British private of the Peninsular age, with all the virtues, and all the limitations of his class. He is stocky in body, stubborn in temper, untaught and primitive in nature. He seems to have had no education. His horizon is singularly limited. He sees little beyond the files to right and left of him. The major who commands the battalion is the biggest figure in his world. His endurance is wonderful. Laden like a donkey, with ill-fitting boots and half-filled stomach, he can splash along the muddy Spanish roads, under the falling rain, or sweat beneath the Spanish midsummer heats, from gray dawn to gathering dusk. He will toil on, indeed, with dogged courage until his brain reels, his eyes grow blind, and the over-wrought muscles can no longer stir the leaden feet. Harris is loyal to his comrades; cherishes an undoubting confidence in his officers; believes that, man for man, any British regiment can beat twice its numbers of any other nation; while his own particular regiment, the 95th, will cheerfully take in hand four times that ratio of foes. Harris has no hate for a Frenchman; he respects and likes him indeed, but he always expects to thrash him, and having shot his French foe he is quite prepared to explore his pockets in search of booty.

For the British private in the Peninsula was by no means an angel in a red coat. His vices, like his virtues, were of a primitive sort. He drank, he swore, and alas, he plundered. If the valour which raged at the great breach of Badajos, or swept up the slope of rugged stones at San Sebastian, was of almost incredible fire, so the brutality which plundered and ravished and slew after the city was carried, was of almost incredible fierceness. Harris had no education or almost none; yet he learned to write, and write well. His style, it is true, is that of the uneducated man. He is most sensitive to things that touch himself. He is conscious of the weight of his knapsack, of the blisters on his feet, of the hunger in his stomach, and he drags all these emotions into his tale. Yet Harris had, somehow, by gift of nature, an unusual literary faculty. He sees, and he makes you see. It is true the area of his vision is narrow. It is almost filled up, as we have said, by his right- and left-hand files. It never goes beyond the battalion. But on that narrow canvas he paints with the minuteness and fidelity of a Dutch artist.

Sergeant-major Anton is really an economical and domestically inclined Scotchman, whom chance has thrust into the ranks of the Royal Highlanders; and who, finding himself a soldier, devotes himself to the business with that hard-headed and unsentimental thoroughness which makes the Lowland Scot about the most formidable fighting man the world knows. For Anton is a Lowlander; heavy-footed, heavy-bodied, dour, with nothing of a Highlander's excitability or clan-sentiment. A story is current of how, in storming a kopje in South Africa, a Highland soldier dislodged a Boer, and, with threatening bayonet, brought him to a stand against a wall of rock. As he lingered for the final and fatal lunge, another eager Scot called out "Oot o' the way, Jock, and gie me room tae get a poke at him." "Na, na, Tarn," shouted his frugal and practically-minded comrade, "awa' wi' ye and find a Boer tae yersel'."

There is a touch of this severely practical spirit in Anton, and in this, no doubt, he reflects his regiment. Given a French battery to be stormed, here are men who, with bent heads, wooden faces, and steady bayonets, will push on into the very flame of the guns, and each man will do his separate part with a conscientious thoroughness that no foe can withstand. The story of the fight on the hillside at Toulouse illustrates this stern quality in Scottish soldiership. But the domestic side of Anton's nature is always visible. He was one of the few married men in his regiment, and he is never wearied of describing what snug nests he built for his mate and himself in the intervals betwixt marching and fighting, or when the troops had gone into winter quarters. The value of Anton's book, indeed, lies largely in the light it sheds on the fortunes and sufferings of the hardy women, sharp of tongue and strong of body, who marched in the rear of Wellington's troops; and who, to their honour be it recorded, were usually faithful wives to the rough soldiers whose fortunes they shared. Anton, it is amusing to note, is the only one of the group who makes deliberate — and, it may be added, singularly unhappy — attempts at fine writing. He indulges in frequent apostrophes to the reader, to posterity, to his native country, and to the universe at large. In his many-jointed sentences linger echoes of ancient sermons; far-off flavours of the Shorter Catechism are discoverable in them. Anton, however, can be simple and direct when he has an actual tale of fighting to tell. He forgets his simplicity only when he moralises over the battlefield the next day.

Mercer is much the ablest and most accomplished writer of the four. He belonged to the scientific branch of the army, the artillery, and he had studied his art with the thoroughness of a scholar. That Mercer was a cool and gallant soldier of the finest type cannot be doubted. He has, indeed, a fine military record, and rose to the rank of general, and held command of the 9th Brigade of Royal Artillery. But Mercer was a many-sided man in a quite curious degree. He was a scholar; a lover of books; a country gentleman, with a country gentleman's delight in horse-flesh and crops. He was, moreover, an artist, with a Ruskinesque, not to say a Turneresque, sense of colour and form. A fine landscape was for him a feast, only rivalled by the joy of a good book. He lingers on the very edge of Quatre Bras, while the thunder of cannon shakes the air, and while his own guns are floundering up a steep hill path, to note and describe the far-stretching landscape, the glow of the evening sky, the Salvator-like trees, the sparkle of glassy pools, &c. Mercer is so good an artillery officer that he sees every buckle in the harness of his horses, and every button on the uniforms of his men; and yet he is sensitive to every tint and change in the landscape through which his guns are galloping.

On the morning after Waterloo, his face still black with its smoke, and his ears stunned with its roar, he picks his way across the turf, thick with the bodies of the slain, into the garden of Hougoumont. The bodies of the dead lie there, too; but Mercer is almost intoxicated with the cool verdure of the trees, with the chant of a stray nightingale, and even with "the exuberant vegetation of turnips and cabbages," as well as with the scent of flowers! It is this combination of keen artistic sensibility with the finest type of courage — courage which, if gentle in form, was yet of the ice-brook's temper — which makes Mercer interesting. Here was a man who might have fished with Izaak Walton, or discussed hymns with Cowper, or philosophy with Coleridge; yet this pensive, gentle, artistic, bookish man fought G Battery at Waterloo till two-thirds of his troop were killed, and has written the best account of the great battle, from the human and personal side, to be found in English literature.

Here, then, are four human documents, of genuine historic value, as well as of keen personal interest. They have their defects. There is no perspective in their pages. To Rifleman Harris, for example, the state of his boots is of as much importance, and is described with as much detail, as the issue of the battle. These memoirs will not give the reader the battle as a whole; still less the campaign; least of all will they give the politics behind the campaign. But a magic is in them, the magic of reality and of personal experience. They seem to put the reader in the actual battle-line, to fill his nostrils with the scent of gunpowder, to make his eyes tingle with the pungency of ancient battle-smoke.

It may be added that these books give pictures of such battle landscapes as will never be witnessed again. They belong to the period when war had much more of the picturesque and human element than it has today. "Brown Bess" was short of range, and the fighting-lines came so near to each other that each man could see his foeman's face, and hear his shout or oath. War appealed to every sense. It filled the eyes. It registered itself in drifting continents of smoke. It deafened the ear with blast of cannon and ring of steel. It adorned itself in all the colours of the rainbow. The uniforms of Napoleon's troops, as they were drawn up on the slopes of La Belle Alliance, were a sort of debauch of colour. Houssaye gives a catalogue of the regiments — infantry of the line in blue coats, white breeches, and gaiters; heavy cavalry with glittering cuirasses and pennoned lances; chasseurs in green and purple and yellow; hussars with dolmans and shakos of all tints — sky-blue, scarlet, green, and red; dragoons with white shoulder-belts and turban-helmets of tigerskin, surmounted by a gleaming cone of brass; lancers in green, with silken cords on their helmets; carabineers, giants of six feet, clad in white, with breastplates of gold and lofty helmets with red plumes; grenadiers in blue, faced with scarlet, yellow epaulettes, and high bearskin caps; the red lancers — red-breeched, red-capped, with floating white plumes half a yard long; the Young Guard; the Old Guard, with bearskin helmets, blue trousers and coats; the artillery of the Guard, with bearskin helmets, &c.

Such a host, looked at from the picturesque point of view, was a sort of human rainbow, with a many-coloured gleam of metal — gold and silver, steel and brass — added. And colour counts at least in attracting recruits. Harris joined the 95th because his eyes were dazzled with the "smartness" of its uniform. Lord Roberts has told the world how he joined the Bengal Horse Artillery purely because he found their white buckskin breeches, and the leopard skin and red plumes on the men's helmets, irresistible! Napoleon, it will be remembered, turned the spectacular aspect of his army to martial use. On the morning of

Waterloo he brought his troops over the slope of the hill in eleven stately columns; he spread them out like a mighty glittering fan in the sight of the coolly watching British. To foes of more sensitive imagination the spectacle of that vast and iris-tinted host might well have chilled their courage. But the British — whether to their credit or their discredit may be disputed — keep their imagination and their courage in separate compartments. They are not liable to be discouraged, still less put to rout, by the most magnificent display of what may be called the millinery of war.

But that aspect of war has faded, never to revive. Khaki kills the picturesque. Battle has grown grey, remote, invisible. It consists of trenches miles long, in which crouch unseen riflemen, shooting at moving specks of grey, distant thousands of yards; or in guns perched on hills five miles apart bellowing to each other across the intervening valleys. It is not merely that in a battle of today a soldier cannot see the features of the man he kills; he probably does not see him at all. The Highlanders at the Modder marched, panted, thirsted, killed, and were killed, for eight hours, and never saw a Boer! The soldier today sees neither the pinpricks of flame nor the whiff of grey smoke which tell that somebody is shooting at him. For these are days of smokeless powder and long-range rifles. The man shot at only learns that circumstance as he catches the air-scurry of the passing bullet, and the atmosphere about him grows full of what one half-terrified war correspondent calls "little whimpering air-devils."

The interest of these books is that they bring back to us living pictures, as seen through living human eyes, of the great battles of a century ago — battles which have grown obsolete in fashion, but which changed the currents of the world's history, and of whose gain we are the heirs today.

It is curious, in a sense even amusing, to note how diversely their famous commander impressed these four soldiers, each occupied in recording for the benefit of posterity what he saw. Anton apparently never sees Wellington. The human horizon for the Scottish sergeant is filled with the colonel of his regiment. Harris gravely records how he saw the great Duke take his hat off on the field of Vimiero; for the rest, he held the ordinary view of the rank and file of the Peninsula that the Duke's long nose on a battlefield was worth 10,000 men. Kincaid says he was so anxious to see the Duke when he joined the army that, as he puts it, "I never should have forgiven the Frenchman that killed me before I effected it." He was soon gratified, but seems quite unable to give any description of the great soldier. He contemplated him with the sort of frightened awe with which the youngest boy at Eton would look at "the head" arrayed in his official robes; a vision to be contemplated from a safe distance, without the least desire for a nearer and personal acquaintance.

Mercer came closer to the great Duke, and regards him with a cooler and therefore a severer judgment. Mercer had boundless confidence in Wellington as a battle-leader, but not the least affection for him as a man, and it is plain he had no special reasons for affection. Wellington had many fine moral qualities, but anxious consideration for other people, or even calm justice in his dealings with them, is not to be included in their catalogue. The famous general order he issued after the retreat from Burgos is an example of the undiscriminating harshness with which Wellington could treat an entire army. And that element of harshness — of swift, impatient, relentless discipline that could not stay to discriminate, to weigh evidence, or even to hear it — was one great defect of Wellington as a general. About his soldiers he had as little human feeling as a good chess-player has about his pawns. Mercer never came into intercourse with the Duke but with disaster to himself, a disaster edged with injustice.

When his troop was in France, Mercer says he ran an equal risk of falling under the Duke's displeasure for systematically plundering the farmers, or for not plundering them! If a commander of a battery allowed his horses to look in worse condition than those of another battery he was relentlessly punished. "The quick eye of the Duke would see the difference. He asked no questions, attended to no justification, but condemned the unfortunate captain as unworthy of the command he held, and perhaps sent him from the army." But the official amount of forage supplied was quite insufficient for the purpose of keeping the horses in high condition. Other troops supplemented the supply by "borrowing" from the farmers, and there was no resource but to imitate them, or to risk professional ruin by presenting at parade horses inferior in look to those of other troops nourished on mere felony. Wellington forgave neither the unlicensed "borrowing" of the officers nor the want of condition in their horses. Yet one fault or the other was inevitable.

The Duke, it seems, "had no love for the artillery," and all his harshness was expended on that branch of the service. "The Duke of Wellington's ideas of discipline," says Mercer, "are rigid; his modes of administering them are summary, and he is frequently led into acts of the grossest injustice." Thus the owner of a building where some of Mercer's men were quartered — a thorough rogue — complained to the Duke that the lead piping of his house had been plundered and sold by the guilty British gunners. Wellington made no inquiry, took no evidence. A staff officer rode to Mercer's quarters one day with a copy of this complaint, on the margin of which was written in the Duke's own handwriting: "Colonel Scovell will find out whose troop this is, and they shall pay double." This was the first intimation the unfortunate Mercer had received of the charge against him. The Frenchman pretended to estimate his loss at 7000 francs, and Mercer was advised, in high quarters, to pay this sum in order to escape the Duke's wrath. Mercer appealed to Sir George Wood, who told him his only chance lay in evading payment as long as he could; then the Duke might be caught in a more amiable mood. The actual thief — one of the French villagers — was discovered and convicted; but this circumstance, Mercer records, "has not in the least altered my position with the Duke of Wellington; for none dare tell him the story; and even Sir Edward Barnes, who kindly attempted it, met with a most ungracious rebuff!"

The French scoundrel, meanwhile, was dunning Mercer to get his 7000 francs. The situation remained thus for weeks, till the audacious Frenchman ventured on a second interview with the Duke. The Duke had dismounted, as it happened, in a very ill humour, at the door of his hotel, and the Frenchman pursued him up the grand staircase with his complaint. The Duke turned roughly upon him, "What the devil do you want, sir?" The Frenchman presented his bill with a flourish, whereupon the Duke exclaimed to his aide-de-camp, "Pooh! kick the rascal downstairs!" The Frenchman and his bill thus vanished from the scene; but Mercer's comment is "that I eventually escaped paying a heavy sum for depredations committed by others is due, not to the Duke's sense of justice, but only to the irritability of his temper."

On another occasion Sir Augustus Fraser, meeting him, said, "Mercer, you are released from arrest." Mercer stared: but on inquiry, discovered that he had been officially under arrest for a fortnight without knowing it.

At a review, just before passing the saluting point, a horse in the rear division of his battery got its leg over the trace. The limber gunners leaped smartly off, put things straight, and jumped to their places again; but the division, with their 18-pounders, had to trot to regain place, and were just pulling up when they reached the saluting point. The precise and rhythmical order of the troop was a little disturbed, and Wellington, in a burst of wrath, put Sir Augustus Fraser himself, who was in command of all the artillery, the major in command of the brigade, and Mercer, the captain of the guilty troop, under arrest, where — happily all unconscious — they remained for a fortnight. Later Mercer wished to apply for leave of absence, but Sir George Wood declined to present the request, as he said, "'It would not be prudent just now to remind the Duke of me in any way.' Rather hard and unjust this," is Mercer's comment.

Mercer, however, tells one story, which shows that the Duke of Wellington was capable of sly satire at the expense of the French. An English officer walking on the boulevard was rudely pushed into the gutter by a French gentleman, whom the Englishman promptly knocked down. The Frenchman, it turned out, was a marshal. He complained to the Duke, but could not identify the officer who had knocked him down. The Duke thereupon issued a general order, desiring that "British officers would, in future, abstain from beating marshals of France."

Part One – From Torres Vedras to Waterloo

Chapter One – A Young Soldier

Kincaid, the author of *Adventures in the Rifle Brigade*, was born at Dalheath, near Falkirk, in 1787. He held a lieutenant's commission in the North York Militia, but in 1809, when only twenty-two years old, joined, as a volunteer, the second battalion of the famous 95th — the "Rifles" in the immortal Light Division. His first military service was of an unhappy sort. He took part in the Walcheren expedition, and, in spite of a cheerful temper and a good constitution, fell a victim to the swamp-bred agues and fevers which destroyed that ill-led and ill-fated expedition. He emerged from his first campaign with shattered health and no glory. In 1811 his battalion was ordered to the Peninsula, and with it Kincaid marched and fought from the lines of Torres Vedras to Waterloo. In the hard fighting of those stern days the Rifles played a brilliant part. Kincaid kept guard in the great hill-defences of Torres Vedras, joined in the pursuit of Massena, when that general fell suddenly back, shared in the fury of the breaches at Ciudad Rodrigo, and in the yet wilder assault on the great breach at Badajos, and took part in all the great battles of those years from Fuentes to Vittoria. He survived the stubborn and bloody combats in the Pyrenees, fought at Toulouse, Quatre Bras, and on the famous ridge at Waterloo. His battalion stood almost in the centre of Wellington's battle-line on that fierce day, and the most desperate fighting of the day eddied round it.

Kincaid was thus a gallant soldier, in a gallant regiment, and played a part in great events. But his promotion was slow; he only received his captain's commission in 1826. He was more fortunate, indeed, after he left the army than while he served in it. He was given a place in the Yeomen of the Guard in 1844, was knighted in 1852, and died in 1862, aged seventy-five.

Kincaid's *Adventures in the Rifle Brigade* is a book of great merits and of great faults. It is brisk, stirring, and picturesque, and paints with great vividness the life of a subaltern in a fighting regiment and during fighting times. But the book lacks order. Dates are dropped into it, or are left out of it, with the most airy caprice. It has no intelligible relationship to history. It never gives the reader a glimpse of the history-making events which serve as a background to the marching and the fighting of the Rifles. Kincaid, in a word, races through his campaigns as a youth might race across the hills in a harrier-chase; or, rather, as a boy with a lively sense of humour, might saunter through a fair — without a plan, except to get all the fun he can, and stopping, now to laugh at a clown, now to stare at a mimic tragedy, now to exchange a jest with some other boy. His choice of incident is determined absolutely by the "fun" they include — the flavour of humour, or the gleam of the picturesque, which he can discover in them. He makes no pretension, that is, to connected and adequate narrative. But his record of adventures is always amusing, often vivid, and sometimes has a certain thrilling quality which, after the lapse of so many years, still keeps its power.

Kincaid's tale is best served by re-grouping its incidents under distinct heads. In his earlier chapters, for example, he gives curiously interesting sketches of what may be called the non-fighting side of a soldier's life — the marches, the bivouacs; the gossip of the camp fires; the hardships of muddy roads, of rain-filled skies, or of dust and heat and thirst, of non-existent rations, and of sleepless nights which the soldier has to endure. So the reader gets a glimpse the orthodox historians quite fail to give of the hardy, resourceful, much-enduring British soldier of the Peninsula. Kincaid may be left to tell all this in his own words, though with generous condensation.

Kincaid dismisses, as not worth remembering or recording, all the tame days of his life before he became a soldier on active service, and plunges abruptly into his tale:

"I joined the 2nd Battalion Rifle Brigade (then the 95th), at Hythe Barracks, in the spring of 1809, and, in a month after, we proceeded to form a part of the expedition to Holland, under the Earl of Chatham.

"With the usual quixotic feelings of a youngster, I remember how desirous I was, on the march to Deal, to impress the minds of the natives with a suitable notion of the magnitude of my importance, by carrying a donkey-load of pistols in my belt, and screwing my naturally placid countenance up to a pitch of ferocity beyond what it was calculated to bear.

"We embarked in the Downs, on board the *Hussar* frigate, and afterwards removed to the *Namur*, a seventy-four, in which we were conveyed to our destination. We landed on the island of South Beeveland, where we remained about three weeks, playing at soldiers, smoking mynheer's long clay pipes, and drinking his vrow's butter-milk, for which I paid liberally with my precious blood to their infernal mosquitoes; not to mention that I had all the extra valour shaken out of me by a horrible ague, which commenced a campaign on my carcass, and compelled me to retire upon Scotland, for the aid of my native air, by virtue of which it was ultimately routed.

"I shall not carry my first chapter beyond my first campaign, as I am anxious that my reader should not expend more than his first breath upon an event which cost too many their last.

"I rejoined the battalion, at Hythe, in the spring of 1810, and, finding that the company to which I belonged had embarked to join the first battalion in the Peninsula, and that they were waiting at Spithead for a fair wind, I immediately applied, and obtained permission, to join them. We anchored in the Tagus in September; no thanks to the ship, for she was a leaky one, and wishing foul winds to the skipper, for he was a bad one.

"To look at Lisbon from the Tagus, there are few cities in the universe that can promise so much, and none, I hope, that can keep it so badly. I only got on shore one day for a few hours, and as I never again had an opportunity of correcting the impression, I have no objection to its being considered an uncharitable one; but I wandered for a time amid the abominations of its streets and squares, in the vain hope that I had got involved among a congregation of stables and outhouses; but I was at length compelled to admit it as the miserable apology for the fair city that I had seen from the harbour.

"It pleased the great disposer of naval events to remove us to another and a better ship, and to send us off for Figuera next day with a foul wind. Sailing at the rate of one mile in two hours, we reached Figuera's Bay at the end of eight days, and were welcomed by about a hundred hideous-looking Portuguese women, whose joy was so excessive that they waded up to their arm-pits through a heavy surf, and insisted on carrying us on shore on their backs! I never clearly ascertained whether they had been actuated by the purity of love or gold."

Kincaid joined Wellington's forces at what might well have seemed a very gloomy juncture. The British army was in full retreat. The star of

Massena shone in the ascendant. Talavera and Busaco had been fought, and fought apparently in vain. Spain was abandoned, Portugal invaded. Wellington seemed to be retreating to his ships. The secret of the great lines of Torres Vedras, which were to finally arrest Massena's advance, and save not only Portugal, but the Peninsula — perhaps Europe — had been so well kept that even Wellington's own forces were in ignorance of their existence. Yet Kincaid shows an easy and careless unconsciousness of the disquieting aspect the campaign wore. It was enough for him that he marched and fought with his regiment, and shared all its fortunes. He scarcely looks beyond the files of his own company, and has no doubt whatever that the French will be satisfactorily thrashed in the end!

"We proceeded next morning to join the army; and as our route lay through the city of Coimbra we came to the magnanimous resolution of providing ourselves with all manner of comforts and equipments for the campaign on our arrival there; but when we entered it at the end of the second day, our disappointment was quite eclipsed by astonishment at finding ourselves the only living things in the city, which ought to have been furnished with twenty thousand souls.

"Lord Wellington was then in the course of his retreat from the frontiers of Spain to the lines of Torres Vedras, and had compelled the inhabitants on the line of march to abandon their homes, and to destroy or carry away everything that could be of service to the enemy. It was a measure that ultimately saved their country, though ruinous and distressing to those concerned, and on no class of individuals did it bear harder, for the moment, than our own little detachment, a company of rosy-cheeked, chubbed youths, who, after three months' feeding on ship's dumplings, were thus thrust, at a moment of extreme activity, in the face of an advancing foe, supported by a pound of raw beef, drawn every day fresh from the bullock, and a mouldy biscuit.

"The difficulties we encountered were nothing out of the usual course of old campaigners; but, untrained and unprovided as I was, I still looked back upon the twelve or fourteen days following the battle of Busaco as the most trying I have ever experienced, for we were on our legs from daylight until dark, in daily contact with the enemy; and, to satisfy the stomach of an ostrich, I had, as already stated, only a pound of beef, a pound of biscuit, and one glass of rum. A brother-officer was kind enough to strap my boat-cloak and portmanteau on the mule carrying his heavy baggage, which, on account of the proximity of the foe, was never permitted to be within a day's march of us, so that, in addition to my simple uniform, my only covering every night was the canopy of heaven, from whence the dews descended so refreshingly that I generally awoke, at the end of an hour, chilled, and wet to the skin; and I could only purchase an equal length of additional repose by jumping up and running about until I acquired a sleeping quantity of warmth. Nothing in life can be more ridiculous than seeing a lean, lank fellow start from a profound sleep at midnight, and begin lashing away at the Highland fling as if St. Andrew himself had been playing the bagpipes; but it was a measure that I very often had recourse to, as the cleverest method of producing heat. In short, though the prudent general may preach the propriety of light baggage in the enemy's presence, I will ever maintain that there is marvellous small personal comfort in travelling so fast and so lightly as I did.

"The Portuguese farmers will tell you that the beauty of their climate consists in their crops receiving from the nightly dews the refreshing influence of a summer's shower, and that they ripen in the daily sun. But they are a sordid set of rascals! Whereas I speak with the enlightened views of a man of war, and say, that it is poor consolation to me, after having been deprived of my needful repose, and kept all night in a fever, dancing wet and cold, to be told that I shall be warm enough in the morning? It is like frying a person after he has been boiled; and I insisted upon it, that if their sun had been milder and their dews lighter I should have found it much more pleasant.

"Having now brought myself regularly into the field, under the renowned Wellington, should this narrative, by any accident, fall into the hands of others who served there, and who may be unreasonable enough to expect their names to be mentioned in it, let me tell them that they are most confoundedly mistaken! Every man may write a book for himself, if he likes; but this is mine; and, as I borrow no man's story, neither will I give any man a particle of credit for his deed, as I have got so little for my own that I have none to spare. Neither will I mention any regiment but my own, if I can possibly avoid it, for there is none other that I like so much, and none else so much deserves it; for we were the light regiment of the Light Division, and fired the first and last shot in almost every battle, siege, and skirmish in which the army was engaged during the war.

"In stating the foregoing resolution, however, with regard to regiments, I beg to be understood as identifying our old and gallant associates, the 43rd and 52nd, as a part of ourselves, for they bore their share in everything, and I love them as I hope to do my better half (when I come to be divided); wherever we were, they were; and although the nature of our arm generally gave us more employment in the way of skirmishing, yet, whenever it came to a pinch, independent of a suitable mixture of them among us, we had only to look behind to see a line, in which we might place a degree of confidence, almost equal to our hopes in heaven; nor were we ever disappointed. There never was a corps of riflemen in the hands of such supporters!"

On October 12, Wellington entered the lines of Torres Vedras, and Massena found his advance barred by frowning lines of trenched and gun-crowned hills, the screen behind which his great antagonist had vanished. During the last few days of the retreat and pursuit the pace of events quickened; the British rear-guard was sharply pressed, and Kincaid, for once grows consecutive and orderly in his narrative:

"October 1, 1810. — We stood to our arms at daylight this morning, on a hill in front of Coimbra; and, as the enemy soon after came on in force, we retired before them through the city. The civil authorities, in making their own hurried escape, had totally forgotten that they had left a jail full of rogues unprovided for, and who, as we were passing near them, made the most hideous screaming for relief. Our quarter-master-general very humanely took some men, who broke open the doors, and the whole of them were soon seen howling along the bridge into the wide world, in the most delightful delirium, with the French dragoons at their heels.

"We retired the same night through Condacia, where the commissariat were destroying quantities of stores that they were unable to carry off. They handed out shoes and shirts to any one that would take them, and the streets were literally running ankle deep with rum, in which the soldiers were dipping their cups and helping themselves as they marched along. The commissariat, some years afterwards, called for a return of the men who had received shirts and shoes on this occasion, with a view of making us pay for them, but we very briefly replied that the one-half were dead, and the other half would be d—d before they would pay anything.

"We retired this day to Leria, and, at the entrance of the city, saw an English and a Portuguese soldier dangling by the bough of a tree — the first summary example I had ever seen of martial law.

"We halted one night near the convent of Batalha, one of the finest buildings in Portugal. It has, I believe, been clearly established, that a living man in ever so bad health is better than two dead ones; but it appears that the latter will vary in value according to circumstances, for we found here, in very high preservation, the body of King John of Portugal, who founded the edifice in commemoration of some victory, God knows how long ago; and though he would have been reckoned a highly valuable antique, within a glass case, in an apothecary's hall in England, yet he was held so cheap in his own house, that the very finger which most probably pointed the way to the victory alluded to, is now in the baggage of the Rifle Brigade. Reader, point not thy finger at me, for I am not the man.

"Retired on the morning of a very wet, stormy day to Allenquer, a small town on the top of a mountain, surrounded by still higher ones; and, as the enemy had not shown themselves the evening before, we took possession of the houses, with a tolerable prospect of being permitted the unusual treat of eating a dinner under cover. But by the time that the pound of beef was parboiled, and while an officer of dragoons was in the act of reporting that he had just patrolled six leagues to the front, without seeing any signs of an enemy, we saw the indefatigable rascals, on the mountains opposite our windows, just beginning to wind round us, with a mixture of cavalry and infantry; the wind blowing so strong that the long tail of each particular horse stuck as stiffly out in the face of the one behind, as if the whole had been strung upon a cable and dragged by the leaders. We turned out a few companies, and kept them in check while the division was getting under arms, spilt the soup as usual, and, transferring the smoking solids to the haversack, for future mastication, we continued our retreat.

"Our long retreat ended at midnight, on our arrival at the handsome little town of Arruda, which was destined to be the piquet post of our division, in front of the fortified lines. The quartering of our division, whether by night or by day, was an affair of about five minutes. The quarter-master-general preceded the troops, accompanied by the brigade-majors and the quartermasters of regiments; and after marking off certain houses for his general and staff, he split the remainder of the town between the majors of brigades; they, in their turn, provided for their generals and staff, and then made a wholesale division of streets among the quarter-masters of regiments, who, after providing for their commanding officers and staff, retailed the remaining houses, in equal proportions, among the companies; so that, by the time that the regiment arrived, there was nothing to be done beyond the quarter-master's simply telling each captain, 'Here's a certain number of houses for you.'

"Like all other places on the line of march, we found Arruda totally deserted; and its inhabitants had fled in such a hurry, that the keys of their house doors were the only things they carried away, so that when we got admission through our usual key — transmitting a rifle-ball through the keyhole: it opens every lock — we were not a little gratified to find that the houses were not only regularly furnished, but most of them had some food in the larder, and a plentiful supply of good wines in the cellar; and, in short, that they only required a few lodgers capable of appreciating the good things which the gods had provided; and the deuce is in it if we were not the very folks who could!

"Those who wish a description of the lines of Torres Vedras, must part. I know nothing, excepting that I was told that one end of them rested on the Tagus, and the other somewhere on the sea; and I saw, with my own eyes, a variety of redoubts and fieldworks on the various hills which stand between. This, however, I do know, that we have since kicked the French out of more formidable-looking and stronger places; and, with all due deference be it spoken, I think that the Prince of Essling ought to have tried his luck against them, as he could only have been beaten by fighting, as he afterwards was without it! And if he thinks that he would have lost as many men by trying, as he did by not trying, he must allow me to differ in opinion with him.

"In very warm or very wet weather it was customary to put us under cover in the town during the day, but we were always moved back to our bivouac on the heights during the night; and it was rather amusing to observe the different notions of individual comfort, in the selection of furniture, which officers transferred from their town house to their no house on the heights. A sofa, or a mattress, one would have thought most likely to be put in requisition; but it was not unusual to see a full-length looking-glass preferred to either.

"We certainly lived in clover while we remained here; everything we saw was our own, seeing no one there who had a more legitimate claim; and every field was a vineyard. Ultimately it was considered too much trouble to pluck the grapes, as there were a number of poor native thieves in the habit of coming from the rear every day to steal some, so that a soldier had nothing to do but to watch one until he was marching off with his basket full, when he would very deliberately place his back against that of the Portuguese, and relieve him of his load, without wasting any words about the bargain. The poor wretch would follow the soldier to the camp, in the hope of having his basket returned, as it generally was, when emptied."

Massena held on to his position in front of the great lines he dared not attack till November 12, then he fell back to Santarem, whence he could still keep Wellington blockaded. He held this position till March 1811, nearly five months in all — months of cold, rain, and hunger — a miracle of stubborn and sullen endurance. Kincaid, acting on his usual principle that all time not occupied in actively doing something is to be counted as nonexistent, passes over the tale of these months in a dozen lines. His narrative only becomes full again when Wellington sallies out of his hilly stronghold and presses in pursuit of Massena. We then have graphic pictures of the hardships of a soldier's life:

"Massena, conceiving any attack upon our lines to be hopeless, as his troops were rapidly mouldering away with sickness and want, at length began to withdraw them nearer to the source of his supplies. He abandoned his position, opposite to us, on the night of November 9, leaving some stuffed-straw gentlemen occupying their usual posts. Some of them were cavalry, some infantry, and they seemed such respectable representatives of their spectral predecessors, that, in the haze of the following morning, we thought that they had been joined by some well-fed ones from the rear; and it was late in the day before we discovered the mistake, and advanced in pursuit.

"It was late ere we halted for the night, on the side of the road, near to Allenquer, and I got under cover in a small house, which looked as if it had been honoured as the headquarters of the tailor-general of the French army, for the floor was strewed with variegated threads, various complexioned buttons, with particles and remnants of cabbage; and, if it could not boast of the flesh and fowl of Noah's ark, there was an abundance of the creeping things which it were to be wished that that commander had not left behind.

"On our arrival at Valle, on November 12, we found the enemy behind the Rio Maior, occupying the heights of Santarem, and exchanged some shots with their advanced posts. In the course of the night we experienced one of those tremendous thunderstorms which used to precede the Wellington victories, and which induced us to expect a general action on the following day. I had disposed myself to sleep in a beautiful green hollow way, and, before I had time even to dream of the effects of their heavy rains, I found myself floating most majestically towards the river, in a fair way of becoming food for the fishes. I ever after gave those inviting looking spots a wide berth, as I found that they were regular watercourses.

"Next morning our division crossed the river, and commenced a false attack on the enemy's left, with a view of making them show their force; and it was to have been turned into a real attack, if their position was found to be occupied by a rear-guard only; but, after keeping up a smart skirmishing fire the great part of the day, Lord Wellington was satisfied that their whole army was present; we were consequently withdrawn.

"This affair terminated the campaign of 1810. Our division took possession of the village of Valle and its adjacents, and the rest of the army was placed in cantonments, under whatever cover the neighbouring country afforded."

Here are some of Kincaid's pictures of a British army in winter quarters, with one fierce campaign behind it, and another, almost sterner still in character, before it:

"Our battalion was stationed in some empty farm-houses, near the end of the bridge of Santarem, which was nearly half a mile long; and our sentries and those of the enemy were within pistol-shot of each other on the bridge.

"I do not mean to insinuate that a country is never so much at peace as when at open war; but I do say that a soldier can nowhere sleep so soundly, nor is he anywhere so secure from surprise, as when within musket-shot of his enemy.

"We lay four months in this situation, divided only by a rivulet, without once exchanging shots. Every evening, at the hour 'When bucks to dinner go,/ And cits to sup,' it was our practice to dress for sleep: we saddled our horses, buckled on our armour, and lay down, with the bare floor for a bed, and a stone for a pillow, ready for anything, and reckless of everything but the honour of our corps and country; for I will say (to save the expense of a trumpeter) that a more devoted set of fellows were never associated. We stood to our arms every morning at an hour before daybreak, and remained there until a grey horse could be seen a mile off (which is the military criterion by which daylight is acknowledged, and the hour of surprise past), when we proceeded to unharness and to indulge in such luxuries as our toilet and our table afforded.

"Our piquet-post, at the bridge, became a regular lounge for the winter to all manner of folks. I used to be much amused at seeing our naval officers come up from Lisbon riding on mules, with huge ships' spyglasses, like six-pounders, strapped across the backs of their saddles. Their first question invariably was, 'Who is that fellow there?' (pointing to the enemy's sentry close to us), and, on being told that he was a Frenchman, 'Then why the devil don't you shoot him!'

"Repeated acts of civility passed between the French and us during this tacit suspension of hostilities. The greyhounds of an officer followed a hare, on one occasion, into their lines, and they very politely returned them. I was one night on piquet at the end of the bridge when a ball came from the French sentry and struck the burning billet of wood round which we were sitting, and they sent in a flag of truce next morning to apologise for the accident, and to say that it had been done by a stupid fellow of a sentry, who imagined that people were advancing upon him. We admitted the apology, though we knew well enough that it had been done by a malicious rather than a stupid fellow from the situation we occupied.

"General Junot, one day reconnoitring, was severely wounded by a sentry, and Lord Wellington, knowing that they were at that time destitute of everything in the shape of comfort, sent to request his acceptance of anything that Lisbon afforded that could be of any service to him; but the French general was too much of a politician to admit the want of anything."

Chapter Two – Retreats and Pursuits

The campaign of 1811-12 is not the least memorable of the immortal campaigns in the Peninsula. It saw Fuentes, Albuera, and Salamanca fought; it includes the great sieges of Ciudad Rodrigo and of Badajos; it witnessed the failure at Burgos. We give Kincaid's account of these great events in other chapters; in this we are simply grouping his pictures of soldiers on the march — in retreat or pursuit — with the hardships and combats which attend such movements. This campaign is specially rich in such pictures. It begins with the fierce marches in which Wellington pursued Massena beyond the Portuguese frontier, and closes with the disastrous and memorable retreat from Burgos:

"The campaign of 1811 commenced on March 6, by the retreat of the enemy from Santarein.

"Lord Wellington seemed to be perfectly acquainted with their intentions, for he sent to apprise our piquets the evening before that they were going off, and to desire that they should feel for them occasionally during the night, and give the earliest information of their having started. It was not, however, until daylight that we were quite certain of their having gone, and our division was instantly put in motion after them, passing through the town of Santarem, around which their camp fires were still burning.

"Santarem is finely situated, and probably had been a handsome town. I had never seen it in prosperity, and it now looked like a city of the plague, represented by empty dogs and empty houses; and, but for the tolling of a convent bell by some unseen hand, its appearance was altogether inhuman. We halted for the night near Pyrnes. This little town, and the few wretched inhabitants who had been induced to remain in it, under the faithless promises of the French generals, showed fearful signs of a late visit from a barbarous and merciless foe. Young women were lying in their houses brutally violated; the streets were strewn with broken furniture, intermixed with the putrid carcasses of murdered peasants, mules, and donkeys, and every description of filth, that filled the air with pestilential nausea. The few starved male inhabitants who

32

were stalking amid the wreck of their friends and property, looked like so many skeletons who had been permitted to leave their graves for the purpose of taking vengeance on their oppressors, and the mangled body of every Frenchman who was unfortunate or imprudent enough to stray from his column showed how religiously they performed their mission.

"March 8 — We overtook their rear-guard this evening, snugly put up for the night in a little village, the name of which I do not recollect, but a couple of six-pounders, supported by a few of our rifles, induced them to extend their walk.

"March 11 — As it is possible that some of my readers might never have had the misfortune to experience the comforts of a bivouac, and as the one which I am now in contains but a small quantity of sleep, I shall devote a waking hour for their edification.

"When a regiment arrives at its ground for the night it is formed in columns of companies at full, half, or quarter distance, according to the space which circumstances will permit it to occupy. The officer commanding each company then receives his orders; and, after communicating whatever may be necessary to the men, he desires them to 'pile arms, and make themselves comfortable for the night.' Now, I pray thee, most sanguine reader, suffer not thy fervid imagination to transport thee into Elysian fields at the pleasing exhortation conveyed in the concluding part of the captain's address, but rest thee contentedly in the one where it is made, which in all probability is a ploughed one, and that, too, in a state of preparation to take a model of thy very beautiful person, under the melting influence of a shower of rain. The soldiers of each company have a hereditary claim to the ground next to their arms, as have their officers to a wider range on the same line, limited to the end of a bugle sound, if not by a neighbouring corps, or one that is not neighbourly, for the nearer a man is to his enemy the nearer he likes to be to his friends. Suffice it, that each individual knows his place as well as if he had been born on the estate, and takes immediate possession accordingly. In a ploughed or a stubble field there is scarcely a choice of quarters; but whenever there is a sprinkling of trees it is always an object to secure a good one, as it affords shelter from the sun by day and the dews by night, besides being a sort of home or signpost for a group of officers, as denoting the best place of entertainment; for they hang their spare clothing and accoutrements among the branches, barricade themselves on each side with their saddles, canteens, and portmanteaus, and, with a blazing fire in their front, they indulge, according to their various humours, in a complete state of gipsyfication.

"There are several degrees of comfort to be reckoned in a bivouac, two of which will suffice.

"The first, and worst, is to arrive at the end of a cold, wet day, too dark to see your ground, and too near the enemy to be permitted to unpack the knapsacks or to take off accoutrements; where, unencumbered with baggage or eatables of any kind, you have the consolation of knowing that things are now at their worst, and that any change must be for the better. You keep yourself alive for a while in collecting material to feed your fire with. You take a smell at your empty calabash, which recalls to your remembrance the delicious flavour of its last drop of wine. You curse your servant for not having contrived to send you something or other from the baggage (though you know that it was impossible). You then d— the enemy for being so near you, though, probably, as in the present instance, it was you that came so near them. And, finally, you take a whiff at the end of a cigar, if you have one, and keep grumbling through the smoke, like distant thunder through a cloud, until you tumble into a most warlike sleep.

"The next, and most common one, is when you are not required to look quite so sharp, and when the light baggage and provisions come in at the heel of the regiment. If it is early in the day, the first thing to be done is to make some tea, the most sovereign restorative for jaded spirits. We then proceed to our various duties. The officers of each company form a mess of themselves. One remains in camp to attend to the duties of the regiment; a second attends to the mess; he goes to the regimental butcher and bespeaks a portion of the only purchasable commodities — hearts, livers, and kidneys; and also to see whether he cannot do the commissary out of a few extra biscuits, or a canteen of brandy; and the remainder are gentlemen at large for the day. But while they go hunting among the neighbouring regiments for news, and the neighbouring houses for curiosity, they have always an eye to their mess, and omit no opportunity of adding to the general stock.

"Dinner-hour, for fear of accident, is always the hour when dinner can be got ready; and the 14th section of the articles of war is always most rigidly attended to by every good officer parading himself round the camp-kettle at the time fixed, with his haversack in his hand. A haversack on service is a sort of dumb waiter. The mess have a good many things in common, but the contents of the haversack are exclusively the property of its owner.

"After doing justice to the dinner, if we feel in a humour for additional society, we transfer ourselves to some neighbouring mess, taking our cups and whatever we mean to drink along with us, for in those times there is nothing to be expected from our friends beyond the pleasure of their conversation; and, finally, we retire to rest. To avoid inconvenience by the tossing off of the bedclothes, each officer has a blanket sewed up at the side, like a sack, into which he scrambles, and, with a green sod or a smooth stone for a pillow, composes himself to sleep, and, under such a glorious reflecting canopy as the heavens, it would be a subject of mortification to an astronomer to see the celerity with which he tumbles into it. Habit gives endurance, and fatigue is the best nightcap; no matter that the veteran's countenance is alternately stormed with torrents of rain, heavy dews, and hoar-frosts; no matter that his ears are assailed by a million mouths of chattering locusts, and by some villainous donkey, who every half-hour pitches a bray note, which is instantly taken up by every mule and donkey in the army, and sent echoing from regiment to regiment, over hill and valley, until it dies away in the distance; no matter that the scorpion is lurking beneath his pillow, the snake winding his slimy way by his side, and the lizard galloping over his face, wiping his eyes with its long, cold tail.

"All are unheeded, until the warning voice of the brazen instrument sounds to arms. Strange it is that the ear which is impervious to what would disturb the rest of the world besides, should alone be alive to one, and that, too, a sound which is likely to soothe the sleep of the citizens, or at most to set them dreaming of their loves. But so it is. The first note of the melodious bugle places the soldier on his legs, like lightning; when, muttering a few curses at the unseasonableness of the hour, he plants himself on his alarm post, without knowing or caring about the cause.

"Such is a bivouac; and our sleep-breaker having just sounded, the reader will find what occurred by reading on.

"March 12 — We stood to our arms before daylight. Finding that the enemy had quitted the position in our front, we proceeded to follow them; and had not gone far before we heard the usual morning's salutation of a couple of shots between their rear and our advanced guard. On driving in their outposts, we found their whole army drawn out on the plain, near Redinha, and instantly quarrelled with them on a large scale."

Here is a picture of one of the almost constant skirmishes which marked Wellington's advance and Massena's slow and stubborn retreat:

"As everybody has read *Waverley* and the *Scottish Chiefs*, and knows that one battle is just like another, inasmuch as they always conclude by one or both sides running away, and as it is nothing to me what this or t'other regiment did, nor do I care three buttons what this or t'other person thinks he did, I shall limit all my descriptions to such events as immediately concerned the important personage most interested in this history.

"Be it known, then, that I was one of a crowd of skirmishers who were enabling the French ones to carry the news of their own defeat through a thick wood at an infantry canter when I found myself all at once within a few yards of one of their regiments in line, which opened such a fire that had I not, rifleman-like, taken instant advantage of the cover of a good fir-tree, my name would have unquestionably been transmitted to posterity by that night's gazette. And however opposed it may be to the usual system of drill, I will maintain, from that day's experience, that the cleverest method of teaching a recruit to stand at attention is to place him behind a tree and fire balls at him; as had our late worthy disciplinarian, Sir David Dundas himself, been looking on, I think that even he must have admitted that he never saw any one stand so fiercely upright as I did behind mine, while the balls were rapping into it as fast as if a fellow had been hammering a nail on the opposite side, not to mention the numbers that were whistling past within the eighth of an inch of every part of my body, both before and behind, particularly in the vicinity of my nose, for which the upper part of the tree could barely afford protection.

"This was a last and a desperate stand made by their rear-guard, for their own safety, immediately above the town, as their sole chance of escape depended upon their being able to hold the post until the only bridge across the river was clear of the other fugitives. But they could not hold it long enough; for, while we were undergoing a temporary sort of purgatory in their front, our comrades went working round their flanks, which quickly sent them flying, with us intermixed, at full cry down the streets.

"When we reached the bridge, the scene became exceedingly interesting, for it was choked up by the fugitives, who were, as usual, impeding each other's progress, and we did not find that the application of our swords to those nearest to us tended at all towards lessening their disorder, for it induced about a hundred of them to rush into an adjoining house for shelter, but that was getting regularly out of the frying-pan into the fire, for the house happened to be really in flames, and too hot to hold them, so that the same hundred were quickly seen unkennelling again, half-cooked, into the very jaws of their consumers.

"John Bull, however, is not a bloodthirsty person, so that those who could not better themselves, had only to submit to a simple transfer of personal property to ensure his protection. We, consequently, made many prisoners at the bridge, and followed their army about a league beyond it, keeping up a flying fight until dark.

"March 13 — Arrived on the hill above Condacia in time to see that handsome little town in flames. Every species of barbarity continued to mark the enemy's retreating steps. They burnt every town or village through which they passed, and if we entered a church which, by accident, had been spared, it was to see the murdered bodies of the peasantry on the altar.

"Our post that night was one of terrific grandeur. The hills behind were in a blaze of light with the British camp-fires, as were those in our front with the French ones. Both hills were abrupt and lofty, not above eight hundred yards asunder, and we were in the burning village in the valley beyond. The roofs of houses every instant falling in, and the sparks and flames ascending to the clouds. The streets were strewed with the dying and the dead, some had been murdered and some killed in action, which, together with the half-famished wretches whom we had saved from burning, contributed in making it a scene which was well calculated to shake a stout heart, as was proved in the instance of one of our sentries, a well-known 'devil-may-care' sort of fellow. I know not what appearances the burning rafters might have reflected on the neighbouring trees at the time, but he had not been long on his post before he came running into the piquet, and swore, by all the saints in the calendar, that he saw six dead Frenchmen advancing upon him with hatchets over their shoulders!

"We found by the buttons on the coats of some of the fallen foe, that we had this day been opposed to the French 95th Regiment (the same number as we were then), and I cut off several of them, which I preserved as trophies."

Here is another picture of a brilliant skirmish at the passage of the Ceira. In this combat Wellington showed himself keener in vision and swifter in stroke than Ney, and inflicted on that general both disgrace and loss. Ney was, as a result, relieved of his command of the French rear-guard, and sent to France under something like a cloud. Here he joined Napoleon, and took part in the perils and horrors of the Russian campaign — once more, there, commanding a French rear-guard in retreat.

"March 15 — We overtook the enemy a little before dark this afternoon. They were drawn up behind the Ceira, at Fez d'Aronce, with their rear-guard, under Marshal Ney, imprudently posted on our side of the river, a circumstance which Lord Wellington took immediate advantage of; and, by a furious attack, dislodged them in such confusion that they blew up the bridge before half of their own people had time to get over. Those who were thereby left behind, not choosing to put themselves to the pain of being shot, took to the river, which received them so hospitably that few of them ever quitted it.

"About the middle of the action, I observed some inexperienced light troops rushing up a deep roadway to certain destruction, and ran to warn them out of it, but I only arrived in time to partake the reward of their indiscretion, for I was instantly struck with a musketball above the left ear, which deposited me at full length in the mud.

"I know not how long I lay insensible, but, on recovering, my first feeling was for my head, to ascertain if any part of it was still standing, for it appeared to me as if nothing remained above the mouth; but, after repeated applications of all my fingers and thumbs to the doubtful parts, I at length proved to myself satisfactorily, that it had rather increased than diminished by the concussion; and jumping on my legs, and hearing, by the whistling of the balls from both sides, that the rascals who had got me into the scrape had been driven back and left me there, I snatched my cap, which had saved my life, and which had been spun off my head to the distance of ten or twelve yards, and joined them a short distance in the rear, when one of them, a soldier of the 60th, came and told me that an officer of ours had been killed a short time before, pointing to the spot where I myself had fallen, and that he had tried to take his jacket off, but that the advance of the enemy had prevented him. I told him that I was the one that had been killed, and that I was deucedly obliged to him for his kind intentions, while I felt still more so to the enemy for their timely advance, otherwise, I have no doubt, but my friend would have taken a fancy to my trousers also, for I found that he had absolutely unbuttoned my jacket.

"There is nothing so gratifying to frail mortality as a good dinner when most wanted and least expected. It was perfectly dark before the action finished, but, on going to take advantage of the fires which the enemy had evacuated, we found their soup kettles in full operation, and every man's mess of biscuit lying beside them, in stockings, as was the French mode of carrying them; and it is needless to say how unceremoniously we proceeded to do the honours of the feast. It ever after became a saying among the soldiers, whenever they were on short allowance, 'Well d— my eyes, we must either fall in with the French or the commissary today, I don't care which.'

"March 19 — We, this day, captured the aide-de-camp of General Loison, together with his wife, who was dressed in a splendid hussar uniform. He was a Portuguese, and a traitor, and looked very like a man who would be hanged. She was a Spaniard, and very handsome, and looked very like a woman who would get married again.

"March 20 — We had now been three days without anything in the shape of bread, and meat without it after a time becomes almost loathsome. Hearing that we were not likely to march quite so early as usual this morning, I started before daylight to a village about two miles off, in the face of the Sierra d'Estrella, in the hopes of being able to purchase something, as it lay out of the hostile line of movements. On my arrival there, I found some nuns who had fled from a neighbouring convent, waiting outside the building of the village oven for some Indian-corn leaven, which they had carried there to be baked, and, when I explained my pressing wants, two of them, very kindly, transferred me their shares, for which I gave each a kiss and a dollar between. They took the former as an unusual favour; but looked at the latter, as much as to say, 'Our poverty, and not our will, consents.' I ran off with my half-baked dough, and joined my comrades, just as they were getting under arms.

"March 31 — At daylight, this morning, we moved to our right, along the ridge of mountains, to Guarda; on our arrival there, we saw the imposing spectacle of the whole of the French army winding through the valley below, just out of gunshot. On taking possession of one of the villages which they had just evacuated, we found the body of a well-dressed female, whom they had murdered by a horrible refinement in cruelty. She had been placed upon her back, alive, in the middle of the street, with the fragment of a rock upon her breast, which it required four of our men to remove.

"April 1 — We overtook the enemy this afternoon in position behind Coa, at Sabugal, with their advanced posts on our side of the river. I was sent on piquet for the night, and had my sentries within half musket-shot of theirs; it was wet, dark, and stormy when I went, about midnight, to visit them, and I was not a little annoyed to find one missing. Recollecting who he was, a steady old soldier, and the last man in the world to desert his post, I called his name aloud, when his answering voice, followed by the discharge of a musket, reached me nearly at the same time, from the direction of one of the French sentries; and, after some inquiry, I found that, in walking his lonely round, in a brown study, no doubt, he had each turn taken ten or twelve paces to his front, and only half that number to the rear, until he had gradually worked himself up to within a few yards of his adversary; and it would be difficult to say which of the two was most astonished — the one at hearing a voice, or the other a shot so near, but all my rhetoric, aided by the testimony of the sergeant and the other sentries, could not convince the fellow that he was not on the identical spot on which I had posted him."

On April 3, 1811, was fought the battle of Sabugal, which is told elsewhere. We take up Kincaid's sketches of a soldier's bivouac and marching experiences after Fuentes, during the pause while Ciudad Rodrigo was being blockaded:

"Our battalion occupied Atalya, a little village at the foot of the Sierra de Gata, and in front of the river Vadilla. On taking possession of my quarter, the people showed me an outhouse, which, they said, I might use as a stable, and I took my horse into it, but, seeing the floor strewed with what appeared to be a small brown seed, heaps of which lay in each corner, as if shovelled together in readiness to take to market, I took up a handful, out of curiosity, and truly, they were a curiosity, for I found that they were all regular fleas, and that they were proceeding to eat both me and my horse, without the smallest ceremony. I rushed out of the place, and knocked them down by fistfuls, and never yet could comprehend the cause of their congregating together in such a place."

Marmont, who now commanded the French army, charged with the defence of Ciudad Rodrigo, advanced, towards the end of September, for its relief, and Wellington at once fell back. Kincaid's cheerful spirits can extract fun out of even a night march and a retreat!

"About the middle of the night we received an order to stand to our arms with as little noise as possible, and to commence retiring, the rest of the array having been already withdrawn, unknown to us; an instance of the rapidity and uncertainty of our movements which proved fatal to the liberty of several amateurs and followers of the army, who, seeing an army of sixty thousand men lying asleep around their camp-fires, at ten o'clock at night, naturally concluded that they might safely indulge in a bed in the village behind until daylight, without the risk of being caught napping; but, long ere that time they found themselves on the high-road to Ciudad Rodrigo, in the rude grasp of an enemy. Amongst others, was the chaplain of our division, whose outward man conveyed no very exalted notion of the respectability of his profession, and who was treated with greater indignity than usually fell to the lot of prisoners, for, after keeping him a couple of days, and finding that, however gifted he might have been in spiritual lore, he was as ignorant as Dominie Sampson on military matters; and, conceiving good provisions to be thrown away upon him, they stripped him nearly naked and dismissed him, like the barber in *Gil Bias*, with a kick in the breech, and sent him into us in a woeful state.

"In every interval between our active services we indulged in all manner of childish trick and amusement with an avidity and delight of which it is impossible to convey an adequate idea. We lived united, as men always are who are daily staring death in the face on the same side, and who, caring little about it, look upon each new day added to their lives as one more to rejoice in.

"We invited the villagers every evening to a dance at our quarters alternately. A Spanish peasant girl has an address about her which I have never met with in the same class of any other country; and she at once enters into society with the ease and confidence of one who had been accustomed to it all her life. We used to flourish away at the bolero, fandango, and waltz, and wound up early in the evening with a supper of roasted chestnuts.

"Our village belles, as already stated, made themselves perfectly at home in our society, and we, too, should have enjoyed theirs for a season; but when month after month and year after year continued to roll along, without producing any change, we found that the cherry cheek and sparkling eye of rustic beauty furnished but a very poor apology for the illuminated portion of Nature's fairest works, and ardently longed for an opportunity of once more feasting our eyes on a lady."

After the glory of Salamanca came, by way of anticlimax, the inglorious failure at Burgos. Kincaid's battalion took part in the toils and suffering of the retreat from Burgos. There is no note of grumbling in his tale. Yet seldom has an army suffered more than during those bitter November days, when Wellington's soldiers, with the discouraging memory of the failure at Burgos chilling their imaginations, toiled in retreat along muddy roads, across swollen rivers, through blinding and incessant rain, almost without food; while fiercely on their rear hung the pursuing French cavalry. Wellington made a brief halt on November 14 at Salamanca, and we take up Kincaid's story at this point:

"November 7 — Halted this night at Alba de Tormes, and next day marched into quarters in Salamanca, where we rejoined Lord Wellington with the army from Burgos.

"On the 14th the British army concentrated on the field of their former glory, in consequence of a part of the French army having effected the passage of the river above Alba de Tormes. On the 15th the whole of the enemy's force having passed the river a cannonade commenced early in the day; and it was the general belief that, ere night, a second battle of Salamanca would be recorded. But as all the French armies in Spain were now united in our front, and outnumbered us so far, Lord Wellington, seeing no decided advantage to be gained by risking a battle, at length ordered a retreat, which we commenced about three in the afternoon. Our division halted for the night at the entrance of a forest about four miles from Salamanca.

"The heavy rains which usually precede the Spanish winter had set in the day before; and as the roads in that part of the country cease to be roads for the remainder of the season, we were now walking nearly knee deep in a stiff mud, into which no man could thrust his foot with the certainty of having a shoe at the end of it when he pulled it out again; and that we might not be miserable by halves, we had this evening to regale our chops with the last morsel of biscuit that they were destined to grind during the retreat.

"We cut some boughs of trees to keep us out of the mud, and lay down to sleep on them, wet to the skin; but the cannonade of the afternoon had been succeeded after dark by a continued firing of musketry, which led us to believe that our piquets were attacked, and, in momentary expectation of an order to stand to our arms, we kept ourselves awake the whole night, and were not a little provoked when we found next morning that it had been occasioned by numerous stragglers from the different regiments shooting at the pigs belonging to the peasantry, which were grazing in the wood.

"November 16 — Retiring from daylight until dark through the same description of roads. The French dragoons kept close behind, but did not attempt to molest us. It still continued to rain hard, and we again passed the night in a wood. I was very industriously employed during the early part of it feeling, in the dark, for acorns as a substitute for bread.

"November 17 — We were much surprised in the course of the forenoon to hear a sharp firing commence behind us on the very road by which we were retiring; and it was not until we reached the spot that we learnt that the troops, who were retreating by a road parallel to ours, had left it too soon, and enabled some French dragoons, under cover of the forest, to advance unperceived to the flank of our line of march, who, seeing an interval between two divisions of infantry, which was filled with light baggage and some passing officers, dashed at it and made some prisoners in the scramble of the moment, amongst whom was Lieutenant-General Sir Edward Paget.

"Our division formed on the heights above Samunoz to cover the passage of the rivulet, which was so swollen with the heavy rains, as only to be passable at particular fords. While we waited there for the passage of the rest of the army, the enemy, under cover of the forest, was, at the same time, assembling in force close around us; and the moment that we began to descend the hill, towards the rivulet, we were assailed by a heavy fire of cannon and musketry, while their powerful cavalry were in readiness to take advantage of any confusion which might have occurred. We effected the passage, however, in excellent order, and formed on the opposite bank of the stream, where we continued under a cannonade and engaged in a sharp skirmish until dark.

"When the firing ceased, we received the usual order 'to make ourselves comfortable for the night,' and I never remember an instance in which we had so much difficulty in obeying it; for the ground we occupied was a perfect flat, which was flooded more than ankle-deep with water, excepting here and there, where the higher ground around the roots of trees presented circles of a few feet of visible earth, upon which we grouped ourselves. Some few fires were kindled, at which we roasted some bits of raw beef on the points of our swords, and ate them by way of a dinner. There was plenty of water to apologise for the want of better fluids, but bread sent no apology at all.

"It made my very heart rejoice to see my brigadier's servant commence boiling some chocolate and frying a beef-steak. I watched its progress with a keenness which intense hunger alone could inspire, and was on the very point of having my desires consummated, when the general, getting uneasy at not having received any communication relative to the movements of the morning, and, without considering how feelingly my stomach yearned for a better acquaintance with the contents of his frying-pan, desired me to ride to General Alten for orders. I found the general at a neighbouring tree; but he cut off all hopes of my timely return, by desiring me to remain with him until he received the report of an officer whom he had sent to ascertain the progress of the other divisions.

"While I was toasting myself at his fire, so sharply set that I could have eaten one of my boots, I observed his German orderly dragoon at an adjoining fire stirring up the contents of a camp-kettle, that once more revived my departing hopes, and I presently had the satisfaction of seeing him dipping in some basins, presenting one to the general, one to the aide-de-camp, and a third to myself. The mess which it contained I found, after swallowing the whole at a draught, was neither more nor less than the produce of a piece of beef boiled in plain water; and though it would have been enough to have physicked a dromedary at any other time, yet, as I could then have made a good hole in the dromedary himself, it sufficiently satisfied my cravings to make me equal to anything for the remainder of the day.

"On November 19 we arrived at the convent of Caridad, near Ciudad Rodrigo, and once more experienced the comforts of our baggage and provisions. My boots had not been off since the 13th, and I found it necessary to cut them to pieces to get my swollen feet out of them.

"Up to this period Lord Wellington had been adored by the army, in consideration of his brilliant achievements, and for his noble and manly bearing in all things; but, in consequence of some disgraceful irregularities which took place during the retreat, he immediately after issued an order conveying a sweeping censure on the whole army. His general conduct was too upright for even the finger of malice itself to point at; but as his censure on this occasion was not strictly confined to the guilty, it afforded a handle to disappointed persons, and excited a feeling against him on the part of individuals which has probably never since been obliterated.

"It began by telling us that we had suffered no privations; and, though this was hard to be digested on an empty stomach, yet, taking it in its more liberal meaning, that our privations were not of an extent to justify any irregularities, which I readily admit; still, as many regiments were not guilty of any irregularities, it is not to be wondered if such should have felt at first a little sulky to find, in the general reproof, that no loophole whatever had been left for them to creep through; for I believe I am justified in saying that neither our own, nor the two gallant corps associated with us, had a single man absent that we could not satisfactorily account for. But it touched us still more tenderly in not excepting us from his general charge of inexpertness in camp arrangements; for it was our belief, and in which we were in some measure borne out by circumstances, that had he placed us at the same moment in the same field with an equal number of the best troops in France, that he would not only have seen our fires as quickly lit, but every Frenchman roasting on them to the bargain, if they waited long enough to be dressed, for there perhaps never was, nor ever again will be, such a war-brigade as that which was composed of the 43rd, 52nd, and the Rifles."

1812 found the Rifles once more taking part in marches which taxed the endurance of the soldiers to the uttermost; but this time the temper of the troops was gay and exultant in the highest degree. They were taking part in the great movement which thrust the French back to Vittoria. The elation of coming and assured victory was in the soldiers' blood. The Rifles, after days of toilsome marches through wild and mountainous country, at last reached the fruitful valley of the Ebro. Here is a pleasant campaign scene:

"We started at daylight on June 15, through a dreary region of solid rock, bearing an abundant crop of loose stones, without a particle of soil or vegetation visible to the naked eye in any direction. After leaving nearly twenty miles of this horrible wilderness behind us, our weary minds clogged with an imaginary view of nearly as much more of it in our front, we found ourselves all at once looking down upon the valley of the Ebro, near the village of Arenas, one of the richest, loveliest, and most romantic spots that I ever beheld. The influence of such a scene on the mind can scarcely be believed. Five minutes before we were all as lively as stones. In a moment we were all fruits and flowers; and many a pair of legs, that one would have thought had not a kick left in them, were, in five minutes after, seen dancing across the bridge to the tune of 'The Downfall of Paris,' which struck up from the bands of the different regiments.

"I lay down that night in a cottage garden, with my head on a melon, and my eye on a cherry-tree, and resigned myself to a repose which did not require a long courtship.

"We resumed our march at daybreak on the 16th. The road, in the first instance, wound through orchards and luxurious gardens, and then closed in to the edge of the river, through a difficult and formidable pass, where the rocks on each side, arising to a prodigious height, hung over each other in fearful grandeur, and in many places nearly met together over our heads.

"After following the course of the river for nearly two miles, the rocks on each side gradually expanded into another valley, lovely as the one we had left, and where we found the fifth division of our army lying encamped. They were still asleep; and the rising sun, and a beautiful

46

morning, gave additional sublimity to the scene; for there was nothing but the tops of the white tents peeping above the fruit trees; and an occasional sentinel pacing his post, that gave any indication of what a nest of hornets the blast of a bugle could bring out of that apparently peaceful solitude.

"We were welcomed into every town or village through which we passed by the peasant girls, who were in the habit of meeting us with garlands of flowers, and dancing before us in a peculiar style of their own; and it not unfrequently happened, that while they were so employed with one regiment, the preceding one was diligently engaged in pulling down some of their houses for firewood, a measure which we were sometimes obliged to have recourse to, where no other fuel could be had, and for which they were ultimately paid by the British Government; but it was a measure that was more likely to have set the poor souls dancing mad than for joy, had they foreseen the consequences of our visit."

At this stage the march brought the British into actual contact with the enemy, and there ensued much brisk skirmishing, in which the Rifles found huge enjoyment:

"On the morning of the 18th, we were ordered to march to San Milan, a small town about two leagues off; and where, on our arrival on the hill above it, we found a division of French infantry, as strong as ourselves, in the act of crossing our path. The surprise, I believe, was mutual, though I doubt whether the pleasure was equally so; for we were red-hot for an opportunity of retaliating for the Salamanca retreat; and, as the old saying goes, 'There is no opportunity like the present.' Their leading brigade had nearly passed before we came up, but not a moment was lost after we did. Our battalion, dispersing among the brushwood, went down the hill upon them; and, with a destructive fire, broke through their line of march, supported by the rest of the brigade. Those that had passed made no attempt at a stand, but continued their flight, keeping up as good a fire as their circumstances would permit; while we kept hanging on their flank and rear, through a good rifle country, which enabled us to make considerable havoc among them. Their general's aide-de-camp, amongst others, was mortally wounded; and a lady, on a white horse, who probably was his wife, remained beside him, until we came very near. She appeared to be in great distress; but, though we called to her to remain, and not to be alarmed, yet she galloped off as soon as a decided step became necessary. The object of her solicitude did not survive many minutes after we reached him."

Chapter Three – Some Famous Battles

Kincaid shared in all the bloody fights of the Peninsula, from Sabugal to Toulouse. His descriptions of these fights are hasty and planless; they give no hint of the strategy behind them or of the results which followed them. But they are always vivid, racy, and rich in personal incident, and we give in this chapter some transcripts from them.

Sabugal was the last combat fought on Portuguese soil in Massena's sullen retreat from the lines of Torres Vedras. Massena was never so dangerous as in retreat, and Ney, with all his fiery valour, commanded his rear-guard. The French, too, were in a mood of almost reckless savagery, and they greatly exceeded in numbers the force pursuing them. It may be imagined, then, what an incessant splutter of fierce and angry skirmishes raged betwixt Wellington's advance-guard and the French rear. Yet the veterans on both sides maintained a singularly cool and business-like attitude towards each other, an attitude not unflavoured with gleams of unprofessional friendliness. Thus as the French were falling back after the disastrous fight at Redinha, night fell while the skirmishers of the Rifles were still eagerly pressing on the tired French rear-guard. The officer commanding the French suddenly held up his sword in the grey dusk with a white handkerchief tied to it. An officer of the Rifles went forward to parley, when the Frenchman explained that he thought both sides needed a rest after a hard day's work. To this the officers of the Rifles cheerfully agreed, and politely invited the Frenchman and his subalterns to share their rations. This proposal was accepted; the French and English officers sat merrily round a common fire, and shared a common meal; then parted, and before daybreak became pursuers and pursued again! Sabugal was described by Wellington himself as "one of the most glorious actions British troops ever engaged in"; but it was little better than a gallant blunder. The day was one of drifting fog and blinding rain. Wellington's plan was with three divisions — a force 10,000 strong — to envelop and crush Massena's left wing, commanded by Regnier, but Erskine, who commanded the Light Division, failed to understand his orders, wandered off with his cavalry in the fog, and left Beckwith with four companies of the Rifles and the 43rd lying sheltered near the ford across the Coa. When Wellington's general attack was developed, Beckwith was to cross the river and attack. A staff officer stumbled upon him early in the day, before the other troops had moved, and demanded, with a note of anger in his voice, why he did not attack? Beckwith instantly led his men across the stream, and with one bayonet battalion and four companies of Rifles, proceeded to attack 12,000 French infantry supported by cavalry and guns! And in a combat so strange, against chances so apparently hopeless, the handful of British won! Here is Kincaid's story:

"April 3, 1811 — Early this morning our division moved still farther to its right, and our brigade led the way across a ford, which took us up to the middle; while the balls from the enemy's advanced posts were hissing in the water around us, we drove in their light troops and commenced a furious assault upon their main body. Thus far all was right; but a thick, drizzling rain now came on, in consequence of which the third division, which was to have made a simultaneous attack to our left, missed their way, and a brigade of dragoons, under Sir William Erskine, who were to have covered our right, went the Lord knows where, but certainly not into the fight, although they started at the same time that we did, and had the 'music' of our rifles to guide them; and even the second brigade of our division could not afford us any support for nearly an hour, so that we were thus unconsciously left with about fifteen hundred men, in the very impertinent attempt to carry a formidable position on which stood as many thousands.

"The weather, which had deprived us of the aid of our friends, favoured us so far as to prevent the enemy from seeing the amount of our paltry force; and the conduct of our gallant fellows, led on by Sir Sidney Beckwith, was so truly heroic, that, incredible as it may seem, we had the best of the fight throughout. Our first attack was met by such overwhelming numbers, that we were forced back and followed by three heavy columns, before which we retired slowly, and keeping up a destructive fire, to the nearest rising ground, where we re-formed and instantly charged their advancing masses, sending them flying at the point of the bayonet, and entering their position along with them, where we were assailed by fresh forces. Three times did the very same thing occur. In our third attempt we got possession of one of their howitzers, for which a desperate struggle was making, when we were at the same moment charged by infantry in front and cavalry on the right, and again compelled to fall back; but, fortunately at this moment we were reinforced by the arrival of the second brigade, and with their aid we once more stormed their position and secured the well-earned howitzer, while the third division came at the same time upon their flank, and they were driven from the field in the greatest disorder.

"Lord Wellington's despatch on this occasion did ample justice to Sir Sidney Beckwith and his brave brigade. Never were troops more judiciously or more gallantly led. Never was a leader more devotedly followed.

"In the course of the action a man of the name of Knight fell dead at my feet, and though I heard a musket ball strike him, I could neither find blood nor wound. There was a little spaniel belonging to one of our officers running about the whole time, barking at the balls, and I saw him once smelling at a live shell, which exploded in his face without hurting him."

It may be added that, when the fight was over, round that fiercely disputed howitzer 300 dead bodies were found piled!

An amusing instance of the cool and business-like temper with which the veterans of the Rifles fought occurred in this combat. A rifleman named Flinn had covered a Frenchman, and was in the act of drawing the trigger, when a hare leaped out of the fern in front of him. Flinn found this game more tempting; he took quick aim at it, and shot it. His officer rebuked him when the fight was over for that wasted shot. "Sure, your honour," was his reply, "we can kill a Frenchman any day, but it isn't always I can bag a hare for your supper."

On May 3, 1811, began the confused manoeuvring and fierce combats, stretching through two days, known as the battle of Fuentes d'Onore. In the middle of the fight Wellington had to change his front, swing his right wing back across the open plain then in possession of the triumphant French cavalry to a ridge at right angles to his former front. The Light Division formed part of the force executing this movement. It was formed in three squares, flanking each other. Masses of French cavalry eddied furiously round them as they marched. But the stern and disciplined ranks of the Light Division never wavered. They moved, says

Napier, "in the most majestic manner"; and, he adds, that "all the cavalry that ever charged under Tamerlane or Genghis Khan would have failed to break their lines." Kincaid's account is graphic, and betrays no consciousness of the exceptional nature of the deed performed by his division:

"May 5, 1811 — The day began to dawn, this fine May morning, with a rattling fire of musketry on the extreme right of our position, which the enemy had attacked, and to which point our division was rapidly moved.

"Our battalion was thrown into a wood, a little to the left and front of the division engaged, and was instantly warmly opposed to the French skirmishers; in the course of which I was struck with a musket ball on the left breast, which made me stagger a yard or two backward, and, as I felt no pain, I concluded that I was dangerously wounded; but it turned out to be owing to my not being hurt. While our operations here were confined to a tame skirmish, and our view to the oaks with which we were mingled, we found, by the evidence of our ears, that the division which we had come to support was involved in a more serious onset, for there was a successive rattle of artillery, the wild hurrah of charging squadrons, and the repulsing volley of musketry; until Lord Wellington, finding his right too much extended, directed that division to fall back behind the small river Touronne, and ours to join the main body of the army. The execution of our movement presented a magnificent military spectacle, as the plain between us and the right of the army was by this time in possession of the French cavalry, and, while we were retiring through it with the order and precision of a common field-day, they kept dancing around us, and every instant threatening a charge, without daring to execute it.

"We took up our new position at a right angle with the then right of the British line, on which our left rested, and with our right on the Touronne. The enemy followed our movement with a heavy column of infantry; but, when they came near enough to exchange shots, they did not seem to like our looks, as we occupied a low ridge of broken rocks, against which even a rat could scarcely have hoped to advance alive; and they again fell back, and opened a tremendous fire of artillery, which was returned by a battery of our guns.

"The battle continued to rage with fury in and about the village, while we were lying by our arms under a burning hot sun, some stray cannon-shot passing over and about us, whose progress we watched for want of other employment. One of them bounded along in the direction of an 'amateur,' whom we had for some time been observing, securely placed, as he imagined, behind a piece of rock, which stood about five feet above the ground, and over which nothing but his head was shown, sheltered from the sun by an umbrella. The shot in question touched the ground three or four times between us and him; he saw it coming lowered his umbrella, and withdrew his head. Its expiring bound carried it into the very spot where he had that instant disappeared. I hope he was not hurt; but the thing looked so ridiculous that it excited a shout of laughter, and we saw no more of him.

"A little before dusk, in the evening, our battalion was ordered forward to relieve the troops engaged in the village, part of which still remained in possession of the enemy, and I saw, by the mixed nature of the dead, in every part of the streets, that it had been successively in possession of both sides. The firing ceased with the daylight, and I was sent, with a section of men, in charge of one of the streets for the night. There was a wounded sergeant of Highlanders lying on my post. A ball had passed through the back part of his head, from which the brain was oozing, and his only sign of life was a convulsive hiccough every two or three seconds. I sent for a medical friend to look at him, who told me that he could not survive; I then got a mattress from the nearest house, placed the poor fellow on it, and made use of one corner as a pillow for myself, on which, after the fatigues of the day, and though called occasionally to visit my sentries, I slept most soundly. The Highlander died in the course of the night.

"When we stood to our arms at daybreak next morning, we found the enemy busy throwing up a six-gun battery immediately in front of our company's post, and we immediately set to work, with our whole hearts and souls, and placed a wall, about twelve feet thick, between us, which, no doubt, still remains there in the same garden, as a monument of what can be effected in a few minutes by a hundred modern men, when their personal safety is concerned, not but that the proprietor, in the midst of his admiration, would rather see a good bed of garlic on the spot manured with the bodies of the architects.

"When the sun began to shine on the pacific disposition of the enemy, we proceeded to consign the dead to their last earthly mansions, giving every Englishman a grave to himself, and putting as many Frenchmen into one as it could conveniently accommodate. Whilst in the superintendence of this melancholy duty, and ruminating on the words of the poet:

There's not a form of all that lie
Thus ghastly, wild and bare,
Tost, bleeding, in the stormy sky,
Black in the burning air,
But to his knee some infant clung,
But on his heart some fond heart hung!

"I was grieved to think that the souls of deceased warriors should be so selfish as to take to flight in their regimentals, for I never saw the body of one with a rag on after battle.

"The day after one of those negative sort of victories is always one of intense interest. The movements on each side are most jealously watched, and each side is diligently occupied in strengthening such points as the fight of the preceding day had proved to be the most vulnerable. They had made a few prisoners, chiefly Guardsmen and Highlanders, whom they marched past the front of our position, in the most ostentatious way, on the forenoon of the 6th; and, the day following, a number of their regiments were paraded in the most imposing manner for review. They looked uncommonly well, and we were proud to think that we had beaten such fine-looking fellows so lately!"

In the tangled and hurried marches which preceded the battle of Salamanca, the Rifles took, of course, an active part. They were probably the quickest-footed and most hardy regiment under Wellington's command. But in the great battle itself Kincaid's battalion played a small part, being held in reserve. Kincaid's account is both amusing and interesting:

"Hitherto we had been fighting the description of battle in which John Bull glories so much — gaining a brilliant and useless victory against great odds. But we were now about to contend for fame on equal terms; and, having tried both, I will say, without partiality, that I would rather fight one man than two any day; for I have never been quite satisfied that the additional quantum of glory altogether compensated for the proportionate loss of substance; a victory of that kind being a doubtful and most unsatisfactory one to the performers, with each occupying the same ground after that they did before; and the whole merit resting with the side which did not happen to begin it.

"Marmont came down upon us the first night with a thundering cannonade, and placed his army *en masse* on the plain before us, almost within gunshot. I was told that, while Lord Wellington was riding along the line, under a fire of artillery, and accompanied by a numerous staff, a brace of greyhounds in pursuit of a hare passed close to him. He was at the moment in earnest conversation with General Castanos; but the instant he observed them he gave the view hallo and went after them at full speed, to the utter astonishment of his foreign accompaniments. Nor did he stop until he saw the hare killed; when he returned and resumed the commander-in-chief as if nothing had occurred.

"I was sent on piquet on the evening of the 19th, to watch a portion of the plain before us; and, soon after sunrise on the following morning, a cannonade commenced behind a hill to my right; and though the combatants were not visible, it was evident that they were not dealing in blank-cartridge, as mine happened to be the pitching-post of all the enemy's round shot. While I was attentively watching its progress, there arose all at once, behind the rising ground to my left, a yell of the most terrific import; and, convinced that it would give instantaneous birth to as hideous a body, it made me look with an eye of lightning at the ground around me; and, seeing a broad deep ditch within a hundred yards, I lost not a moment in placing it between my piquet and the extraordinary sound. I had scarcely effected the movement when Lord Wellington, with his staff, and a cloud of French and English dragoons and horse artillery intermixed, came over the hill at full cry, and all hammering at each other's heads, in one confused mass over the very ground I had that instant quitted. It appeared that his lordship had gone there to reconnoitre, covered by two guns and two squadrons of cavalry, who by some accident were surprised and charged by a superior body of the enemy, and sent tumbling in upon us in the manner described.

"A piquet of the 43rd had formed on our right, and we were obliged to remain passive spectators of such an extraordinary scene going on within a few yards of us, as we could not fire without an equal chance of shooting some of our own side. Lord Wellington and his staff, with the two guns, took shelter for a moment behind us, while the cavalry went sweeping along our front, where, I suppose, they picked up some reinforcement, for they returned almost instantly in the same confused mass; but the French were now the fliers; and, I must do them the justice to say, that they got off in a manner highly creditable to themselves. I saw one, in particular, defending himself against two of ours; and he would have made his escape from both, but an officer of our dragoons came down the hill, and took him in the flank at full speed, sending man and horse rolling headlong on the plain.

"I was highly interested all this time in observing the distinguished characters which this unlooked-for turn-up had assembled around us. Marshal Beresford and the greater part of the staff remained with their swords drawn, and the Duke himself did not look more than half-pleased, while he silently despatched some of them with orders. General Alten and his huge German orderly dragoon, with their swords drawn, cursed the whole time to a very large amount; but, as it was in German, I had not the full benefit of it. He had an opposition swearer in Captain Jenkinson of the artillery, who commanded the two guns, and whose oaths were chiefly aimed at himself for his folly, as far as I could understand, in putting so much confidence in his covering party, that he had not thought it necessary to unfix the catch which horse-artillerymen, I believe, had to prevent their swords quitting the scabbards when they are not wanted, and which on this occasion prevented their jumping forth when they were so unexpectedly called for.

"The straggling enemy had scarcely cleared away from our front when Lord Combermere came from the right with a reinforcement of cavalry; and our piquet was at the same moment ordered to join the battalion.

"The movements which followed presented the most beautiful military spectacle imaginable. The enemy were endeavouring to turn our left; and, in making a counteracting movement, the two armies were marching in parallel lines close to each other on a perfect plain, each ready to take advantage of any opening of the other, and exchanging round shot as they moved along. Our division brought up the rear of the infantry, marching with the order and precision of a field-day, in open column of companies, and in perfect readiness to receive the enemy in any shape, who, on their part, had a huge cavalry force close at hand and equally ready to pounce upon us.

"July 22 — A sharp fire of musketry commenced at daylight in the morning; but as it did not immediately concern us and was nothing unusual we took no notice of it, but busied ourselves in getting our arms and our bodies disengaged from the rust and the wet engendered by the storm of the past night. About ten o'clock our division was ordered to stand to their arms. The enemy were to be seen in motion on the opposite ridges, and a straggling fire of musketry, with an occasional gun, acted as a sort of prelude to the approaching conflict. We heard, about this time, that Marmont had just sent to his *ci-devant* landlord in Salamanca to desire that he would have the usual dinner ready for himself and staff at six o'clock; and so satisfied was 'mine host' of the infallibility of the French Marshal, that he absolutely set about making the necessary preparations.

"There assuredly never was an army so anxious as ours was to be brought into action on this occasion. They were a magnificent body of well-tried soldiers, highly equipped, and in the highest health and spirits, with the most devoted confidence in their leader, and an invincible confidence in themselves. The retreat of the four preceding days had annoyed us beyond measure, for we believed that we were nearly equal to the enemy in point of numbers, and the idea of our retiring before an equal number of any troops in the world was not to be endured with common patience.

"We were kept the whole of the forenoon in the most torturing state of suspense through contradictory reports. One passing officer telling us that he had just heard the order given to attack, and the next asserting with equal confidence that he had just heard the order to retreat; and it was not until about two o'clock in the afternoon that affairs began to wear a more decided aspect; and when our own eyes and ears at length conveyed the wished-for tidings that a battle was inevitable, for we saw the enemy beginning to close upon our right, and the cannonade had become general along the whole line. Lord Wellington about the same time ordered the movement which decided the fate of the day — that of bringing the third division from beyond the river on our left rapidly to our extreme right, turning the enemy in their attempt to turn us, and commencing the offensive with the whole of his right wing.

"The effect was instantaneous and decisive, for although some obstinate and desperate fighting took place in the centre, with various success, yet the victory was never for a moment in doubt, and the enemy were soon in full retreat, leaving seven thousand prisoners, two eagles, and eleven pieces of artillery in our hands. Had we been favoured with two hours' more daylight, their loss would have been incalculable, for they committed a blunder at starting which they never got time to retrieve, and their retreat was therefore commenced in such disorder, and with a river in their rear, that nothing but darkness could have saved them.

"The third division, under Sir Edward Pakenham, the artillery, and some regiments of dragoons, particularly distinguished themselves. But our division, very much to our annoyance, came in for a very slender portion of this day's glory. We were exposed to a cannonade the whole of the afternoon, but, as we were not permitted to advance until very late, we had only an opportunity of throwing a few straggling shot at the fugitives before we lost sight of them m the dark, and then bivouacked for the night near the village of Huerta (I think it was called).

"We started after them at daylight next morning, and crossing at a ford of the Tormes we found their rear-guard, consisting of three regiments of infantry, with some cavalry and artillery, posted on a formidable height above the village of Serna. General Bock, with his brigade of heavy German dragoons, immediately went at them, and putting their cavalry to flight, he broke through their infantry, and took or destroyed the whole of them. This was one of the most gallant charges recorded in history. I saw many of these fine fellows lying dead along with their horses, on which they were still astride, with the sword firmly grasped in the hand, as they had fought the instant before, and several of them still wearing a look of fierce defiance, which death itself had been unable to quench."

In the mountain march which turned the French right, and drove Joseph's whole army, burdened with the plunder of a kingdom, back into the fatal valley of Vittoria, the Rifles had a full share. In the actual fighting of June 21, 1813, their part was brilliant. They fired the first shot in the fight; they were first across the river; they were first up the central hill of Arinez, where the fury of the great battle culminated; and they captured the first gun taken. Barnard's daring advance with his riflemen really enabled the third and seventh divisions to carry the bridge of Mendoza. Barnard opened so cruel a flank fire on the French guns and infantry guarding the bridge that they fell back in confusion, and the

British crossed practically without confusion. It is needless to add that the hardy and active Rifles led in the pursuit of the defeated French far into the night after the battle, and early on the succeeding day:

"June 21, 1813 — Our division got under arms this morning before daylight, passed the base of the mountain by its left, through the camp of the fourth division, who were still asleep in their tents, to the banks of the river Zadora, at the village of Tres Puentes. The opposite side of the river was occupied by the enemy's advanced posts, and we saw their army on the hills beyond, while the spires of Vittoria were visible in the distance. We felt as if there was likely to be a battle; but as that was an event we were never sure of until we found ourselves actually in it, we lay for some time just out of musket-shot, uncertain what was likely to turn up, and waiting for orders. At length a sharp fire of musketry was heard to our right, and on looking in that direction we saw the head of Sir Rowland Hill's corps, together with some Spanish troops, attempting to force the mountain which marked the enemy's left. The three battalions of our regiment were, at the same moment, ordered forward to feel the enemy, who lined the opposite banks of the river, with whom we were quickly engaged in a warm skirmish. The affair with Sir Rowland Hill became gradually warmer, but ours had apparently no other object than to amuse those Avho were opposite to us for the moment, so that for about two hours longer it seemed as if there would be nothing but an affair of outposts.

"About twelve o'clock, however, we were moved rapidly to our left, followed by the rest of the division, till we came to an abrupt turn of the river, where we found a bridge, unoccupied by the enemy, which we immediately crossed and took possession of what appeared to me to be an old field-work on the other side. We had not been many seconds there before we observed the bayonets of the third and seventh divisions glittering above the standing corn, and advancing upon another bridge which stood about a quarter of a mile farther to our left, and where, on their arrival, they were warmly opposed by the enemy's light troops, who lined the bank of the river (which we ourselves were now on), in great force, for the defence of the bridge. As soon as this was observed by our division, Colonel Barnard advanced with our battalion, and took them in flank with such a furious fire as quickly dislodged them, and thereby opened a passage for these two divisions free of expense, which must otherwise have cost them dearly. What with the rapidity of our movement, the colour of our dress, and our close contact with the enemy before they would abandon their post, we had the misfortune to be identified with them for some time by a battery of our own guns, who, not observing the movement, continued to serve it out indiscriminately, and all the while admiring their practice upon us; nor was it until the red coats of the third division joined us that they discovered their mistake.

"On the mountain to our extreme right the action continued to be general and obstinate, though we observed that the enemy were giving ground slowly to Sir Rowland Hill. The passage of the river by our division had turned the enemy's outpost at the bridge on our right, where we had been engaged in the morning, and they were now retreating, followed by the fourth division. The plain between them and Sir Rowland Hill was occupied by the British cavalry, who were now seen filing out of a wood, squadron after squadron, galloping into form as they gradually cleared it. The hills behind were covered with spectators, and the third and the light divisions, covered by our battalion, advanced rapidly upon a formidable hill in front of the enemy's centre, which they had neglected to occupy in sufficient force.

"In the course of our progress our men kept picking off the French vedettes, who were imprudent enough to hover too near us; and many a horse, bounding along the plain, dragging his late rider by the stirrup-irons, contributed in making it a scene of extraordinary and exhilarating interest.

"Old Picton rode at the head of the third division, dressed in a blue coat and a round hat, and swore as roundly all the way as if he had been wearing two cocked ones. Our battalion soon cleared the hill in question of the enemy's light troops; but we were pulled up on the opposite side of it by one of their lines, which occupied a wall at the entrance of a village immediately under us.

"During the few minutes that we stopped there, while a brigade of the third division was deploying into line, two of our companies lost two officers and thirty men, chiefly from the fire of artillery bearing on the spot from the French position. One of their shells burst immediately under my nose, part of it struck my boot and stirrupiron, and the rest of it kicked up such a dust about me that my charger refused to obey orders; and while I was spurring and he capering I heard a voice behind me, which I knew to be Lord Wellington's, calling out, in a tone of reproof, 'Look to keeping your men together, sir'; and though, God knows, I had not the remotest idea that he was within a mile of me at the time, yet so sensible was I that circumstances warranted his supposing that I was a young officer cutting a caper, by way of bravado, before him, that worlds would not have tempted me to look round at the moment. The French fled from the wall as soon as they received a volley from part of the third division, and we instantly dashed down the hill and charged them through the village, capturing three of their guns; the first, I believe, that were taken that day. They received a reinforcement, and drove us back before our supports could come to our assistance; but, in the scramble of the moment, our men were knowing enough to cut the traces and carry off the horses, so that when we retook the village immediately after the guns still remained in our possession.

"The battle now became general along the whole line, and the cannonade was tremendous. At one period we held on one side of a wall, near the village, while the French were on the other, so that any person who chose to put his head over from either side was sure of getting a sword or a bayonet up his nostrils. This situation was, of course, too good to be of long endurance. The victory, I believe, was never for a moment doubtful. The enemy were so completely out-generalled, and the superiority of our troops was such, that to carry their positions required little more than the time necessary to march to them. After forcing their centre the fourth division and our own got on the flank and rather in rear of the enemy's left wing, who were retreating before Sir Rowland Hill, and who, to effect their escape, were now obliged to fly in one confused mass. Had a single regiment of our dragoons been at hand, or even a squadron, to have forced them into shape for a few minutes, we must have taken from ten to twenty thousand prisoners. After marching alongside of them for nearly two miles, and as a disorderly body will always move faster than an orderly one, we had the mortification to see them gradually heading us, until they finally made their escape.

"Our elevated situation at this time afforded a good view of the field of battle to our left, and I could not help being struck with an unusual appearance of unsteadiness and want of confidence among the French troops. I saw a dense mass of many thousands occupying a good defensible post, who gave way in the greatest confusion before a single

61

line of the third division, almost without feeling them. If there was nothing in any other part of the position to justify the movement, and I do not think there was, they ought to have been flogged, every man, from the general downwards.

"The ground was particularly favourable to the retreating foe, as every half mile afforded a fresh and formidable position, so that from the commencement of the action to the city of Vittoria, a distance of six or eight miles, we were involved in one continued hard skirmish. On passing Vittoria, however, the scene became quite new and infinitely more amusing, as the French had made no provision for a retreat; and Sir Thomas Graham having seized upon the great road to France, the only one left open was that leading by Pampeluna; and it was not open long, for their fugitive army and their myriads of followers, with baggage, guns, carnages, &c., being all precipitated upon it at the same moment, it got choked up about a mile beyond the town, in the most glorious state of confusion; and the drivers, finding that one pair of legs was worth two pair of wheels, abandoned it all to the victors.

"It is much to be lamented, on those occasions, that the people who contribute most to the victory should profit the least by it; not that I am an advocate for plunder — on the contrary, I would much rather that all our fighting was for pure love; but as everything of value falls into the hands of the followers and scoundrels who skulk from the ranks for the double purpose of plundering and saving their dastardly carcasses, what I regret is that the man who deserts his post should thereby have an opportunity of enriching himself with impunity, while the true man gets nothing; but the evil, I believe, is irremediable. Sir James Kempt, who commanded our brigade, in passing one of the captured waggons in the evening, saw a soldier loading himself with money, and was about to have him conveyed to the camp as a prisoner, when the fellow begged hard to be released, and to be allowed to retain what he had got, telling the general that all the boxes in the waggon were tilled with gold. Sir James, with his usual liberality, immediately adopted the idea of securing it as a reward to his brigade for their gallantry; and, getting a fatigue party, he caused the boxes to be removed to his tent, and ordered an officer and some men from each regiment to parade there next morning to receive their proportions of it; but when they opened the boxes they found them filled with 'hammers, nails, and horse-shoes!'

"As not only the body, but the mind, had been in constant occupation since three o'clock in the morning, circumstances no sooner permitted about ten at night than I threw myself on the ground, and fell into a profound sleep, from which I did not awake until broad daylight, when I found a French soldier squatted near me, intensely watching for the opening of my 'shutters.' He had contrived to conceal himself there during the night; and when he saw that I was awake, he immediately jumped on his legs, and very obsequiously presented me with a map of France, telling me that as there was now a probability of our visiting his native country, he could make himself very useful, and would be glad if I would accept of his services. I thought it unfair, however, to deprive him of the present opportunity of seeing a little more of the world himself; and therefore sent him to join the rest of the prisoners, which would insure him a trip to England, free of expense."

On the rough and shaggy field of the Pyrenees, with its deep and tangled valleys and wind-scourged summits, where Soult was maintaining a gallant and obstinate fight against Wellington, the British endured and achieved much. Kincaid's account of the carrying of the Great Rhune, of the passage of the Bidassoa and of the Nivelle, and of all the fighting which led up to Toulouse, is worth giving:

"November 10, 1813 — Petite La Rhune was allotted to our division as their first point of attack; and, accordingly, on the loth being the day fixed, we moved to our ground at midnight on the 9th. The abrupt ridges in the neighbourhood enabled us to lodge ourselves, unperceived, within half musket-shot of their piquets; and we had left every description of animal behind us in camp, in order that neither the barking of dogs nor the neighing of steeds should give indication of our intentions. Our signal of attack was to be a gun from Sir John Hope, who had now succeeded Sir Thomas Graham in the command of the left wing of the army.

"We stood to our arms at dawn of day, which was soon followed by the signal gun; and each commanding officer, according to previous instructions, led gallantly off to his point of attack. The French must have been, no doubt, astonished to see such an armed force spring out of the ground almost under their noses, but they were nevertheless prepared behind their entrenchments, and caused us some loss in passing the short space between us; but the whole place was carried within the time required to walk over it, and in less than half-an-hour from the commencement of the attack it was in our possession, with all their tents left standing.

"Petite La Rhune was more of an outpost than a part of their position, the latter being a chain of stupendous mountains in its rear; so that, while our battalion followed their skirmishers into the valley between, the remainder of our division were forming for the attack on the mam position and waiting for the co-operation of the other divisions, the thunder of whose artillery, echoing along the valleys, proclaimed that they were engaged far and wide on both sides of us. About midday our division advanced to the grand attack on the most formidable-looking part of the whole of the enemy's position, and, much to our surprise, we carried it with more ease and less loss than the outpost in the morning, a circumstance which we could only account for by supposing that it had been defended by the same troops, and that they did not choose to sustain two hard beatings on the same day. The attack succeeded at every point, and in the evening we had the satisfaction of seeing the left wing of the army marching into St. Jean de Luz."

Barnard, the gallant leader of the Rifles, was shot through the breast when pressing in pursuit of the broken French, who had been driven from the Little Rhune. He fell from his horse, and it was evident that the lung was pierced, for blood and air issued from the wound, while blood ran from the fallen man's mouth. "Do you think I am dying?" asked Barnard coolly of an officer bending over him. "Did you ever see a man so wounded recover?" He was told there were cases of recovery from such a wound. "Then," said Barnard, "if any man can recover, I know that I shall." And he did, his resolve not to die materially helping him to survive. For so much does a cool and strong will count!

Kincaid's account of Toulouse is singularly brief. The Rifles were placed so as to connect Picton's left with the Spaniards under Freire, who were to attack the shoulder of Mont Rave. Thus Kincaid was able to watch, and afterwards describe, the memorable rout of the Spaniards, which forms the most picturesque feature of the battle. The Rifles themselves were engaged in a sharp musketry fire with the convent, and as they advanced a great open sewer had to be crossed and held. The Rifles, according to the regimental record, suffered more from the odours of the sewer than from the bullets of the French:

"We crossed the river, and advanced sufficiently near to the enemy's position to be just out of reach of their fire, where we waited until dispositions were made for the attack.

"On our side of the river the Spanish army, which had never hitherto taken an active part in any of our general actions, now claimed the post of honour, and advanced to storm the strongest part of the heights. Our division was ordered to support them in the low grounds, and at the same time to threaten a point of the canal; and Picton, who was on our right, was ordered to make a false attack on the canal. These were all that were visible to us. The remaining divisions of the army were in continuation to the left.

"The Spaniards, anxious to monopolise all the glory, I rather think, moved on to the attack a little too soon, and before the British divisions, on their left were in readiness to co-operate. However, be that as it may, they were soon in a blaze of fire, and began walking through it at first with a great show of gallantry and determination; but their courage was not altogether screwed up to the sticking-point, and the nearer they came to the critical pass the less prepared they seemed to meet it, until they all finally faced to the right-about, and came back upon us as fast as their heels could carry them, pursued by the enemy.

"We instantly advanced to their relief, and concluded that they would have rallied behind us, but they had no idea of doing anything of the kind, for when with Cuesta and some or the other Spanish generals they had been accustomed, under such circumstances, to run a hundred miles at a time; so that, passing through the intervals of our division, they went clear off to the rear, and we never saw them more. The moment the French found us interpose between them and the Spaniards they retired within their works.

"The only remark that Lord Wellington was said to have made on their conduct, after waiting to see whether they would stand after they got out of the reach of the enemy's shot, was, 'Well, d—n me, if ever I saw ten thousand men run a race before!' How ever, notwithstanding their disaster, many of their officers certainly evinced great bravery, and on their account it is to be regretted that the attack was made so soon, for they would otherwise have carried their point with little loss, either of life or credit, as the British divisions on the left soon after stormed and carried all the other works, and obliged those who had been opposed to the Spaniards to evacuate theirs without firing another shot.

"When the enemy were driven from the heights, they retired within the town, and the canal then became their line of defence, which they maintained the whole of the next day; but in the course of the following night they left the town altogether, and we took possession of it on the morning of the 12th.

"The inhabitants of Toulouse hoisted the white flag, and declared for the Bourbons the moment that the French army had left it; and, in the course of the same day, Colonel Cooke arrived from Paris with the extraordinary news of Napoleon's abdication. Soult has been accused of having been in possession of that fact prior to the battle of Toulouse; but, to disprove such an assertion, it can only be necessary to think, for a moment, whether he would not have made it public the day after the battle, while he yet held possession of the town, as it would not only have enabled him to keep it, but, to those who knew no better, it might have given him a shadow of claim to the victory, if he chose to avail himself of it — and I have known a victory claimed by a French marshal on more slender grounds. In place of knowing it then, he did not even believe it now; and we were absolutely obliged to follow him a day's march beyond Toulouse before he agreed to an armistice."

Chapter Four – The Imminent Deadly Breach

Of the three great and memorable sieges of the Peninsula — Ciudad Rodrigo, Badajos, and San Sebastian — Kincaid took part in the first two, and has left a curiously interesting account of his experiences in them. Wellington's capture of Ciudad Rodrigo was a very swift and dazzling stroke of war. The place was a great frontier fortress; it held vast magazines of warlike material. While in French hands it barred Wellington's advance into Spain. If captured, it would furnish a secure base for such an advance.

Marmont and Soult, each in command of an army stronger than that under Wellington, kept watch over the great fortress. To pluck it from their very hands would have been judged beforehand an impossible thing. Yet Wellington did it! He achieved the feat by a combination of secrecy, audacity, and speed rarely excelled in war. He hid his preparations beneath a veil of profoundest silence and mystery. Then, when his foes had been thrown completely off their guard, he leaped on the doomed fortress; and almost before the thunder of his guns had reached the ears of Soult and of Marmont the fortress was lost! Wellington had everything against him. His supplies were scanty, his siege train miserable. The weather was bitter, and rains incessant, the ground rocky. Yet the siege never faltered nor paused. Wellington broke ground on January 8; he stormed the city on January 19. Never was a great warlike operation conceived more subtly, or executed with greater fire and swiftness.

Kincaid has a special right to tell the tale of this siege. He shared in the hardships of the trenches, and led the storming party at one of the breaches.

"January 8, 1812. — The campaign of 1812 commenced with the siege of Ciudad Rodrigo, which was invested by our division on the 8th of January.

"There was a smartish frost, with some snow on the ground, and, when we arrived opposite the fortress, about midday, the garrison did not appear to think that we were in earnest, for a number of their officers came out, under the shelter of a stone wall, within half musket-shot, and amused themselves in saluting and bowing to us in ridicule; but, ere the day was done, some of them had occasion to wear the laugh on the opposite side of the countenance.

"We lay by our arms until dark, when a party, consisting of a hundred volunteers from each regiment, under Colonel Colborne of the 52nd, stormed and carried the Fort of St. Francisco, after a short, sharp action, in which the whole of its garrison were taken or destroyed. The officer who commanded it was a chattering little fellow, and acknowledged himself to have been one of our saluting friends of the morning. He kept incessantly repeating a few words of English which he had picked up during the assault, and the only ones, I fancy, that were spoken, viz., 'dem eyes, b—t eyes!' and, in demanding the meaning of them, he required that we should also explain why we stormed a place without first besieging it; for, he said, that another officer would have relieved him of his charge at daylight, had we not relieved him of it sooner.

"The enemy had calculated that this outwork would have kept us at bay for a fortnight or three weeks; whereas its capture the first night enabled us to break ground at once, within breaching distance of the walls of the town. They kept up a very heavy fire the whole night on the working parties; but, as they aimed at random, we did not suffer much, and made such good use of our time that, when daylight enabled them to see what we were doing, we had dug ourselves under tolerable cover.

"In addition to ours, the first, third, and fourth divisions were employed in the siege. Each took the duties for twenty-four hours alternately, and returned to their cantonments during the interval. We were relieved by the first division, under Sir Thomas Graham, on the morning of the 9th, and marched to our quarters.

"January 12 — At ten o'clock this morning we resumed the duties of the siege. It still continued to be dry, frosty weather; and, as we were obliged to ford the Agueda, up to the middle, every man carried a pair of iced breeches into the trenches with him.

"My turn of duty did not arrive until eight in the morning, when I was ordered to take thirty men with shovels to dig holes for ourselves, as near as possible to the walls, for the delectable amusement of firing at the embrasures for the remainder of the night. The enemy threw frequent fire-balls among us, to see where we were; but, as we always lay snug until their blaze was extinguished, they were not much the wiser, except by finding, from having some one popped off from their guns every instant, that they had got some neighbours whom they would have been glad to get rid of. We were relieved as usual at ten next morning, and returned to our cantonments.

"January 16 — Entered on our third day's duty, and found the breaching batteries in full operation, and our approaches close to the walls on every side. When we arrived on the ground I was sent to take command of the Highland company which we had at that time in the regiment, and which was with the left wing, under Colonel Cameron. I found them on piquet, between the right of the trenches and the river, half of them posted at a mud cottage and the other half in a ruined convent close under the walls. It was a very tolerable post when at it; but it is no joke travelling by daylight up to within a stone's throw of a wall on which there is a parcel of fellows who have no other amusement but to fire at everybody they see.

"We could not show our noses at any point without being fired at; but, as we were merely posted there to protect the right flank of the trenches from any sortie, we did not fire at them, and kept as quiet as could be, considering the deadly blast that was blowing around us. There are few situations in life where something cannot be learnt, and I myself stand indebted to my twenty-four hours' residence there for a more correct knowledge of martial sounds than in the study of my whole lifetime besides. They must be an unmusical pair of ears that cannot inform the wearer whether a cannon or a musket played last, but the various notes, emanating from their respective mouths, admit of nice distinctions. My party was too small and too well sheltered to repay the enemy for the expense of shells and round shot; but the quantity of grape and musketry aimed at our particular heads made a good concert of first and second whistles, while the more sonorous voice of the round shot, travelling to our friends on the left, acted as a thorough bass; and there was not a shell, that passed over us to the trenches, that did not send back a fragment among us as soon as it burst, as if to gratify a curiosity that I was far from expressing.

"Everything is by comparison in this world, and it is curious to observe how men's feelings change with circumstances. In cool blood a man would rather go a little out of his way than expose himself to unnecessary danger; but we found, this morning, that by crossing the river where we then were and running the gantlet for a mile exposed to the fire of two pieces of artillery, that we should be saved the distance of two or three miles in returning to our quarters. After coming out of such a furnace as we had been frying in, the other fire was not considered a fire at all, and passed without a moment's hesitation.

"January 19, 1812 — We moved to the scene of operations about two o'clock this afternoon; and, as it was a day before our regular turn, we concluded that we were called there to lend a hand in finishing the job we had begun so well. Nor were we disappointed, for we found that two practicable breaches had been effected, and that the place was to be stormed in the evening by the third and light divisions, the former by the right breach, and the latter by the left, while some Portuguese troops were to attempt an escalade on the opposite sides of the town.

"About eight o'clock in the evening our division was accordingly formed for the assault, behind a convent, near the left breach.

"At a given signal the different columns advanced to the assault; the night was tolerably clear, and the enemy evidently expected us, for as soon as we turned the corner of the convent wall, the space between us and the breach became one blaze of light with their fireballs, which, while they lighted us on to glory, lightened not a few of their lives and limbs; for the whole glacis was in consequence swept by a well-directed fire of grape and musketry, and they are the devil's own brooms; but our gallant fellows walked through it to the point of attack, with the most determined steadiness, excepting the Portuguese sack-bearers, most of whom lay down behind their bags, to wait the result, while the few that were thrown into the ditch looked so like dead bodies, that, when I leapt into it, I tried to avoid them.

"The advantage of being on a storming party is considered as giving the prior claim to be 'put out of pain,' for they receive the first fire, which is generally the best, not to mention that they are also expected to receive the earliest salutations from the beams of timber, hand-grenades, and other missiles which the garrison are generally prepared to transfer from the top of the wall, to the tops of the heads of their foremost visitors. But I cannot say that I myself experienced any such preference, for every ball has a considerable distance to travel, and I have generally found them equally ready to pick up their man at the end as at the beginning of their flight.

"We had some difficulty at first in finding the breach, as we had entered the ditch opposite to a ravelin, which we mistook for a bastion. I tried first one side of it and then the other, and seeing one corner of it a good deal battered, with a ladder placed against it, I concluded that it must be the breach, and calling to the soldiers near me to follow, I mounted with the most ferocious intent, carrying a sword in one hand and a pistol in the other; but, when I got up, I found nobody to fight with, except two of our own men, who were already laid dead across the top of the ladder. I saw in a moment that I had got into the wrong box, and was about to descend again, when I heard a shout from the opposite side that the breach was there; and, moving in that direction, I dropped myself from the ravelin, and landed in the ditch, opposite to the foot of the breach, where I found the head of the storming party just beginning to fight their way into it. The combat was of short duration, and, in less than half-an-hour from the commencement of the attack, the place was in our possession.

"After carrying the breach, we met with no further opposition, and moved round the ramparts to see that they were perfectly clear of the enemy, previous to entering the town. I was fortunate enough to take the left-hand circuit, by accident, and thereby escape the fate which befell a great portion of those who went to the right, and who were blown up, along with some of the third division, by the accidental explosion of a magazine.

"I was highly amused, in moving round the ramparts, to find some of the Portuguese troops just commencing their escalade, on the opposite side near the bridge, in ignorance of the place having already fallen. Gallantly headed by their officers, they had got some ladders placed against the wall, while about two thousand voices from the rear were cheering with all their might for mutual encouragement; and, like most other troops under similar circumstances, it appeared to me that their feet and their tongues went at a more equal pace after we gave them the hint. On going a little farther we came opposite to the ravelin which had been my chief annoyance during my last day's piquet. It was still crowded by the enemy, who had now thrown down their arms and endeavoured to excite our pity by virtue of their being 'Pauvres Italianos'; but our men had somehow imbibed a horrible antipathy to the Italians, and every appeal they made in that name was invariably answered with: 'You're Italians, are you? then d—n you, here's a shot for you'; and the action instantly followed the word.

"We continued our course round the ramparts until we met the head of the column which had gone by the right, and then descended into the town. At the entrance of the first street, a French officer came out of a door and claimed my protection, giving me his sword. He told me that there was another officer in the same house who was afraid to venture out, and entreated that I would go in for him. I, accordingly, followed him up to the landing-place of a dark stair, and, while he was calling to his friend by name to come down 'as there was an English officer present who would protect him,' a violent screaming broke through a door at my elbow. I pushed it open, and found the landlady struggling with an English soldier, whom I immediately transferred to the bottom of the stair head foremost. The French officer had followed me in at the door, and was so astonished at all he saw, that he held up his hands, turned up the whites of his eyes, and resolved himself into a state of most eloquent silence.

"As the other officer could not be found, I descended into the street again with my prisoner; and, finding the current of soldiers setting towards the centre of the town, I followed the stream, which conducted me into the great square, on one side of which the late garrison were drawn up as prisoners, and the rest of it was filled with British and Portuguese intermixed without any order or regularity. I had been there but a very short time, when they all commenced firing, without any ostensible cause; some fired in at the doors and windows, some at the roofs of houses, and others at the clouds; and at last some heads began to be blown from their shoulders in the general hurricane, when the voice of Sir Thomas Picton, with the power of twenty trumpets, began to proclaim damnation to everybody, while Colonel Barnard, Colonel Cameron, and some other active officers, were carrying it into effect with a strong hand; for seizing the broken barrels of muskets which were lying about in great abundance, they belaboured every fellow most unmercifully about the head who attempted either to load or fire, and finally succeeded in reducing them to order. In the midst of the scuffle, however, three of the houses in the square were set on fire; and the confusion was such that nothing could be done to save them; but, by the extraordinary exertions of Colonel Barnard during the whole of the night, the flames were prevented from communicating to the adjoining buildings.

"We succeeded in getting a great portion of our battalion together by one o'clock in the morning, and withdrew with them to the ramparts, where we lay by our arms until daylight.

"There is nothing in this life half so enviable as the feelings of a soldier after a victory. Previous to a battle there is a certain sort of something that pervades the mind which is not easily denied; it is neither akin to joy or fear, and, probably, anxiety may be nearer to it than any other word in the dictionary; but, when the battle is over, and crowned with victory, he finds himself elevated for a while into the regions of absolute bliss! It had ever been the summit of my ambition to attain a post at the head of a storming party — my wish had now been accomplished and gloriously ended; and I do think that, after all was over, and our men laid asleep on the ramparts, that I strutted about as important a personage, in my own opinion, as ever trod the face of the earth; and, had the ghost of the renowned Jack-the-Giant-Killer itself passed that way at the time, I venture to say that I would have given it a kick in the breech without the smallest ceremony. But, as the sun began to rise, I began to fall from the heroics; and, when he showed his face, I took a look at my own and found that I was too unclean a spirit to worship, for I was covered with mud and dirt, with the greater part of my dress torn to rags.

"The fifth division, which had not been employed in the siege, marched in and took charge of the town on the morning of the 20th, and we prepared to return to our cantonments. Lord Wellington happened to be riding in at the gate at the time that we were marching out, and had the curiosity to ask the officer of the leading company what regiment it was; for there was scarcely a vestige of uniform among the men, some of whom were dressed in Frenchmen's coats, some in white breeches and huge jack-boots, some with cocked hats and queues; most of their swords were fixed on the rifles, and stuck full of hams, tongues, and loaves of bread, and not a few were carrying bird-cages! There never was a better masked corps!

"Among other things carried from Ciudad Rodrigo, one of our men had the misfortune to carry his death in his hands, under the mistaken shape of amusement. He thought that it was a cannonball, and took it for the purpose of playing at the game of nine-holes, but it happened to be a live shell. In rolling it along it went over a bed of burning ashes, and ignited without his observing it. Just as he had got it between his legs, and was in the act of discharging it a second time, it exploded, and nearly blew him to pieces."

The story of the siege of Badajos is darker and more tragical than that of the capture of Ciudad Rodrigo. The defences of Badajos were much more formidable than those of the sister fortress, the garrison was more numerous, the defence more stubborn and skilful. Phillipon, the commander of the assailed city, has, indeed, won enduring fame by the skill and valour of his defence. Yet the siege only lasted twenty days. It was begun on March 16; on April 6 the city was stormed. It was carried by a night assault; but the breaches were imperfect, and the art of Phillipon had made the Great Breach practically impregnable. But the fierce and unquailing valour with which the British stormers flung themselves on the breaches, and died on their rough and blood-splashed slopes, makes one of the most thrilling stories in the history of war. All the attacks on the breeches failed; but Picton carried the castle by escalcade, and Leith forced his way over the bastion of St. Vincent, where no breach existed, and where the scarp was thirty feet high; and so the town was carried. It was one of the Rifles of whom Napier tells the story, that in his resolution to win, he thrust himself beneath the chained swordblades at the summit of the Great Breach, and there suffered the enemy to dash his head to pieces with the ends of their muskets. Of Major O'Hare, who led the stormers of the Rifles, a grim story is told. As his men were moving off in the darkness he shook hands with a brother officer, and said: 'A Lieutenant-Colonel or cold meat in a few hours.' He fell, shot dead on the breach itself ten minutes afterwards.

As Kincaid led one of the storming parties at Ciudad Rodrigo, a lighter part was assigned to him at Badajos. He commanded a strong party whose business it was to line the glacis and keep down the fire from the ramparts. He tells the tale briefly:

"On the 17th of March 1812, the third, fourth, and light divisions encamped around Badajos, embracing the whole of the inland side of the town on the left bank of the Guadiana, and commenced breaking ground before it immediately after dark the same night.

"The elements on this occasion adopted the cause of the besieged, for we had scarcely taken up our ground when a heavy rain commenced, and continued, almost without intermission, for a fortnight; in consequence thereof the pontoon bridge, connecting us with our supplies from Elvas, was carried away by the rapid increase of the river, and the duties of the trenches were otherwise rendered extremely harassing. We had a smaller force employed than at Rodrigo, and the scale of operations was so much greater that it required every man to be actually in the trenches six hours every day, and the same length of time every night, which, with the time required to march to and from them, through fields more than ankle-deep in a stiff mud, left us never more than eight hours out of the twenty-four in camp, and we never were dry the whole time.

"One day's trench work is as like another as the days themselves, and like nothing better than serving an apprenticeship to the double calling of gravedigger and gamekeeper, for we found ample employment both for the spade and the rifle.

"The Portuguese artillery, under British officers, was uncommonly good. I used to be much amused in looking at a twelve-gun breaching-battery of theirs. They knew the position of all the enemy's guns which could bear upon them, and had one man posted to watch them, to give notice of what was coming, whether a shot or a shell, who accordingly kept calling out, 'Bomba, balla, balla, bomba,' and they ducked their heads until the missile passed; but sometimes he would see a general discharge from all arms, when he threw himself down, screaming out, 'Jesus, todos, todos!' meaning 'everything.'

"An officer of ours was sent one morning before daylight with ten men to dig holes for themselves opposite to one of the enemy's guns which had been doing a great deal of mischief the day before, and he had soon the satisfaction of knowing the effect of his practice by seeing them stopping up the embrasure with sand-bags. After waiting a little he saw them beginning to remove the bags, when he made his men open upon it again, and they were instantly replaced without the guns being fired. Presently he saw the huge cocked hat of a French officer make its appearance on the rampart near the embrasure, but knowing by experience that the head was somewhere in the neighbourhood, he watched until the flash of a musket through the long grass showed the position of the owner, and calling one of his best shots, he desired him to take deliberate aim at the spot, and lent his shoulder as a rest to give it more elevation. Bang went the shot, and it was the finishing flash for the Frenchman, for they saw no more of him, although his cocked hat maintained its post until dark.

"In proportion as the grand crisis approached, the anxiety of the soldiers increased, not on account of any doubt or dread as to the result, but for fear that the place should be surrendered without standing an assault; for, singular as it may appear, although there was a certainty of about one man out of every three being knocked down, there were, perhaps, not three men in the three divisions who would not rather have braved all the chances than receive it tamely from the hands of the enemy. So great was the rage for passports into eternity in our battalion on that occasion that even the officers' servants insisted on taking their places in the ranks, and I was obliged to leave my baggage in charge of a man who had been wounded some days before.

"On the 6th of April three practicable breaches had been effected, and arrangements were made for assaulting the town that night: the third division by escalade at the castle, a brigade of the fifth division by escalade at the opposite side of the town, while the fourth and light divisions were to storm the breaches. The whole were ordered to be formed for the attack at eight o'clock.

"April 6, 1812 — Our division formed for the attack of the left breach in the same order as at Ciudad Rodrigo. The command of it had now devolved upon our commandant, Colonel Barnard. I was then the acting adjutant of four companies, under Colonel Cameron, who were to line the crest of the glacis, and to fire at the ramparts and the top of the left breach.

"The enemy seemed aware of our intentions. The fire of artillery and musketry, which for three weeks before had been incessant, both from the town and trenches, had now entirely ceased as if by mutual consent, and a death-like silence of nearly an hour preceded the awful scene of carnage.

"The signal to advance was made about nine o'clock, and our four companies led the way. Colonel Cameron and myself had reconnoitred the ground so accurately by daylight that we succeeded in bringing the head of our column to the very spot agreed on, opposite to the left breach, and then formed line to the left without a word being spoken, each man lying down as he got into line, with the muzzle of his rifle over the edge of the ditch, between the palisades, all ready to open. It was tolerably clear above, and we distinctly saw their heads lining the ramparts, but there was a sort of haze on the ground which, with the colour of our dress, prevented them from seeing us, although only a few yards asunder. One of their sentries, however, challenged us twice, "Qui vive," and, receiving no reply, he fired off his musket, which was followed by their drums beating to arms; but we still remained perfectly quiet, and all was silence again for the space of five or ten minutes, when the head of the forlorn hope at length came up, and we took advantage of the first fire while the enemy's heads were yet visible.

"The scene that ensued furnished as respectable a representation of hell itself as fire and sword and human sacrifices could make it, for in one instant every engine of destruction was in full operation. It is in vain to attempt a description of it. We were entirely excluded from the right breach by an inundation which the heavy rains had enabled the enemy to form, and the two others were rendered totally impracticable by their interior defences.

"The five succeeding hours were therefore passed in the most gallant and hopeless attempts on the part of individual officers, forming up fifty or a hundred men at a time at the foot of the breach, and endeavouring to carry it by desperate bravery; and, fatal as it proved to each gallant band in succession, yet, fast as one dissolved, another was formed. We were informed about twelve at night that the third division had established themselves in the castle; but as its situation and construction did not permit them to extend their operations beyond it at the moment, it did not in the least affect our opponents at the breach, whose defence continued as obstinate as ever.

"I was near Colonel Barnard after midnight, when he received repeated messages from Lord Wellington to withdraw from the breach and to form the division for a renewal of the attack at daylight; but as fresh attempts continued to be made, and the troops were still pressing forward into the ditch, it went against his gallant soul to order a retreat while yet a chance remained; but after heading repeated attempts himself, he saw that it was hopeless, and the order was reluctantly given about two o'clock in the morning. We fell back about three hundred yards, and re-formed all that remained to us.

"Our regiment alone had to lament the loss of twenty-two officers killed and wounded, ten of whom were killed, or afterwards died of their wounds. We had scarcely got our men together when we were informed of the success of the fifth division in their escalade, and that the enemy were, in consequence, abandoning the breaches, and we were immediately ordered forward to take possession of them. On our arrival we found them entirely evacuated, and had not occasion to fire another shot; but we found the utmost difficulty and even danger in getting in in the dark, even without opposition. As soon as we succeeded in establishing our battalion inside, we sent piquets into the different streets and lanes leading from the breach, and kept the remainder in hand until day should throw some light on our situation.

"When I was in the act of posting one of the piquets a man of ours brought me a prisoner, telling me that he was the governor; but the other immediately said that he had only called himself so the better to ensure his protection, and then added that he was the colonel of one of the French regiments, and that all his surviving officers were assembled at his quarters, in a street close by, and would surrender themselves to any officer who would go with him for that purpose. I accordingly took two or three men with me, and, accompanying him there, found fifteen or sixteen of them assembled, and all seeming very much surprised at the unexpected termination of the siege. They could not comprehend under what circumstances the town had been lost, and repeatedly asked me how I had got in; but I did not choose to explain further than simply telling them that I had entered at the breach, coupling the information with a look which was calculated to convey somewhat more than I knew myself; for, in truth, when I began to recollect that a few minutes before had seen me retiring from the breach under a fanciful overload of degradation, I thought that I had now as good a right as any man to be astonished at finding myself lording it over the officers of a French battalion; nor was I much wiser than they were as to the manner of its accomplishment.

"They were all very much dejected, excepting their major, who was a big, jolly-looking Dutchman, with medals enough on his left breast to have furnished the window of a tolerable toy-shop. His accomplishments were after the manner of Captain Dugald Dalgetty; and while he cracked his joke he was not inattentive to the cracking of the corks from the many wine bottles which his colonel placed on the table successively, along with some cold meat, for general refreshment, prior to marching into captivity, and which I, though a free man, was not too proud to join them in.

"When I had allowed their chief a reasonable time to secure what valuables he wished about his person, he told me that he had two horses in the stable, which, as he would no longer be permitted to keep, he recommended me to take; and as a horse is the only thing on such occasions that an officer can permit himself to consider a legal prize, I caused one of them to be saddled, and his handsome black mare thereby became my charger during the remainder of the war.

"In proceeding with my prisoners towards the breach I took, by mistake, a different road to that I came; and as numbers of Frenchmen were lurking about for a safe opportunity of surrendering themselves, about a hundred additional ones added themselves to my column as we moved along, jabbering their native dialect so loudly as nearly to occasion a dire catastrophe, as it prevented me from hearing some one challenge in my front; but, fortunately, it was repeated and I instantly answered; for Colonel Barnard and Sir Colin Campbell had a piquet of our men drawn across the street on the point of sending a volley into us, thinking that we were a rallied body of the enemy.

"The whole of the garrison were marched off as prisoners to Elvas, about ten o'clock in the morning, and our men were then permitted to fall out to enjoy themselves for the remainder of the day, as a reward for having kept together so long as they were wanted. The whole of the three divisions were by this time loose in the town, and the usual frightful scene of plunder commenced, which the officers thought it necessary to avoid for the moment by retiring to the camp.

"We went into the town on the morning of the 8th to endeavour to collect our men, but only succeeded in part, as the same extraordinary scene of plunder and rioting still continued. Wherever there was anything to eat or drink, the only saleable commodities, the soldiers had turned the shopkeepers out of doors and placed themselves regularly behind the counter, selling off the contents of the shop. By-and-by another and a stronger party would kick those out in their turn, and there was no end to the succession of self-elected shopkeepers, until Lord Wellington found that to restore order severe measures must be resorted to. On the third day he caused a Portuguese brigade to be marched in and kept standing to their arms in the great square, where the provost-marshal erected a gallows and proceeded to suspend a few of the delinquents, which very quickly cleared the town of the remainder, and enabled us to give a more satisfactory account of our battalion than we had hitherto been able to do.

"The third day after the fall of the town, I rode, with Colonel Cameron, to take a bathe in the Guadiana, and, in passing the verge of the camp of the fifth division, we saw two soldiers standing at the door of a small shed, or outhouse, shouting, waving their caps, and making signs that they wanted to speak to us. We rode up to see what they wanted, and found that the poor fellows had each lost a leg. They told us that a surgeon had dressed their wounds on the night of the assault, but that they had ever since been without food or assistance of any Kind, although they, each day, had opportunities of soliciting the aid of many of their comrades, from whom they could obtain nothing but promises. In short, surrounded by thousands of their countrymen within call, and not more than three hundred yards from their own regiment, they were unable to interest any one in their behalf, and they were literally starving. It is unnecessary to say that we instantly galloped back to camp and had them removed to the hospital.

"On the morning of the 7th, when some of our officers were performing the last duties to their fallen comrades, one of them had collected the bodies of four young officers who had been slain. He was in the act of digging a grave for them, when an officer of the Guards arrived on the spot, from a distant division of the army, and demanded tidings of his brother, who was at that moment lying a naked lifeless corpse under his very eyes. The officer had the presence of mind to see that the corpse was not recognised, and, wishing to spare the other's feelings, told him that his brother was dangerously wounded, but he would hear more of him by going out to the camp; and thither the other immediately bent his steps, with a seeming presentiment of the sad intelligence that awaited him."

One curious incident in the siege of Badajos may be related. The day after the assault two Spanish ladies, the younger a beautiful girl of fourteen, appealed for help to two officers of the Rifles, who were passing through one of the streets of the town. Their dress was torn, their ears, from which rings had been roughly snatched, were bleeding, and to escape outrage or death they cast themselves on the protection of the first British officers they met. One of the officers was Captain Harry Smith of the Rifles. Two years later he married the girl he had saved in a scene so wild. Captain Harry Smith, in after years, served at the Cape as Sir Harry, and this Spanish girl, as Lady Smith, gave her name to the historic town which Sir George White defended with such stubborn valour. The two great sieges of Badajos and of Ladysmith are separated from each other by nearly a century; but there exists this interesting human link betwixt them.

Chapter Five – In the Pyrenees

The great battles and sieges, of course, arrest the attention of the historian, and their tale has been told over and over again. But what may be called the unrecorded marches and skirmishes of the campaign have genuine interest; and Kincaid, as we have seen, describes these with great vividness. Another set of such pictures is supplied by the campaign in the Pyrenees, where the soldiers marched and fought in wild and sunless ravines, on the wild-blown crests of mighty hills, or in deep and roadless valleys. Here are some of Kincaid's Pyrenean reminiscences. The month is July 1813. Wellington is pushing the broken French back through the hill passes towards the French frontiers:

"We advanced along the banks of the Bidassoa, through a succession of beautiful little fertile valleys, thickly studded with clean, respectable-looking farmhouses and little villages, and bounded by stupendous, picturesque, and well-wooded mountains, until we came to the hill next to the village of Bera, which we found occupied by a small force of the enemy, who, after receiving a few shots from our people, retired through the village into their position behind it. Our line of demarcation was then clearly seen. The mountain which the French army occupied was the last ridge of the Pyrenees; and their sentries stood on the face of it, within pistol-shot of the village of Bera, which now became the advanced post of our division. The left wing of the army, under Sir Thomas Graham, now commenced the siege of St. Sebastian; and as Lord Wellington had, at the same time, to cover both that and the blockade of Pampeluna, our army occupied an extended position of many miles.

"Marshal Soult having succeeded to the command of the French army, and finding, towards the end of July, that St. Sebastian was about to be stormed, and that the garrison of Pampeluna were beginning to get on short allowance, he determined on making a bold push for the relief of both places; and, assembling the whole of his army, he forced the pass of Maya, and advanced rapidly upon Pampeluna. Lord Wellington was never to be caught napping. His army occupied too extended a position to offer effectual resistance at any of their advanced posts; but, by the time that Marshal Soult had worked his way to the last ridge of the Pyrenees, and within sight of 'the haven of his wishes,' he found his lordship waiting for him, with four divisions of the army, who treated him to one of the most signal and sanguinary defeats that he ever experienced.

"Our division during the important movements on our right was employed in keeping up the communication between the troops under the immediate command of Lord Wellington and those under Sir Thomas Graham, at St. Sebastian. We retired, the first day, to the mountains behind Le Secca; and, just as we were about to lie down for the night, we were again ordered under arms, and continued our retreat in utter darkness, through a mountain path, where, in many places, a false step might have rolled a fellow as far as the other world. The consequence was, that, although we were kept on our legs during the whole of the night, we found, when daylight broke, that the tail of the column had not got a quarter of a mile from their starting-post. On a good broad road it is all very well, but on a narrow, bad road a night march is like a nightmare, harassing a man to no purpose.

"On the 26th, we occupied a ridge of mountain near enough to hear the battle, though not in a situation to sec it; and remained the whole of the day in the greatest torture for want of news. About midnight we heard the joyful tidings of the enemy's defeat, with the loss of four thousand prisoners. Our division proceeded in pursuit at daylight on the following morning. We moved rapidly by the same road on which we had retired; and, after a forced march, found ourselves, when near sunset, on the flank of their retiring column on the Bidassoa, near the bridge of Janca, and immediately proceeded to business.

"The sight of a Frenchman always acted like a cordial on the spirits of a rifleman; and the fatigues of the day were forgotten, as our three battalions extended among the brushwood, and went down to 'knock the dust out of their hairy knapsacks,'[1] as our men were in the habit of expressing themselves; but, in place of knocking the dust out of them, I believe that most of their knapsacks were knocked in the dust; for the greater part of those who were not floored along with their knapsacks, shook them oft', by way of enabling the owner to make a smarter

---

[1] The French knapsack is made of unshorn goatskin.

scramble across that portion of the road on which our leaden shower was pouring; and, foes as they were, it was impossible not to feel a degree of pity for their situation; pressed by an enemy in the rear, an inaccessible mountain on their right, and a river on their left, lined by an invisible foe, from whom there was no escape but the desperate one of running the gantlet.

"We advanced next morning, and occupied our former post at Bera. The enemy still continued to hold the mountain of Echelar, which, as it rose out of the right end of our ridge, was, properly speaking, a part of our property, and we concluded that a sense of justice would have induced them to leave it of their own accord in the course of the day; but, when towards the afternoon, they showed no symptoms of quitting, our division, leaving their kettles on the fire, proceeded to eject them. As we approached the mountain, the peak of it caught a passing cloud, that gradually descended in a thick fog and excluded them from our view. Our three battalions, however, having been let loose, under Colonel Barnard, we soon made ourselves 'Children of the Mist'; and, guided to our opponents by the whistling of their balls, made them descend from their 'high estate'; and, handing them across the valley into their own position, we then retired to ours, where we found our tables ready spread, and a comfortable dinner waiting for us.

"This was one of the most gentleman-like day's fighting that I ever experienced, although we had to lament the vacant seats of one or two of our messmates.

"August 22 — I narrowly escaped being taken prisoner this morning, very foolishly. A division of Spaniards occupied the ground to our left, beyond the Bidassoa; and having mounted my horse to take a look at their post, I passed through a small village, and then got on a rugged path winding along the edge of the river, where I expected to find their outposts. The river at that place was not above knee-deep, and about ten or twelve yards across; and though I saw a number of soldiers gathering chestnuts from a row of trees which lined the opposite bank, I concluded that they were Spaniards, and kept moving onwards; but, observing at last, that I was an object of greater curiosity than I ought to be to people who had been in the daily habit of seeing the uniform, it induced me to take a more particular look at my neighbours, when, to my consternation, I saw the French eagle ornamenting the front of every cap. I instantly wheeled my horse to the right about; and seeing that I had a full quarter of a mile to traverse at a walk, before I could get clear of them, I began to whistle, with as much unconcern as I could muster, while my eye was searching like lightning for the means of escape in the event of their trying to cut me off. I had soon the satisfaction of observing that none of them had firelocks, which reduced my capture to the chances of a race! For, though the hill on my right was inaccessible to a horseman, it was not so to a dismounted Scotchman; and I therefore determined, in case of necessity, to abandon my horse, and show them what I could do on my own bottom at a pinch. Fortunately they did not attempt it; and I could scarcely credit my good luck when I found myself once more in my own tent."

No fighting in the whole Peninsular campaign was more stubborn than that which took place in the Pyrenees towards the close of 1813. Soult showed great skill and audacity as a general. He was fighting to keep the invader's foot from profaning the "sacred" soil of France, and his genius shines at its brightest in the combats fought in the wild country betwixt San Sebastian and Bayonne. But Wellington's troops were veterans, flushed with victory and full of pride in themselves and confidence in their leader; and they were irresistible. One or two of Kincaid's sketches of fighting in the Pyrenees may be given:

"The ensuing month passed by without producing the slightest novelty, and we began to get heartily tired of our situation. Our souls, in fact, were strung for war, and peace afforded no enjoyment, unless the place did, and there was none to be found in a valley of the Pyrenees, which the ravages of contending armies had reduced to a desert. The labours of the French on the opposite mountain had, in the first instance, been confined to fortification; but, as the season advanced, they seemed to think that the branch of a tree, or a sheet of canvas, was too slender a barrier between them and a frosty night, and their fortified camp was gradually becoming a fortified town of regular brick, and mortar. Though we were living under the influence of the same sky, we did not think it necessary to give ourselves the same trouble, but reasoned on their proceedings like philosophers, and calculated, from the aspect of the times, that there was a probability of a speedy transfer of property, and that it might still be reserved for us to give their town a name; nor were we disappointed. Late on the night of the 7th of October, Colonel

Barnard arrived from headquarters with the intelligence that the next was to be the day of trial. Accordingly, on the morning of the 8th, the fourth division came up to support us, and we immediately marched down to the foot of the enemy's position, shook off our knapsacks before their faces, and went at them.

"The action commenced by five companies of our third battalion advancing, under Colonel Ross, to dislodge the enemy from a hill which they occupied in front of their entrenchments; and there never was a movement more beautifully executed, for they walked quietly and steadily up, and swept them regularly off without firing a single shot until the enemy had turned their backs, when they then served them out with a most destructive discharge. The movement excited the admiration of all who witnessed it, and added another laurel to the already crowded wreath which adorned the name of that distinguished officer.

"At the first look of the enemy's position it appeared as if our brigade had got the most difficult task to perform; but as the capture of this hill showed us a way round the flank of their entrenchments, we carried one after the other until we finally gained the summit, with very little loss. Our second brigade, however, were obliged to take 'the bull by the horns' on their side, and suffered more severely; but they rushed at everything with a determination that defied resistance, carrying redoubt after redoubt at the point of the bayonet, until they finally joined us on the summit of the mountain, with three hundred prisoners in their possession.

"We now found ourselves firmly established within the French territory, with a prospect before us that was truly refreshing, considering that we had not seen the sea for three years, and that our views for months had been confined to fogs and the peaks of mountains. On our left the Bay of Biscay lay extended as far as the horizon, while several of our ships of war were seen sporting upon her bosom. Beneath us lay the pretty little town of St. Jean de Luz, which looked as if it had just been framed out of the Liliputian scenery of a toyshop. The town of Bayonne, too, was visible in the distance, and the view to the right embraced a beautiful, well-wooded country, thickly studded with towns and villages, as far as the eye could reach.

"On the morning of the 9th we turned out as usual an hour before daylight. The sound of musketry to our right in our own hemisphere announced that the French and Spaniards had resumed their unfinished argument of last night relative to the occupation of La Rhune; while at the same time 'from our throne of clouds' we had an opportunity of contemplating, with some astonishment, the proceedings of the nether world. A French ship of war, considering St. Jean de Luz no longer a free port, had endeavoured, under cover of the night, to steal alongshore to Bayonne, and when daylight broke they had an opportunity of seeing that they were not only within sight of their port, but within sight of a British gun-brig, and if they entertained any doubts as to which of the two was nearest, their minds were quickly relieved on that point by finding that they were not within reach of their port, and strictly within reach of the guns of the brig, while two British frigates were bearing down with a press of canvas. The Frenchman returned a few broadsides. He was double the size of the one opposed to him, but, conceiving his case to be hopeless, he at length set fire to the ship and took to his boats. We watched the progress of the flames, until she finally blew up and disappeared in a column of smoke. The boats of our gun-brig were afterwards seen employed in picking up the odds and ends.

"The French, after leaving La Rhune, established their advanced post on Petite La Rhune, a mountain that stood as high as most of its neighbours; but, as its name betokens, it was but a child to its gigantic namesake, of which it seemed as if it had at a former period formed a part; but having been shaken off like a useless galoche, it now stood gaping, open-mouthed, at the place it had left (and which had now become our advanced post), while the enemy proceeded to furnish its jaws with a set of teeth, or, in other words, to face it with breastworks, &c., a measure which they invariably had recourse to in every new position.

"Encamped on the face of La Rhune, we remained a whole month idle spectators of their preparations, and dearly longing for the day that should afford us an opportunity of penetrating into the more hospitable-looking low country beyond them; for the weather had become excessively cold, and our camp stood exposed to the utmost fury of the almost nightly tempest. Oft have I in the middle of the night awoke from a sound sleep and found my tent on the point of disappearing in the air like a balloon, and, leaving my warm blankets, been obliged to snatch the mallet and rush out in the midst of a hailstorm to peg it down. I think that

I now see myself looking like one of those gay creatures of the elements who dwelt, as Shakespeare has it, among the rainbows!

"By way of contributing to the warmth of my tent, I dug a hole inside, which I arranged as a fireplace, carrying the smoke underneath the walls, and building a turf-chimney outside. I was not long in proving the experiment, and, finding that it went exceedingly well, I was not a little vain of the invention. However, it came on to rain very hard while I was dining at a neighbouring tent, and on my return to my own I found the fire not only extinguished, but a fountain playing from the same place up to the roof, watering my bea and baggage, and all sides of it, most refreshingly.

"It is very singular that, notwithstanding our exposure to all the severities of the worst of weather, we tad not a single sick man in the battalion while we remained there."

To this period belongs the stern fighting near Bayonne betwixt December 9 and 13, 1813.

"We turned out at daylight on the 10th, but as there was a thick drizzling rain which prevented us from seeing anything, we soon turned in again. My servant soon after came to tell me that Sir Lowry Cole and some of his staff had just ascended to the top of the chateau, a piece of information which did not quite please me, for I fancied that the general had just discovered our quarter to be better than his own, and had come for the purpose of taking possession of it. However, in less than five minutes we received an order for our battalion to move up instantly to the support of the piquets; and on my descending to the door to mount my horse, I found Sir Lowry standing there, who asked if we had received any orders, and on my telling him that we had been ordered up to support the piquets, he immediately desired a staff-officer to order up one of his brigades to the rear of the chateau. This was one of the numerous instances in which we had occasion to admire the prudence and forethought of the great Wellington! He had foreseen the attack that would take place, and had his different divisions disposed to meet it.

"The enemy came up to the opposite ridge in formidable numbers, and began blazing at our windows and loopholes and showing some disposition to attempt it by storm; but they thought better of it, and withdrew their columns a short distance to the rear, leaving the nearest hedge lined with their skirmishers. An officer of ours, Mr. Hopewood, and one of our sergeants, had been killed in the field opposite, within twenty yards of where the enemy's skirmishers now were. We were very anxious to get possession of their bodies, but had not force enough to effect it. Several French soldiers came through the hedge at different times with the intention, as we thought, of plundering, but our men shot every one who attempted to go near them, until towards evening, when a French officer approached, waving a white handkerchief and pointing to some of his men who were following him with shovels. Seeing that his intention was to bury them we instantly ceased firing, nor did we renew it again that night.

"The 43rd, from their post at the church, kept up an incessant shower of musketry the whole of the day, at what was conceived at the time to be a very long range; but from the quantity of balls which were afterwards found sticking in every tree where the enemy stood, it was evident that their berth must have been rather uncomfortable. One of our officers, in the course of the day, had been passing through a deep roadway between two banks with hedgerows, when, to his astonishment, a dragoon and his horse tumbled heels over head into the road, as if they had been fired out of a cloud. Neither of them were the least hurt; but it must have been no joke that tempted him to take such a flight. General Alten and Sir James Kempt took up their quarters with us in the chateau; our sentries and those of the enemy stood within pistol-shot of each other in the ravine below.

"On the 12th there was heavy firing and hard fighting all day to our left, but we remained perfectly quiet. Towards the afternoon Sir James Kempt formed our brigade for the purpose of expelling the enemy from the hill next to the chateau, to which he thought them rather too near; but, just as we reached our different points for commencing the attack, we were recalled, and nothing further occurred.

"I went about one o'clock in the morning to visit our different piquets, and seeing an unusual number of fires in the enemy's lines, I concluded that they had lit them to mask some movement; and, taking a patrol with me, I stole cautiously forward and found that they had left the ground altogether. I immediately returned and reported the circumstance to General Alten, who sent off a despatch to apprise Lord Wellington.

"As soon as day began to dawn on the morning of the 13th, a tremendous fire of artillery and musketry was heard to our right. Soult had withdrawn everything from our front in the course of the night, and had now attacked Sir Rowland Hill with his whole force. Lord Wellington, in expectation of this attack, had last night rein forced Sir Rowland Hill with the sixth division; which enabled him to occupy his contracted position so strongly that Soult, unable to bring more than his own front to bear upon him, sustained a signal and sanguinary defeat.

"Lord Wellington galloped into the yard of our chateau soon after the attack had commenced, and demanded, with his usual quickness, what was to be seen? Sir James Kempt, who was spying at the action from an upper window, told him; and, after desiring Sir James to order Sir Lowry Cole to follow him with the fourth division, he galloped off to the scene of action. In the afternoon, when all was over, he called in again on his return to headquarters, and told us, 'that it was the most glorious affair that he had ever seen; and that the enemy had absolutely left upwards of five thousand men killed and wounded on the ground.'"

Chapter Six – Quatre Bras

Napoleon escaped from Elba on January 26, 1815; on March 19 he reached Fontainebleau, and Louis XVIII fled from Paris. Instantly the flames of war were rekindled throughout Europe. England hurried her best troops into the Netherlands, where a great army under Wellington was assembling. Amongst the first of the regiments to embark were naturally the famous Rifles. Kincaid had persuaded himself that his fighting days were ended, and he was peacefully shooting woodcocks in Scotland when summoned to join his regiment at speed. His battalion had sailed, and he caught the first boat leaving Leith for Rotterdam. It took ten days to reach the coast of Holland, and then went helplessly ashore. Kincaid got safely to land, and pushed on to Brussels, when he found his battalion forming part of the fifth division under Picton. A fortnight's pause followed, while the Prussian and English armies watched and listened for the first sign or sound which would show where Napoleon's blow was about to fall. It was the fate of the Rifles to take a gallant part in the stern fight at Quatre Bras, and Kincaid tells the story very graphically:

"As our division was composed of crack regiments under crack commanders, and headed by fire-eating generals, we had little to do the first fortnight after my arrival beyond indulging in all the amusements of our delightful quarter; but, as the middle of June approached, we began to get a little more on the *qui vive*, for we were aware that Napoleon was about to make a dash at some particular point; and, as he was not the sort of general to give his opponent an idea of the when and the where, the greater part of our army was necessarily disposed along the frontier, to meet him at his own place. They were, of course, too much extended to offer effectual resistance in their advanced position; but as our division and the Duke of Brunswick's corps were held in reserve at Brussels, in readiness to be thrust at whatever point might be attacked, they were a sufficient additional force to check the enemy for the time required to concentrate the army.

"We were, the whole of June 15th, on the most anxious lookout for news from the front; but no report had been received prior to the hour of dinner. I went, about seven in the evening, to take a stroll in the park, and meeting one of the Duke's staff he asked me, en passant, whether my pack-saddles were all ready? I told him that they were nearly so, and added, 'I suppose they won't be wanted, at all events, before tomorrow?' to which he replied, in the act of leaving me, 'If you have any preparation to make, I would recommend you not to delay so long.' I took the hint, and, returning to quarters, remained in momentary expectation of an order to move. The bugles sounded to arms about two hours after.

"To the credit of our battalion, be it recorded that, although the greater part were in bed when the assembly sounded, and billeted over the most distant parts of that extensive city, every man was on his alarm-post before eleven o'clock in a complete state of marching order; whereas it was nearly two o'clock in the morning before we were joined by the others.

"As a grand ball was to take place the same night at the Duchess of Richmond's, the order for the assembling of the troops was accompanied by permission for any officer who chose, to remain for the ball, provided that he joined his regiment early in the morning. Several of ours took advantage of it.

"Waiting for the arrival of the other regiments, we endeavoured to snatch an hour's repose on the pavement; but we were every instant disturbed, by ladies as well as gentlemen, some stumbling over us in the dark — some shaking us out of our sleep to be told the news — and not a few conceiving their immediate safety depending upon our standing in place of lying. All those who applied for the benefit of my advice, I recommended to go home to bed, to keep themselves perfectly cool, and to rest assured that, if their departure from the city became necessary (which I very much doubted), they would have at least one whole day to prepare for it, as we were leaving some beef and potatoes behind us, for which, I was sure, we would fight rather than abandon!

"The whole of the division having at length assembled, we were put in motion about three o'clock on the morning of the 16th, and advanced to the village of Waterloo, where, forming in a field adjoining the road, our men were allowed to prepare their breakfasts. I succeeded in getting mine in a small inn on the left-hand side of the village. Lord Wellington joined us about nine o'clock; and from his very particular orders to see that the roads were kept clear of baggage, and everything likely to impede the movements of the troops, I have since been convinced that his lordship had thought it probable that the position of Waterloo might, even that day, have become the scene of action; for it was a good broad road, on which there were neither the quantity of baggage nor of troops moving at the time to excite the slightest apprehension of confusion. Leaving us halted, he galloped on to the front, followed by his staff; and we were soon after joined by the Duke of Brunswick, with his corps of the army.

"His Highness dismounted near the place where I was standing, and seated himself on the roadside, along with his adjutant-general. He soon after despatched his companion on some duty; and I was much amused to see the vacated place immediately filled by an old beggar-man, who, seeing nothing in the black hussar uniform beside him denoting the high rank of the wearer, began to grunt and scratch himself most luxuriously! The Duke showed a degree of courage which few would under such circumstances; for he maintained his post until the return of his officer, when he very jocularly said, 'Well, O—n, you see that your place was not long unoccupied!' How little idea had I, at the time, that the life of the illustrious speaker was limited to three short hours!

"About twelve o'clock an order arrived for the troops to advance, leaving their baggage behind; and though it sounded warlike, yet we did not expect to come in contact with the enemy, at all events, on that day. But, as we moved forward, the symptoms of their immediate presence kept gradually increasing; for we presently met a cartload of wounded Belgians; and, after passing through Genappe, the distant sound of a solitary gun struck on the listening ear. But all doubt on the subject was quickly removed; for, on ascending the rising ground where stands the village of Quatre Bras, we saw a considerable plain in our front, flanked on each side by a wood, and on another acclivity beyond, we could perceive the enemy descending towards us in most imposing numbers.

"Quatre Bras, at that time, consisted of only three or four houses; and, as its name betokens, I believe, stood at the junction of four roads, on one of which we were moving; a second inclined to the right; a third, in the same degree, to the left; and the fourth, I conclude, must have gone backwards; but, as I had not an eye in that direction, I did not see it. The village was occupied by some Belgians, under the Prince of Orange, who had an advanced post in a large farmhouse at the foot of the road, which inclined to the right; and a part of his division also occupied the wood on the same side.

"Lord Wellington, I believe, after leaving us at Waterloo, galloped on to the Prussian position at Ligny, where he had an interview with Blücher, in which they concerted measures for their mutual co-operation. When we arrived at Quatre Bras, however, we found him in a field near the Belgian outpost; and the enemy's guns were just beginning to play upon the spot where he stood, surrounded by a numerous staff.

"We halted for a moment on the brow of the hill; and as Sir Andrew Barnard galloped forward to the headquarter group, I followed, to be in readiness to convey any orders to the battalion. The moment we approached, Lord Fitzroy Somerset, separating himself from the Duke, said, 'Barnard, you are wanted instantly; take your battalion and endeavour to get possession of that village,' pointing to one on the face of the rising ground, down which the enemy were moving; 'but if you cannot do that, secure that wood on the left, and keep the road open for communication with the Prussians.' We instantly moved in the given direction; but, ere we had got half-way to the village, we had the mortification to see the enemy throw such a force into it as rendered any attempt to retake it, with our numbers, utterly hopeless; and as another strong body of them were hastening towards the wood, which was the second object pointed out to us, we immediately brought them to action, and secured it. In moving to that point, one of our men went raving mad, from excessive heat. The poor fellow cut a few extraordinary capers, and died in the course of a few minutes.

"While our battalion reserve occupied the front of the wood, our skirmishers lined the side of the road, which was the Prussian line of communication. The road itself, however, was crossed by such a shower of balls, that none but a desperate traveller would have undertaken a journey on it. We were presently reinforced by a small battalion of foreign light troops, with whose assistance we were in hopes to have driven the enemy a little farther from it; but they were a raw body of men, who had never before been under fire, and, as they could not be prevailed upon to join our skirmishers, we could make no use of them whatever. Sir Andrew Barnard repeatedly pointed out to them which was the French, and which was our side; and, after explaining that they were not to fire a shot until they joined our skirmishers, the word 'March!' was given; but march to them was always the signal to fire, for they stood fast, and began blazing away, chiefly at our skirmishers too, the officers commanding whom were every time sending back to say that we were shooting them: until we were at last obliged to be satisfied with whatever advantages their appearance could give, as even that was of some consequence where troops were so scarce.

"Bonaparte's attack on the Prussians had already commenced, and the fire of artillery and musketry in that direction was tremendous; but the intervening higher ground prevented us from seeing any part of it.

"The plain to our right which we had just quitted had likewise become the scene of a sanguinary and unequal contest. Our division after we left it deployed into line, and, in advancing, met and routed the French infantry; but in following up their advantage they encountered a furious charge of cavalry, and were obliged to throw themselves into squares to receive it. With the exception of one regiment, however, which had two companies cut to pieces, they were not only successful in resisting the attack, but made awful havoc in the enemy's ranks, who, nevertheless, continued their forward career, and went sweeping past them like a whirlwind up to the village of Quatre Bras, to the confusion and consternation of the numerous useless appendages of our army who wore there assembled waiting the result of the battle.

"The forward movement of the enemy's cavalry gave their infantry time to rally; and strongly reinforced with fresh troops, they again advanced to the attack. This was a crisis in which, according to Bonaparte's theory, the victory was theirs by all the Rifles of war, for they held superior numbers both before and behind us; but the gallant old Picton, who had been trained in a different school, did not choose to confine himself to Rifles in those matters. Despising the force in his rear, he advanced, charged, and routed those in his front, which created such a panic among the others that they galloped back through the intervals in his division with no other object in view but their own safety. After this desperate conflict the firing on both sides lulled almost to a calm for nearly an hour, while each was busy in renewing their order of battle.

"The battle, on the side of the Prussians, still continued to rage in an unceasing roar of artillery. About four in the afternoon a troop of their dragoons came, as a patrol, to inquire how it fared with us, and told us in passing that they still maintained their position. Their day, however, was still to be decided, and, indeed, for that matter, so was our own; for, although the firing for the moment had nearly ceased, I had not yet clearly made up my mind which side had been the offensive, which the defensive, or which the winning. I had merely the satisfaction of knowing that we had not lost it; for we had met fairly in the middle of a field (or, rather unfairly, considering that they had two to one), and, after the scramble was over, our division still held the ground they fought on. All doubts on the subject, however, began to be removed about five o'clock. The enemy's artillery once more opened, and on running to the brow of the hill to ascertain the cause, we perceived our old light-division general, Count Alton, at the head of a fresh British division, moving gallantly down the road towards us. It was, indeed, a joyful sight; for, as already mentioned, our division had suffered so severely that we could not help looking forward to a renewal of the action, with such a disparity of force, with considerable anxiety. But this reinforcement gave us new life, and, as soon as they came near enough to afford support, we commenced the offensive, and driving in the skirmishers opposed to us, succeeded in gaining a considerable portion of the position originally occupied by the enemy, when darkness obliged us to desist. In justice to the foreign battalion which had been all day attached to us, I must say that, in this last movement, they joined us cordially and behaved exceedingly well. They had a very gallant young fellow at their head; and their conduct in the earlier part of the day can therefore only be ascribed to its being their first appearance on such a stage.

"Leaving General Alten in possession of the ground which we had assisted in winning, we returned in search of our division, and reached them about eleven at night, lying asleep in their glory on the field where they had fought, winch contained many a bloody trace of the day's work. The firing, on the side of the Prussians, had altogether ceased before dark, but recommenced with redoubled fury about an hour after; and it was then, as we afterwards learnt, that they lost the battle.

"We lay down by our arms near the farmhouse already mentioned, in front of Quatre Bras; and the deuce is in it if we were not in good trim for sleeping, seeing that we had been either marching or fighting for twenty-six successive hours."

In the retreat from Quatre Bras to Waterloo, made necessary by the defeat of Blücher at Ligny, the Rifles formed part of the rear-guard. Says Kincaid:

"June 17 — As last night's fighting only ceased with the daylight, the scene this morning presented a savage, unsettled appearance; the fields were strewed with the bodies of men, horses, torn clothing, and shattered cuirasses; and, though no movements appeared to be going on on either side, yet, as occasional shots continued to be exchanged at different points, it kept every one wide awake. We had the satisfaction of knowing that the whole of our army had assembled on the hill behind in the course of the night.

"About nine o'clock we received the news of Blücher's defeat, and of his retreat to Wavre. Lord Wellington, therefore, immediately began to withdraw his army to the position of Waterloo. Sir Andrew Barnard was ordered to remain as long as possible with our battalion, to mask the retreat of the others; and was told, if we were attacked, that the whole of the British cavalry were in readiness to advance to our relief. I had an idea, however, that a single rifle battalion in the midst of ten thousand dragoons, would come but indifferently off in the event of a general crash, and was by no means sorry when, between eleven and twelve o'clock, every regiment had got clear off, and we followed before the enemy had put anything in motion against us.

"After leaving the village of Quatre Bras, and passing through our cavalry who were formed on each side of the road, we drew up at the entrance of Genappe. The rain at that moment began to descend in torrents, and our men were allowed to shelter themselves in the nearest houses; but we were obliged to turn out again in the midst of it in less than five minutes, as we found the French cavalry and ours already exchanging shots, and the latter were falling back to the more favourable ground behind Genappe; we therefore retired with them *en masse* through the village, and formed again on the rising ground beyond.

"While we remained there we had an opportunity of seeing the different affairs of cavalry; and it did one's heart good to see how cordially the Life Guards went at their work. They had no idea of anything but straightforward fighting, and sent their opponents flying in all directions. The only young thing they showed was in every one who got a roll in the mud (and, owing to the slipperiness of the ground, there were many) going off to the rear, according to their Hyde Park custom, as being no longer fit to appear on parade! I thought at first that they had been all wounded, but, on finding how the case stood, I could not help telling them that theirs was now the situation to verify the old proverb, 'The uglier the better soldier!'

"The roads as well as the fields had now become so heavy that our progress to the rear was very slow; and it was six in the evening before we drew into the position of Waterloo. Our battalion took post in the second line that night, with its right resting on the Namur Road, behind La Haye Sainte, near a small mud cottage, which Sir Andrew Barnard occupied as a quarter. The enemy arrived in front in considerable force about an hour after us, and a cannonade took place in different parts of the line, which ended at dark, and we lay down by our arms. It rained excessively hard the greater part of the night, nevertheless, having succeeded in getting a bundle of hay for my horse, and one of straw for myself, I secured the horse to his bundle, by tying him to one of the men's swords stuck in the ground, and, placing mine under his nose, I laid myself down upon it, and never opened my eyes again until daylight."

Chapter Seven – The Rifles at Waterloo

Nothing in Kincaid's "adventures" is finer than his account of Waterloo. He tells, it is true, only that which took place about himself, and, as the grey and strangling battle-smoke lay for hours on the ridge where Kincaid stood, he could see only a very tiny patch of the great landscape of the battle. Waterloo, for him, might be described as a ring of imprisoning smoke, over which bellowed and echoed constantly the roar of a hundred guns, and out of which, at irregular intervals, broke lines of French infantry — sometimes as a spray of skirmishers, sometimes as massed battalions. Sometimes, by way of change, a column of horsemen — helmeted dragoons, cuirassiers in glittering breastplates, red lancers of the Guard — broke through the fog, rode at the stubborn line of the Rifles, and reeled off into the fog again, pursued by darting musketry volleys. To endure and to repel incessant attacks, hour after hour, was the business of the dwindling companies of the Rifles. The third battalion, to which Kincaid belonged, formed part of Adams's brigade. It stood a hundred yards to the rear of La Haye Sainte, a little to the left of Wellington's centre. The famous sandpit was in the immediate front of the battalion, and was held by three companies of Rifles. On this point in the British line the utmost strength of the French attack horse, foot, and artillery was expended, and no men that day saw fiercer fighting than did Kincaid and his fellow-riflemen. Kincaid, therefore, has this right to tell the story of Waterloo: he fought through the whole of that fateful day in the very heart of the great struggle:

"When I awoke this morning at daylight, I found myself drenched with rain. I had slept so long and so soundly that I had, at first, but a very confused notion of my situation; but having a bright idea that my horse had been my companion when I went to sleep, I was rather startled at finding that I was now alone, nor could I rub my eyes clear enough to procure a sight of him, which was vexatious enough; for, independent of his value as a horse, his services were indispensable, and an adjutant might as well think of going into action without his arms as without such a supporter. But whatever my feelings might have been towards him, it was evident that he had none for me, from having drawn his sword and marched off. The chances of finding him again, amid ten thousand others, were about equal to the odds against the needle in a bundle of hay; but for once the single chance was gained, as, after a diligent search of an hour, he was discovered between two artillery horses, about half a mile from where he broke loose.

"The weather cleared up as the morning advanced; and, though everything remained quiet at the moment, we were confident that the day would not pass off without an engagement, and, therefore, proceeded to put our arms in order, as, also, to get ourselves dried and made as comfortable as circumstances would permit.

"We made a fire against the wall of Sir Andrew Barnard's cottage, and boiled a huge camp-kettle full of tea, mixed up with a suitable quantity of milk and sugar, for breakfast; and, as it stood on the edge of the high-road, where all the bigwigs of the army had occasion to pass, in the early part of the morning, I believe almost every one of them, from the Duke downwards, claimed a cupful. About ten o'clock an unusual bustle was observable among the staff-officers, and we soon after received an order to stand to our arms. The troops who had been stationed in our front during the night were then moved off to the right, and our division" took up its fighting position.

"Our battalion stood on what was considered the left centre of the position. We had our right resting on the Brussels road, about a hundred yards in the rear of the farmhouse of La Haye Sainte, and our left extending behind a broken hedge, which ran along the ridge to the left. Immediately in our front, and divided from La Haye Sainte only by the great road, stood a small knoll, with a sand-hole in its farthest side, which we occupied, as an advanced post, with three companies. The remainder of the division was formed in two lines; the first, consisting chiefly of light troops, behind the hedge, in continuation from the left of our battalion reserve, and the second, about a hundred yards in its rear. The guns were placed in the intervals between the brigades, two pieces were in the roadway on our right, and a rocket brigade in the centre.

"The road had been cut through the rising ground, and was about twenty or thirty feet deep where our right rested, and which, in a manner, separated us from all the troops beyond. The division, I believe, under General Alten occupied the ground next to us, on the right.

"Shortly after we had taken up our ground, some columns, from the enemy's left, were seen in motion towards Hougoumont, and were soon warmly engaged with the right of our army. A cannon ball, too, came from the Lord knows where, for it was not fired at us and took the head off our right-hand man. That part of their position, in our own immediate front, next claimed our undivided attention. It had hitherto been looking suspiciously innocent, with scarcely a human being upon it; but innumerable black specks were now seen taking post at regular distances in its front, and recognising them as so many pieces of artillery, I knew, from experience, although nothing else was yet visible, that they were unerring symptoms of our not being destined to be idle spectators.

"From the moment we took possession of the knoll we had busied ourselves in collecting branches of trees and other things, for the purpose of making an abatis to block up the road between that and the farmhouse, and soon completed one, which we thought looked sufficiently formidable to keep out the whole of the French cavalry; but it was put to the proof sooner than we expected, by a troop of our own light dragoons, who, having occasion to gallop through, astonished us not a little by clearing away every stick of it. We had just time to replace the scattered branches, when the whole of the enemy's artillery opened, and their countless columns began to advance under cover of it."

The attack on Hougoumont, it will be remembered, was intended by Napoleon to be a mere feint, serving to draw off Wellington's attention from the real attack, the onfall of D'Erlon's huge columns on the left centre of the British position, which Napoleon hoped to pierce and destroy. Napoleon's tactics broke down first at Hougoumont, for the feigned attack grew persistent and obstinate, and drew into its madness more than twelve thousand good infantry, and after all failed. D'Erlon's great infantry attack was defeated by the stubbornness of Picton's slender lines, and by the sudden and overwhelming onfall of the Life Guards, Inniskillings, and Greys. Kincaid tells how he watched the French columns taking position for their attack:

"The scene at that moment was grand and imposing, and we had a few minutes to spare for observation. The column destined as 'our' particular 'friends,' first attracted our notice, and seemed to consist of about ten thousand infantry. A smaller body of infantry and one of cavalry moved on their right; and, on their left, another huge column of infantry, and a formidable body of cuirassiers, while beyond them it seemed one moving mass.

"We saw Bonaparte himself take post on the side of the road immediately in our front, surrounded by a numerous staff; and each regiment, as they passed him, rent the air with shouts of 'Vive l'Empereur,' nor did they cease after they had passed, but, backed by the thunder of their artillery, and carrying with them the rub-a-dub of drums and the tantarara of trumpets, in addition to their increasing shouts, it looked at first as if they had some hopes of scaring us off the ground, for it was a singular contrast to the stern silence reigning on our side, where nothing as yet but the voices of our great guns told that we had mouths to open when we chose to use them. Our rifles were, however, in a very few seconds required to play their parts, and opened such a fire on the advancing skirmishers as quickly brought them to a standstill; but their columns advanced steadily through them, although our incessant tiralade was telling in their centre with fearful exactness, and our post was quickly turned in both flanks, which compelled us to fall back and join our comrades behind the hedge, though not before some of our officers and theirs had been engaged in personal combat.

"When the heads of their columns showed over the knoll which we had just quitted, they received such a fire from our first line that they wavered and hung behind it a little; but, cheered and encouraged by the gallantry of their officers, who were dancing and flourishing their swords in front, they at last boldly advanced to the opposite side of our hedge and began to deploy. Our first line, in the meantime, was getting so thinned that Picton found it necessary to bring up his second, but fell in the act of doing it. The command of the division at that critical moment devolved upon Sir James Kempt, who was galloping along the line, animating the men to steadiness. He called to me by name, where I happened to be standing on the right of our battalion, and desired 'that I would never quit that spot.' I told him that 'he might depend upon it'; and in another instant I found myself in a fair way of keeping my promise more religiously than I intended; for, glancing my eye to the right, I saw the next field covered with the cuirassiers, some of whom were making directly for the gap in the hedge where I was standing.

"I had not hitherto drawn my sword, as it was generally to be had at a moment's warning; but from its having been exposed to the last night's rain, it had now got rusted in the scabbard and refused to come forth! I was in a precious scrape. Mounted on my strong Flanders mare, and with my good old sword in my hand, I would have braved all the chances without a moment's hesitation; but I confess that I felt considerable doubts as to the propriety of standing there to be sacrificed without the means of making a scramble for it. My mind, however, was happily relieved from such an embarrassing consideration before my decision was required; for the next moment the cuirassiers were charged by our household brigade, and the infantry in our front, giving way at the same time under our terrific shower of musketry, the flying cuirassiers tumbled in among the routed infantry, followed by the Life Guards, who were cutting away in all directions. Hundreds of the infantry threw themselves down and pretended to be dead, while the cavalry galloped over them, and then got up and ran away. I never saw such a scene in all my life.

"Lord Wellington had given orders that the troops were on no account to leave the position to follow up any temporary advantage; so that we now resumed our post, as we stood at the commencement of the battle, and with three companies again advanced on the knoll. I was told it was very ridiculous at that moment to see the number of vacant spots that were left nearly along the whole of the line, where a great part of the dark-dressed foreign troops had stood, intermixed with the British, when the action began.

"Our division got considerably reduced in numbers during the last attack; but Lord Wellington's fostering hand sent Sir John Lambert to our support with the sixth division, and we now stood prepared for another and a more desperate struggle. Our battalion had already lost three officers killed and six or seven wounded; among the latter were Sir Andrew Barnard and Colonel Cameron.

"Some one asking me what had become of my horse's ear was the first intimation I had of his being wounded; and I now found that, independent of one ear having been shaved close to his head (I suppose by a cannon-shot), a musket-ball had grazed across his forehead and another gone through one of his legs, but he did not seem much the worse for either of them.

"Between two and three o'clock we were tolerably quiet, except from a thundering cannonade; and the enemy had by that time got the range of our position so accurately that every shot brought a ticket for somebody's head. An occasional gun beyond the plain, far to our left, marked the approach of the Prussians; but their progress was too slow to afford a hope of their arriving in time to take any share in the battle. On our right the roar of cannon and musketry had been incessant from the time of its commencement; but the higher ground near us prevented our seeing anything of what was going on."

The anguish of the fight, as far as the Rifles were concerned, came when La Haye Sainte was carried by the French. This gave them cover at half-musket range, whence they could waste the British front with their fire. Their elation at having carried the farmhouse, it may be added, gave them new fire and audacity. They believed they had broken the British centre, that the day was won, that the stubborn British line was about to crumble and flee! And French soldiers are never so dangerous as when the rapture of real or imagined victory is kindling their blood. The pressure on the sadly-thinned lines of the Rifles was cruel, but it was borne with cool and stubborn valour:

"Between three and four o'clock the storm gathered again in our front. Our three companies on the knoll were soon involved in a furious fire. The Germans occupying La Haye Sainte expended all their ammunition and fled from the post. The French took possession of it; and as it flanked our knoll we were obliged to abandon it also and fall back again behind the hedge.

"The loss of La Haye Sainte was of the most serious consequence as it afforded the enemy an establishment within our position. They immediately brought up two guns on our side of it, and began serving out some grape to us; but they were so very near that we destroyed their artillerymen before they could give us a second round.

"The silencing of these guns was succeeded by a very extraordinary scene on the same spot. A strong regiment of Hanoverians advanced in line to charge the enemy out of La Have Sainte; but they were themselves charged by a brigade of cuirassiers, and, excepting one officer, on a little black horse, who went off to the rear like a shot out of a shovel, I do believe that every man of them was put to death in about five seconds. A brigade of British light dragoons advanced to their relief, and a few on each side began exchanging thrusts; but it seemed likely to be a drawn battle between them, without much harm being done, when our men brought it to a crisis sooner than either side anticipated, for they previously had their rifles eagerly pointed at the cuirassiers, with a view of saving the perishing Hanoverians; but the fear of killing their friends withheld them, until the others were utterly overwhelmed, when they instantly opened a terrific fire on the whole concern, sending both sides to flight; so that, on the small space of ground, within a hundred yards of us, where five thousand men had been fighting the instant before, there was not row a living soul to be seen.

"It made me mad to see the cuirassiers in their retreat stooping and stabbing at our wounded men as they lay on the ground. How I wished that I had been blessed with Omnipotent power for a moment, that I might have blighted them!

"The same field continued to be a wild one the whole of the afternoon. It was a sort of duelling-post between the two armies, every half-hour showing a meeting of some kind upon it; but they never exceeded a short scramble, for men's lives were held very cheap there.

"For the two or three succeeding hours there was no variety with us, but one continued blaze of musketry. The smoke hung so thick about, that, although not more than eighty yards asunder, we could only distinguish each other by the flashes of the pieces.

"I shall never forget the scene which the field of battle presented about seven in the evening. I felt weary and worn out, less from fatigue than anxiety. Our division, which had stood upwards of five thousand men at the commencement of the battle, had gradually dwindled down into a solitary line of skirmishers. The 27th Regiment were lying literally dead, in square, a few yards behind us. My horse had received another shot through the leg, and one through the flap of the saddle, which lodged in his body, sending him a step beyond the pension-list. The smoke still hung so thick about us that we could see nothing. I walked a little way to each flank, to endeavour to get a glimpse of what was going on; but nothing met my eye except the mangled remains of men and horses, and I was obliged to return to my post as wise as I went.

"I had never yet heard of a battle in which everybody was killed; but this seemed likely to be an exception, as all were going by turns. We got excessively impatient under the tame similitude of the latter part of the process, and burned with desire to have a last thrust at our respective *vis-à-vis*; for, however desperate our affairs were, we had still the satisfaction of seeing that theirs were worse. Sir John Lambert continued to stand as our support at the head of three good old regiments, one dead (the 27th) and two living ones, and we took the liberty of soliciting him to aid our views; but the Duke's orders on that head were so very particular that the gallant general had no choice.

"Presently a cheer, which we knew to be British, commenced far to the right, and made every one prick up his ears — it was Lord Wellington's long wished for orders to advance; it gradually approached, growing louder as it drew near — we took it up by instinct, charged through the hedge down upon the old knoll, sending our adversaries flying at the point of the bayonet. Lord Wellington galloped up to us at the instant, and our men began to cheer him; but he called out, 'No cheering, my lads, but forward, and complete your victory!'

"This movement had carried us clear of the smoke; and, to people who had been for so many hours enveloped in darkness, in the midst of destruction, and naturally anxious about the result of the day, the scene which now met the eye conveyed a feeling of more exquisite gratification than can be conceived. It was a fine summer's evening, just before sunset. The French were flying in one confused mass. British lines were seen in close pursuit, and in admirable order, as far as the eye could reach to the right, while the plain to the left was filled with Prussians. The enemy made one last attempt at a stand on the rising ground to our right of La Belle Alliance; but a charge from General Adams's brigade again threw them into a state of confusion, which was now inextricable, and their rum was complete. Artillery, baggage, and everything belonging to them fell into our hands. After pursuing them until dark, we halted about two miles beyond the field of battle, leaving the Prussians to follow up the victory.

"This was the last, the greatest, and the most uncomfortable heap of glory that I ever had a hand in, and may the deuce take me if I think that everybody waited there to see the end of it, otherwise it never could have been so troublesome to those who did. We were, take us all in all, a very bad army. Our foreign auxiliaries, who constituted more than half of our numerical strength, with some exceptions, were little better than a raw militia — body without a soul, or like an inflated pillow, that gives to the touch and resumes its shape again when the pressure ceases — not to mention the many who went clear out of the field, and were only seen while plundering our baggage in their retreat.

"Our heavy cavalry made some brilliant charges in the early part of the day; but they never knew when to stop, their ardour in following their advantages carrying them headlong on, until many of them 'burnt their fingers,' and got dispersed or destroyed. Of that gallant corps, the Royal Artillery, it is enough to say that they maintained their former reputation — the first in the world — and it was a serious loss to us in the latter part of the day to be deprived of this more powerful co-operation, from the causes already mentioned.

"If Lord Wellington had been at the head of his old Peninsula army, I am confident that he would have swept his opponents off the face of the earth immediately after their first attack; but, with such a heterogeneous mixture under his command, he was obliged to submit to a longer day.

"The field of battle next morning presented a frightful scene of carnage; it seemed as if the world had tumbled to pieces and three-fourths of everything destroyed in the wreck. The ground running parallel to the front of where we had stood was so thickly strewed with fallen men and horses, that it was difficult to step clear of their bodies; many of the former still alive, and imploring assistance, which it was not in our power to bestow. The usual salutation on meeting an acquaintance of another regiment after an action was to ask who had been hit? but on this occasion it was, 'Who's alive?' Meeting one next morning, a very little fellow, I asked what had happened to them, yesterday? 'I'll be hanged,' says he, 'if I know anything at all about the matter, for I was all day trodden in the mud and galloped over by every scoundrel who had a horse; and, in short, that I only owe my existence to my insignificance.'

"Two of our men, on the morning of the 19th, lost their lives by a very melancholy accident. They were cutting up a captured ammunition waggon for firewood, when one of their swords, striking against a nail, sent a spark among the powder. When I looked in the direction of the explosion, I saw the two poor fellows about twenty or thirty feet up in the air. On falling to the ground, though lying on their backs and bellies, some extraordinary effort of nature, caused by the agony of the moment, made them spring from that position five or six times, to the height of eight or ten feet, just as a fish does when thrown on the ground after being newly caught. It was so unlike a scene in real life that it was impossible to witness it without forgetting, for a moment, the horror of their situation.

"I ran to the spot along with others, and found that every stitch of clothes had been burnt off, and they were black as ink all over. They were still alive, and told us their names, otherwise we could not have recognised them; and, singular enough, they were able to walk off the ground with a little support, but died shortly after.

"About twelve o'clock on the day after the battle we commenced our march for Paris. I shall, therefore, leave my readers at Waterloo, in the hope that, among the many stories of romance to which that and the other celebrated fields gave birth, the foregoing unsophisticated one of an eye-witness may not have been found altogether uninteresting."

Part Two – One of Craufurd's Veterans

Chapter Eight – The King's Shilling

"Rifleman" Harris, an innocent-looking sheep boy, his face brown with the winds and rains of the Dorsetshire Downs, drifted, so to speak, into a soldier's life pretty much as a floating leaf, blown from some rustic valley and fallen into a rustic stream, might drift into a great historic river, furrowed by a thousand keels, and be swept away to unknown seas. His autobiography is curious alike in what it omits and in what it tells. It is so barren of one class of personal details that we are left in ignorance of when the writer was born. He leaves himself in his own volume without a Christian name. We are not told why he enlisted, nor where. Unlike most people undertaking an autobiography, Rifleman Harris appears to have had no interest whatever in himself, and he was incapable of imagining that anybody else would be interested. But he was keenly concerned in all the personal incidents of a soldier's life, and he describes them with a simplicity and a directness, an economy of adjectives, and a felicity of substantives, which makes his *Recollections* one of the freshest and most interesting soldier autobiographies ever written.

He had some good luck as a soldier. He belonged to a famous regiment; he served under some famous commanders; he heard the first shots fired by British muskets in the Peninsula. But he had also much ill-luck. He tramped, perspired, and probably swore, under South American suns in that most ignominious of all expeditions, under the most contemptible leader that ever wore a cocked hat — Whitelocke's fiasco at Buenos Aires. He next served in Portugal, and took part in the fighting at Roliça and Vimiero. Under Sir John Moore he shared in the heroism and the horrors of the dreadful retreat to Corunna, or rather to Vigo. That Harris survived snow and rain and hunger, the inexpressible toils of the long marches, the biting cold of the black unsheltered nights, as well as the sabres of the pursuing French horsemen and the bullets of the French skirmishers, is little less than marvellous. But he did, and landed at Spithead, ragged, barefooted, unshaven, with rusty musket, hollow cheeks, and eyes that had almost gone sightless with mere fatigue —

about as stiff and hardy and unconquerable a bit of soldierly flesh and blood as the world of that day could produce. A British private who had known the shame of Whitelocke's South American expedition and the distress of Moore's immortal retreat might well think he had exhausted all the evil possibilities of a soldier's life. But the unfortunate Harris had one more evil experience. He found a place in the unhappy Walcheren expedition, and crept out of it with wrecked constitution and ague-poisoned blood. He served after this in a veteran battalion; tried hard for service in the Peninsula, but, to his unspeakable disgust, was disqualified by a doctor with an unsympathetic temper and an inelastic conscience, and while still only thirty-two was discharged on a pension of sixpence a day. "For the first time," he says, "since I had been a shepherd-lad on the Blandford downs I found myself in plain clothes and with liberty to go and come where I liked."

But Harris never received a sixpence of his hard-earned pension, bought with blood and sweat. Before the first payment became due Napoleon had escaped from Elba; the veterans were called back to the ranks. Harris, wasted with fever and shaken with ague — legacies from Walcheren swamps — was unable to join, and forfeited his pension. He had to spend the rest of his days making shoes and writing his *Recollections of a Rifleman*. In view of this record, perhaps, the most striking thing in Harris' *Recollections* is their unconquerable good humour. The writer never grumbles. No faintest accent of discontent ever steals into his voice. His cheerfulness is invincible. He is proud of his officers; in the best of temper with his comrades; takes mud, rain, toil, empty stomach, and too heavy knapsack, a couch on the wet grass and under weeping skies, the pain of wounds, and the peril of death, all as part of the day's work, about which nobody has any right to grumble. A soldier's life, he plainly holds, is the pleasantest in the world. No one is better qualified than Rifleman Harris to tell to a modern and ease-loving generation how the men of the Peninsula marched, suffered, fought, and conquered.

Harris's *Recollections* begin with the simplicity and directness of one of Defoe's tales:

"My father was a shepherd, and I was a sheep-boy from my earliest youth. Indeed, as soon almost as I could run I began helping my father to look after the sheep on the downs of Blandford, in Dorsetshire, where I was born. Whilst I continued to tend the flocks and herds under my charge, and occasionally in the long whiter nights to learn the art of making shoes, I grew a hardy little chap, and was one fine day, in the year 1802, drawn as a soldier for the Army of Reserve. Thus, without troubling myself much about the change which was to take place in the hitherto quiet routine of my days, I was drafted into the 66th Regiment of Foot, bade goodbye to my shepherd companions, and was obliged to leave my father without an assistant to collect his flocks, just as he was beginning more than ever to require one; nay, indeed, I may say to want tending and looking after himself, for old age and infirmity were coming on him, his hair was growing as white as the sleet of our downs, and his countenance becoming as furrowed as the ploughed fields around. However, as I had no choice in the matter, it was quite as well that I did not grieve over my fate.

"My father tried hard to buy me off, and would have persuaded the sergeant of the 66th that I was of no use as a soldier from having maimed my right hand (by breaking the forefinger when a child). The sergeant, however, said I was just the sort of little chap he wanted, and off he went, carrying me (amongst a batch of recruits he had collected) away with him."

Harris's earliest experiences as a soldier naturally made the deepest impressions upon him. He found himself in a new world, with new comrades, and under strange new laws — laws with sanctions, swift, inevitable, and terrible behind them. Here is one of his earlier stories:

"Whilst lying at Winchester (where we remained three months), young as I was in the profession, I was picked out amongst others to perform a piece of duty that for many years afterwards remained deeply impressed upon my mind, and gave me the first impression of the stern duties of a soldier's life. A private of the 70th Regiment had deserted from that corps, and afterwards enlisted into several other regiments, indeed I was told at the time (though I cannot answer for so great a number) that sixteen different times he had received the bounty and then stolen off. Being, however, caught at last, he was brought to trial at Portsmouth, and sentenced by general court-martial to be shot.

"The 66th received a route to Portsmouth to be present on the occasion, and as the execution would be a good hint to us young 'uns, there were four lads picked out of our corps to assist in this piece of duty, myself being one of the number chosen.

"Besides these men, four soldiers from three other regiments were ordered on the firing-party, making sixteen in all. The place of execution was Portsdown Hill, near Hilsea Barracks, and the different regiments assembled must have composed a force of about fifteen thousand men, having been assembled from the Isle of Wight, from Chichester, Gosport, and other places. The sight was very imposing, and appeared to make a deep impression on all there. As for myself, I felt that I would have given a good round sum (had I possessed it) to have been in any situation rather than the one in which I now found myself; and when I looked into the faces of my companions, I saw, by the pallor and anxiety depicted in each countenance, the reflection of my own feelings. When all was ready, we were moved to the front, and the culprit was brought out. He made a short speech to the parade, acknowledging the justice of his sentence, and that drinking and evil company had brought the punishment upon him.

"He behaved himself firmly and well, and did not seem at all to flinch. After being blindfolded, he was desired to kneel down behind a coffin which was placed on the ground, and the drum-major of the Hilsea depot, giving us an expressive glance, we immediately commenced loading.

"This was done in the deepest silence, and the next moment we were primed and ready. There was then a dreadful pause for a few moments, and the drum-major, again looking towards us, gave the signal before agreed upon (a flourish of his cane) and we levelled and fired. We had been previously strictly enjoined to be steady and take good aim, and the poor fellow, pierced by several balls, fell heavily upon his back; and as he lay, with his arms pinioned to his sides, I observed that his hands waved for a few moments, like the fins of a fish, when in the agonies of death. The drum-major also observed the movement, and, making another signal, four of our party immediately stepped up to the prostrate body, and placing the muzzles of their pieces to the head, fired, and put him out of his misery. The different regiments then fell back by companies, and the word being given to march past in slow time, when each company came in line with the body the word was given to 'mark time,' and then 'eyes left,' in order that we might all observe the terrible example. We then moved onwards, and marched from the ground to our different quarters.

"The 66th stopped that night about three miles from Portsdown Hill, and in the morning we returned to Winchester. The officer in command that day, I remember, was General Whitelocke, who was afterwards brought to court-martial himself. This was the first time of our seeing that officer. The next meeting was at Buenos Aires, and during the confusion of that day one of us received an order from the fiery Craufurd to shoot the traitor dead if he could see him in the battle, many others of the Rifles receiving the same order from that fine and chivalrous officer.

"The unfortunate issue of the Buenos Aires affair is matter of history, and I have nothing to say about it, but I well remember the impression it made upon us all at the time, and that Sir John Moore was present at Whitelocke's court-martial; General Craufurd, and I think General Auchmuty, Captain Eleder of the Rifles, Captain Dickson, and one of our privates being witnesses.

"So enraged was Craufurd against him, that I heard say he strove hard to have him shot. Whitelocke's father I also heard was at his son's trial, and cried like an infant during the proceedings. Whitelocke's sword was broken over his head, I was told, and for months afterwards, when our men took their glass, they used to give as a toast, 'success to "grey hairs," but bad luck to "Whitelocks."' Indeed, that toast was drunk in all the public-houses around for many a day."

The 66th was shortly afterwards sent to Ireland; and Harris, who had shown himself smart and intelligent, was put into the light company of his regiment. While in Dublin he saw some companies of the famous 95th Rifles marching. They bore the signature of Sir John Moore's soldierly hand on them; and Harris records that "I fell so in love with their smart, dashing, and devil-may-care appearance that nothing would serve me till I was a rifleman myself," and meeting a recruiting party of the regiment, he volunteered into the second battalion. He gives a strangely interesting account of the recruits which formed the raw material out of which Wellington evolved the magnificent soldiers of the Peninsula — men with whom, to use Wellington's own words, he "could go anywhere, and do anything." Rougher, wilder material — half savage and half child-like than these recruits can hardly be imagined. Certainly no such strange human material finds its way into British barracks today:

"This recruiting-party were all Irishmen, and had been sent over from England to collect (amongst others) men from the Irish Militia, and were just about to return to England. I think they were as reckless and devil-may-care a set of men as ever I beheld, either before or since.

"Being joined by a sergeant of the 92nd Highlanders, and a Highland piper of the same regiment (also a pair of real rollicking blades), I thought we should all have gone mad together. We started on our journey, one beautiful morning, in tip-top spirits, from the Royal Oak, at Cashel; the whole lot of us (early as it was) being three sheets in the wind. When we paraded before the door of the Royal Oak, the landlord and landlady of the inn, who were quite as lively, came reeling forth, with two decanters of whisky, which they thrust into the fists of the sergeants, making them a present of decanters and all, to carry along with them, and refresh themselves on the march. The piper then struck up, the sergeants flourished their decanters, and the whole rout commenced a terrific yell. We then all began to dance, and danced through the town, every now and then stopping for another pull at the whisky decanters. Thus we kept it up till we had danced, drank, shouted, and piped thirteen Irish miles, from Cashel to Clonmel. Such a day, I think, I never spent, as I enjoyed with these fellows; and on arriving at Clonmel, we were as 'glorious' as any soldiers in all Christendom need wish to be.

"In about ten days after this, our sergeants had collected together a good batch of recruits, and we started for England. Some few days before we embarked (as if we had not been bothered enough already with the unruly Paddies), we were nearly pestered to death with a detachment of old Irishwomen, who came from different parts (on hearing of their sons having enlisted), in order to endeavour to get them away from us. Following us down to the water's edge, they hung to their offspring and, dragging them away, sent forth such dismal howls and moans that it was quite distracting to hear them. The lieutenant commanding the party, ordered me (being the only Englishman present) to endeavour to keep them back. It was, however, as much as I could do to preserve myself being torn to pieces by them, and I was glad to escape out of their hands.

"At length we got our lads safe on board, and set sail for England. No sooner were we out at sea, however, than our troubles began afresh with these hot-headed Paddies; for, having now nothing else to do, they got up a dreadful quarrel amongst themselves, and a religious row immediately took place, the Catholics reviling the Protestants to such a degree that a general fight ensued. The poor Protestants (being few in number) soon got the worst of it, and as fast as we made matters up among them, they broke out afresh and began the riot again.

"From Bath we marched to Andover, and when we came upon Salisbury Plain, our Irish friends got up a fresh row. At first they appeared uncommonly pleased with the scene, and, dispersing over the soft carpet of the Downs, commenced a series of Irish jigs till at length as one of the Catholics was setting to his partner (a Protestant), he gave a whoop and a leap into the air, and at the same time (as if he couldn't bear the partnership of a heretic any longer), dealt him a tremendous blow with his shillelagh, and stretched him upon the sod. This was quite enough, and the bludgeons immediately began playing away at a tremendous rate.

"The poor Protestants were again quickly disposed of, and then arose a cry of 'Huzza for the Wicklow boys,' 'Huzza for the Connaught boys,' 'Huzza for Munster,' and 'Huzza for Ulster!' They then recommenced the fight as if they were determined to make an end of their soldiering altogether upon Salisbury Plains. We had, I remember, four officers with us, and they did their best to pacify their pugnacious recruits. One thrust himself amongst them, but was instantly knocked down for his pains, so that he was glad enough to escape. After they had completely tired themselves, they began to slacken in their endeavours, and apparently to feel the effect of the blows they dealt each other, and at length suffering themselves to be pacified, the officers got them into Andover.

"Scarcely had we been a couple of hours there, and obtained some refreshment, ere these incorrigible blackguards again commenced quarrelling, and collecting together in the streets, created so serious a disturbance that the officers, getting together a body of constables, seized some of the most violent and succeeded in thrusting them into the town jail; upon this their companions again collected, and endeavoured to break open the prison gates.

"Baffled in this attempt, they rushed through the streets knocking down everybody they met. The drums now commenced beating up for a volunteer corps of the town, which, quickly mustering, drew up in the street before the jail, and immediately were ordered to load with ball. This somewhat pacified the rioters, and our officers persuading them to listen to a promise of pardon for the past, peace was at length restored amongst them."

Harris's first experience of active service was in that obscure and more than half-forgotten expedition to Copenhagen in 1807. Harris found that coming under fire was, on the whole, an exhilarating experience. Certainly the manner in which he bore himself when first he heard the whistle of hostile bullets showed he had the makings of a good soldier.

"The expedition consisted of about 30,000 men, and at the moment of our getting on shore, the whole force set up one simultaneous and tremendous cheer, a sound I cannot describe, it seemed so inspiring. This, indeed, was the first time of my hearing the style in which our men give tongue when they get near the enemy, though afterwards my ears became pretty well accustomed to such sounds.

"As soon as we got on shore the Rifles were pushed forward as the advance, in chain order, through some thick woods of fir, and when we had cleared these woods and approached Copenhagen, sentries were posted on the roads and openings leading towards the town, in order to intercept all comers and prevent all supplies. Such posts we occupied for about three days and nights, whilst the town was being fired on by our shipping. I rather think this was the first time of Congreve rockets being brought into play, and as they rushed through the air in the dark, they appeared like so many fiery serpents, creating, I should think, terrible dismay amongst the besieged.

"As the main army came up, we advanced and got as near under the walls of the place as we could without being endangered by the fire from our own shipping. We now received orders ourselves to commence firing, and the rattling of the guns I shall not easily forget.

"I felt so much exhilarated that I could hardly keep back, and was checked by the commander of the company (Captain Leech), who called to me by name to keep my place. About this time, my front-rank man, a tail fellow named Jack Johnson, showed a disposition as though the firing had on him an effect the reverse of what it had on many others of the company, for he seemed inclined to hang back, and once or twice turned round in my face. I was a rear-rank man, and porting my piece, in the excitement of the moment I swore that if he did not keep his ground, I would shoot him dead on the spot, so that he found it would be quite as dangerous for him to return as to go on.

"I feel sorry to record the want of courage of this man, but I do so with the less pain as it gives me the opportunity of saying that during many years' arduous service, it is the only instance I remember of a British soldier endeavouring to hold back when his comrades were going forward. Indeed, Johnson was never again held in estimation amongst the Rifle corps; for the story got wind that I had threatened to shoot him for cowardice in the field, and Lieutenant Cox mentioned to the colonel that he had overheard my doing so; and such was the contempt the man was held in by the Rifles, that he was soon afterwards removed from amongst us to a veteran battalion."

Chapter Nine – In the Peninsula

Harris's Peninsular experiences began in 1808. The Rifles formed part of a modest force of less than 10,000 men about to sail for a raid on the Spanish colonies in South America. But Napoleon had just effected the highly ingenious but quite felonious transfer of the Spanish crown to the head of his brother Joseph. As a result all Spain rose in revolt against French arms; and what yesterday had been for England an enemy to be plundered, became today an ally to be helped. The expedition which was intended to destroy Spanish colonies was, therefore, despatched to assist in the deliverance of Spain itself.

An even larger share than usual of the national gift for blundering at the beginning of a campaign was shown at the start of the great operations in the Peninsula. The force despatched was utterly inadequate. It was 20,000 men against 120,000. But even this little force was broken into fragments and despatched on totally unrelated adventures. Spencer was sent with 10,000 men to Cadiz; another body of 10,000 was despatched to the Tagus. By a happy chance — perhaps it would be fair to say by a happy flash of insight — Wellesley was given command of this latter expedition; but Sir Harry Burrard was promptly despatched to supersede Wellesley, and Sir Hew Dalrymple to supersede Sir Harry Burrard! Under this delightful arrangement the astonished British army had three distinct commanders within the space of twenty-four hours. Harris describes the long and loitering pause at Cork, where the ships lay for six weeks, without disembarking the unfortunate soldiers. At last, on July 12, 1808, the expedition sailed. The landing-place chosen was the mouth of the Mondego. The Rifles, Harris records with delight, "were the first out of the ships. We were, indeed, always in the front in an advance and in the rear in a retreat." The heats of a Spanish summer lay on the plains and the hills; the roads were mere ribbons of sand, the watercourses were parched; and Harris's first experience of marching under service conditions, and on sandy Spanish roads, was very trying. He says:

"The weight I myself toiled under was tremendous, and I often wonder at the strength I possessed at this period, which enabled me to endure it; for, indeed, I am convinced that many of our infantry sank and died under the weight of their knapsacks alone. For my own part, being a handicraft, I marched under a weight sufficient to impede the free motions of a donkey! for besides my well-filled kit, there was the greatcoat rolled on its top, my blanket and camp kettle, my haversack, stuffed full of leather for repairing the men's shoes, together with a hammer and other tools (the lap-stone I took the liberty of flinging to the devil), ship-biscuit and beef for three days. I also carried my canteen filled with water, my hatchet and rifle, and eighty rounds of ball cartridge in my pouch; this last, except the beef and biscuit, being the best thing I owned, and which I always gave the enemy the benefit of when opportunity offered.

"Altogether the quantity of things I had on my shoulders was enough and more than enough for my wants, sufficient, indeed, to sink a little fellow of five feet seven inches into the earth. Nay, so awkwardly was the load our men bore in those days placed upon their backs, that the free motion of the body was impeded, the head held down from the pile at the back of the neck, and the soldier half beaten before he came to the scratch."

A pleasanter description is given of the march on the following day. He says:

"The next day we again advanced, and being in a state of the utmost anxiety to come up with the French, neither the heat of the burning sun, long miles, nor heavy knapsacks were able to diminish our ardour. Indeed, I often look back with wonder at the light-hearted style, the jollity, and reckless indifference with which men who were destined in so short a time to fall, hurried onwards to the field of strife; seemingly without a thought of anything but the sheer love of meeting the foe and the excitement of the battle."

Harris's *Recollections* have absolutely no chronology, or chronology only of the most distracted and planless character. A clear thread of narrative is to be obtained only by the process of rearranging all his incidents.

The opening skirmish — the first splutter of British muskets in the long Peninsular campaigns — took place on August 15, and naturally the

95th, which formed the British outposts, were the actors in the combat. They erred by over-vehemence. They fell on so eagerly, and pursued so fast and so far, that they presently found themselves charging the entire French army, and were drawn off with some loss. Harris's description is brief:

"It was on the 15th of August when we first came up with the French, and their skirmishers immediately commenced operations by raining a shower of balls upon us as we advanced, which we returned without delay.

"The first man that was hit was Lieutenant Bunbury; he fell pierced through the head with a musket-ball, and died almost immediately. I thought I never heard such a tremendous noise as the firing made on this occasion, and the men on both sides of me, I could occasionally observe, were falling fast. Being overmatched, we retired to a rising ground, or hillock, in our rear, and formed there all round its summit, standing three deep, the front rank kneeling. In this position we remained all night, expecting the whole host upon us every moment. At daybreak, however, we received instructions to fall back as quickly as possible upon the main body. Having done so, we now lay down for a few hours' rest, and then again advanced to feel for the enemy."

Wellington described the affair as "unpleasant" from the general's point of view; but apparently the Rifles found it very enjoyable.

On August 17 Roliça was fought. The British again erred by over-eagerness, the 29th in particular suffering heavy losses owing to the fact that the regiment went straight at the enemy's front instead of turning its flank. The battle, however, was on the British side a bit of characteristic, dogged, and straightforward fighting. The French flank was turned, their front driven in, and they were compelled to fall back from one position to another till they finally abandoned the fight. Here is Harris's account, collated from the different parts of his volume:

"On the 17th, being still in front, we again came up with the French, and I remember observing the pleasing effect afforded by the sun's rays glancing upon their arms as they formed in order of battle to receive us. Moving on in extended order under whatever cover the nature of the ground afforded, together with some companies of the 60th, we began a sharp fire upon them, and thus commenced the battle of Roliça.

"I do not pretend to give a description of this or any other battle I have been present at. All I can do is to tell the things which happened immediately around me, and that, I think, is as much as a private soldier can be expected to do.

"Soon afterwards the firing commenced, and we had advanced pretty close upon the enemy. Taking advantage of whatever cover I could find I threw myself down behind a small bank, where I lay so secure, that although the Frenchmen's bullets fell pretty thickly around, I was enabled to knock several over without being dislodged, in fact, I fired away every round I had in my pouch whilst lying on this spot. At length after a sharp contest we forced them to give ground, and following them up, drove them from their position in the heights, and hung upon their skirts till they made another stand, and then the game began again.

"The 29th Regiment received so terrible a fire that I saw the right wing almost annihilated, and the colonel (I think his name was Lennox[2]) lay sprawling amongst the rest. We had ourselves caught it pretty handsomely, for there was no cover for us, and we were rather too near. The living skirmishers were lying beside heaps of their own dead, but still we had held our own till the battalion regiments came up. 'Fire and retire'[3] is a very good sound, but the Rifles were not over fond of such notes. We never performed that manoeuvre except when it was made pretty plain to us that it was quite necessary; the 29th, however, had got their faring here at this time, and the shock of that fire seemed to stagger the whole line and make them recoil. At the moment a little confusion appeared in the ranks, I thought. Lord Hill was near at hand and saw it, and I observed him come galloping up. He put himself at the head of the regiment and restored them to order in a moment. Pouring a regular and sharp fire upon the enemy he galled them in return; and, remaining with the 29th till he brought them to the charge, quickly sent the foe to the right-about. It seemed to me that few men could have conducted the business with more coolness and quietude of manner under such a storm of balls as he was exposed to. Indeed I have never forgotten him from that day.

---

[2] It was Colonel Lake.

[3] One of the bugle sounds to the skirmishers when hard-pressed.

"At the time I was remarking these matters (loading and firing as I lay), another circumstance divided my attention for a while, and made me forget even the gallant conduct of General Hill. A man near me uttered a scream of agony, and looking from the 29th, who were on my right, to the left, whence the screech had come, I saw one of our sergeants, named Fraser, sitting in a doubled-up position, and swaying backwards and forwards as though he had got a terrible pain in his bowels. He continued to make so much complaint that I arose and went to him, for he was rather a crony of mine.

"'Oh, Harris,' said he, as I took him in my arms, 'I shall die! I shall die! The agony is so great that I cannot bear it.'

"It was, indeed, dreadful to look upon him; the froth came from his mouth, and the perspiration poured from his face. Thank Heaven! he was soon out of pain, and, laying him down, I returned to my place. Poor fellow! He suffered more for the short time that he was dying than any man I think I ever saw in the same circumstances. I had the curiosity to return and look at him after the battle. A musket-ball, I found, had taken him sideways and gone through both groins.

"Within about half-an-hour after this I left Sergeant Fraser, and, indeed, for the time had as completely forgotten him as if he had died a hundred years back. The sight of so much bloodshed around will not suffer the mind to dwell long on any particular casualty, even though it happen to one's dearest friend. There was no time either to think, for all was action with us Rifles just at this moment, and the barrel of my piece was so hot from continual firing that I could hardly bear to touch it, and was obliged to grasp the stock beneath the iron, as I continued to blaze away.

"James Ponton was another crony of mine (a gallant fellow!); he had pushed himself in front of me, and was checked by one of our officers for his rashness. 'Keep back, you Ponton!' the lieutenant said to him more than once. But Ponton was not to be restrained by anything but a bullet when in action. This time he got one which, striking him in the thigh, I suppose cut an artery, for he died quickly. The Frenchmen's balls were flying very wickedly at that moment; and I crept up to Ponton, and took shelter by lying behind, and making a rest for my rifle of his dead body. It strikes me that I revenged his death by the assistance of his carcass. At any rate I tried my best to hit his enemies hard.

"There were two small buildings in our front, and the French, having managed to get into them, annoyed us much from that quarter. A small rise in the ground close before these houses also favoured them; and our men were being handled very severely in consequence. They became angry, and wouldn't stand it any longer. One of the skirmishers jumping up, rushed forward, crying, 'Over boys! — over! over!' when instantly the whole line responded to the cry, 'Over! over! over!' They ran along the grass like wildfire, and dashed at the rise, fixing their sword-bayonets as they ran. The French light bobs could not stand the sight, but turned about and fled, and, getting possession of their ground, we were soon inside the buildings.

"After the battle was over I stepped across to the other house I have mentioned, in order to see what was going on there, for the one I remained in was now pretty well filled with the wounded (both French and English) who had managed to get there for a little shelter. Two or three surgeons also had arrived at this house, and were busily engaged in giving their assistance to the wounded, now also here lying as thickly as in the building which I had left; but what struck me most forcibly was, that from the circumstance of some wine-butts having been left in the apartment, and their having in the engagement been perforated by bullets, and otherwise broken, the red wine had escaped most plentifully, and ran down upon the earthen floor where the wounded were lying, so that many of them were soaked in the wine with which their blood was mingled.

"The Rifles fought well this day, and we lost many men. They seemed in high spirits, and delighted at having driven the enemy before them. Joseph Cochan was by my side loading and firing very industriously about this period of the day. Thirsting with heat and action he lifted his canteen to his mouth, 'Here's to you, old boy,' he said, as he took a pull at its contents. As he did so a bullet went through the canteen, and, perforating his brain, killed him in a moment. Another man fell close to him almost immediately, struck by a ball in the thigh. Indeed, we caught it severely just here, and the old iron was also playing its part amongst our poor fellows very merrily. When the roll was called after the battle, the females who missed their husbands came along the front of the line to inquire of the survivors whether they knew anything about them.

Amongst other names I heard that of Cochan called in a female voice, without being replied to.

"The name struck me, and I observed the poor woman who had called it, as she stood sobbing before us, and apparently afraid to make further inquiries about her husband. No man had answered to his name, or had any account to give of his fate. I myself had observed him fall, as related before, whilst drinking from his canteen; but as I looked at the poor sobbing creature before me, I felt unable to tell her of his death. At length Captain Leech observed her, and called out to the company —

"'Does any man here know what has happened to Cochan? If so, let him speak out at once.'

"Upon this order I immediately related what I had seen, and told the manner of his death. After a while Mrs. Cochan appeared anxious to seek the spot where her husband fell, and, in the hope of still finding him alive, asked me to accompany her over the field. She trusted, notwithstanding what I had told her, to find him yet alive.

"'Do you think you could find it?' said Captain Leech, upon being referred to.

"'I told him I was sure I could, as I had remarked many objects whilst looking for cover during the skirmishing.

"'Go then,' said the captain, 'and show the poor woman the spot, as she seems so desirous of finding the body.'

"I accordingly took my way over the ground we had fought upon, she following and sobbing after me, and, quickly reaching the spot where her husband's body lay, pointed it out to her.

"She now soon discovered all her hopes were in vain; she embraced a stiffened corpse, and after rising and contemplating his disfigured face for some minutes, with hands clasped and tears streaming down her cheeks, she took a prayer-book from her pocket, and, kneeling down, repeated the service for the dead over the body. When she had finished she appeared a good deal comforted, and I took the opportunity of beckoning to a pioneer I saw near with some other men, and together we dug a hole and quickly buried the body. Mrs. Cochan then returned with me to the company to which her husband had been attached, and laid herself down upon the heath near us. She lay amongst some other females who were in the same distressing circumstances with herself, with the sky for her canopy and a turf for her pillow, for we had no tents with us. Poor woman! I pitied her much; but there was no remedy. If she had been a duchess she must have fared the same. She was a handsome woman, I remember, and the circumstance of my having seen her husband fall, and accompanied her to find his body, begot a sort of intimacy between us. What little attention I could pay her during the hardships of the march I did, and I also offered on the first opportunity to marry her. 'She had, however, received too great a shock on the occasion of her husband's death ever to think of another soldier,' she said; she therefore thanked me for my good feeling towards her, but declined my offer, and left us soon afterwards for England.

"After I had left the house I have alluded to in the account of the battle of Roliça, I walked a few paces onwards, when I saw some of the Rifles lying about and resting. I laid myself down amongst them, for I felt fatigued. A great many of the French skirmishers were lying dead just about this spot. I recollect that they had long white frock-coats on, with the eagle in front of their caps. This was one of the places from which they had greatly annoyed us; and, to judge from the appearance of the dead and wounded strewed around, we had returned the compliment pretty handsomely. I lay upon my back, and, resting upon my knapsack, examined the enemy in the distance. Whilst I lay watching them, I observed a dead man directly opposite to me whose singular appearance had not at first caught my eye. He was lying on his side amongst some burnt-up bushes, and whether the heat of the firing here had set these bushes on fire, or from whatever cause they had been ignited, I cannot take upon me to say; but certain it is (for several of my companions saw it as well as myself, and cracked many a joke upon the poor fellow's appearance), that this man, whom we guessed to have been French, was as completely roasted as if he had been spitted before a good kitchen-fire. He was burnt quite brown, every stitch of clothes was singed off, and he was drawn all up like a dried frog. I called the attention of one or two men near me, and we examined him, turning him about with our rifles with no little curiosity. I remember now, with some surprise, that the miserable fate of this poor fellow called forth from us very little sympathy, but seemed only to be a subject of mirth."

Vimiero followed hard on Roliça, being fought only four days afterwards. In this battle the French attacked, and their onfall was marked by high daring and tactical skill. But the British out-fought as their general out-manoeuvred the French, and Junot was only saved from complete destruction by the circumstance that Sir Harry Burrard, at the very moment of victory, displaced Wellesley in command, and ordered the pursuit to cease. The Rifles were in the skirmishing line, and were naturally driven back when the French advanced in mass. The steadfast British line, however, took very badly the retreat of the skirmishers, as Harris, in amusing fashion, records. Harris's account is interesting as a picture of what may be called the domestic details of the fighting, the preparations for it, the rough jesting of the fighting line, the fashion in which individual soldiers fought and died. There is, indeed, an almost Homeric touch in Harris's picture of individual combats. Here is his story of how the Rifles fought at Vimiero:

"It was on the 21st of August that we commenced fighting the battle of Vimiero.

"The French came down upon us in a column, and the Riflemen immediately commenced a sharp fire upon them from whatever cover they could get a shelter behind, whilst our cannon played upon them from our rear. I saw regular lanes torn through their ranks as they advanced, which were immediately closed up again as they marched steadily on. Whenever we saw a round shot thus go through the mass we raised a shout of delight.

"One of our corporals, named Murphy, was the first man in the Rifles who was hit that morning, and I remember more particularly remarking the circumstance from his apparently having a presentiment of his fate before the battle began. He was usually an active fellow, and up to this time had shown himself a good and brave soldier, but on this morning he seemed unequal to his duty. General Fane and Major Travers were standing together on an early part of this day. The general had a spyglass in his hand, and for some time looked anxiously at the enemy. Suddenly he gave the word to fall in, and immediately all was bustle amongst us. The Honourable Captain Pakenham spoke very sharply to Murphy, who appeared quite dejected and out of spirits, I observed. He had a presentiment of death, which is by no means an uncommon circumstance, and I have observed it once or twice since this battle.

"Others beside myself noticed Murphy on this morning, and as we had reason to know he was not ordinarily deficient in courage, the circumstance was talked of after the battle was over. He was the first man shot that day.

"Just before the battle commenced in earnest, and whilst the officers were busily engaged with their companies, shouting the word of command, and arranging matters of moment, Captain Leech ordered a section of our men to move off, at double quick, and take possession of a windmill, which was on our left. I was amongst this section, and set off full cry towards the mill, when Captain Leech espied and roared out to me by name to return — 'Hello there! you Harris!' he called, 'fall out of that section directly. We want you here, my man.' I, therefore, wheeled out of the rank, and returned to him. 'You fall in amongst the men here, Harris,' he said, 'I shall not send you to that post. The cannon will play upon the mill in a few moments like hail; and what shall we do,' he continued laughing, 'without our head shoemaker to repair our shoes?'

"It is long since these transactions took place. But I remember the words of the captain as if they had been uttered but yesterday; for that which was spoken in former years in the field has made a singular impression on my mind. As I looked about me, whilst standing enranked, and just before the commencement of the battle, I thought it the most imposing sight the world could produce. Our lines glittering with bright arms; the stern features of the men, as they stood with their eyes fixed unalterably upon the enemy; the proud colours of England floating over the heads of the different battalions; and the dark cannon on the rising ground, and all in readiness to commence the awful work of death, with a noise that would deafen the whole multitude. Altogether, the sight had a singular and terrible effect upon the feelings of a youth, who, a few short months before, had been a solitary shepherd upon the Downs of Dorsetshire, and had never contemplated any other sort of life than the peaceful occupation of watching the innocent sheep as they fed upon the grassy turf.

"The first cannon shot I saw fired, I remember, was a miss. The artilleryman made a sad bungle, and the ball went wide of the mark. We were all looking anxiously to see the effect of this shot; and another of the gunners (a red-haired man) rushed at the fellow who had fired, and in the excitement of the moment, knocked him head over heels with his fists. 'D—n you for a fool,' he said, 'what sort of a shot do you call that? Let me take the gun.' He accordingly fired the next shot himself, as soon as the gun was loaded, and so truly did he point it at the French column on the hillside, that we saw the fatal effect of the destructive missile by the lane it made and the confusion it caused.

"Our Riflemen (who at the moment were amongst the guns) upon seeing this, set up a tremendous shout of delight, and the battle commencing immediately, we were all soon hard at work.

"I myself was very soon so hotly engaged, loading and firing away, enveloped in the smoke I created, and the cloud which hung about me from the continued fire of my comrades, that I could see nothing for a few minutes but the red flash of my own piece amongst the white vapour clinging to my very clothes. This has often seemed to me the greatest drawback upon our present system of fighting; for whilst in such state, on a calm day, until some friendly breeze of wind clears the space around, a soldier knows no more of his position and what is about to happen in his front, or what has happened (even amongst his own companions) than the very dead lying around.

"Such is my remembrance of the commencement of the battle of Vimiero. The battle began on a fine bright day, and the sun played on the arms of the enemy's battalions, as they came on, as if they had been tipped with gold. The battle soon became general; the smoke thickened around, and often I was obliged to stop firing and dash it aside from my face, and try in vain to get sight of what was going on, whilst groans and shouts and a noise of cannon and musketry appeared almost to shake the very ground. It seemed hell upon earth, I thought.

"A man named John Low stood before me at this moment, and he turned round during a pause in our exertions, and addressed me: 'Harris, you humbug,' he said, 'you have plenty of money about you, I know, for you are always staying about and picking up what you can find on the field. But I think this will be your last field-day, old boy. A good many of us will catch it, I suspect, today.' 'You are right, Low,' I said, 'I have got nine guineas in my pack, and if I get shot today, and you yourself escape, it's quite at your service. In the meantime, however, if you see any symptoms of my wishing to flinch in this business, I hope you will shoot me with your own hand.'

"Low as well as myself survived this battle, and after it was over, whilst we sat down with our comrades and rested, amongst other matters talked over, Low told them of our conversation during the heat of the day, and the money I had collected, and the Rifles from that time had a great respect for me. It is, indeed, singular how a man loses or gains caste with his comrades from his behaviour, and how closely he is observed in the field. The officers, too, are commented upon and closely observed. The men are very proud of those who are brave in the field, and kind and considerate to the soldiers under them. An act of kindness done by an officer has often during the battle been the cause of his life being saved. Nay, whatever folks may say upon the matter, I know from experience that in our army the men like best to be officered by gentlemen, men whose education has rendered them more kind in manners than your coarse officer, sprung from obscure origin, and whose style is brutal and overbearing.

"During the battle I remarked the gallant style in which the 50th, Major Napier's regiment, came to the charge. They dashed upon the enemy like a torrent breaking bounds, and the French, unable even to bear the sight of them, turned and fled. Methinks at this moment I can hear the cheer of the British soldiers in the charge, and the clatter of the Frenchmen's accoutrements, as they turned in an instant, and went off as hard as they could run for it. I remember, too, our feelings towards the enemy on that occasion was the north side of friendly, for they had been firing upon us Rifles very sharply, greatly outnumbering our skirmishers, and appearing inclined to drive us off the face of the earth. Their Lights, and Grenadiers, I, for the first time, particularly remarked on that day. The Grenadiers (the 70th, I think), our men seemed to know well. They were all fine-looking young men, wearing red shoulder-knots and tremendous looking moustaches. As they came swarming upon us, they rained a perfect shower of balls, which we returned quite as sharply. Whenever one of them was knocked over our men called out, 'There goes another of Boney's Invincibles.'

"In the main body immediately in our rear, were the second battalion 52nd, the 50th, the second battalion 43rd, and a German corps, whose number I do not remember, besides several other regiments. The whole line seemed annoyed and angered at seeing the Rifles outnumbered by the Invincibles, and as we fell back, 'firing and retiring,' galling them handsomely as we did so, the men cried out (as it were with one voice) to charge. 'D—n them!' they roared, 'charge! charge!' General Fane, however, restrained their impetuosity. He desired them to stand fast and keep their ground.

"'Don't be too eager, men,' he said, as coolly as if we were on drill-parade in old England; 'I don't want you to advance just yet. Well done, 95th!' he called out, as he galloped up and down the line; 'well done, 43rd, 52nd, and well done all. I'll not forget, if I live, to report your conduct today. They shall hear of it in England, my lads!'

"A man named Brotherwood, of the 95th, at this moment rushed up to the general, and presented him with a green feather, which he had torn out of the cap of a French light-infantry soldier he had killed. 'God bless you, general!' he said; 'wear this for the sake of the 95th.' I saw the general take the feather and stick it in his cocked hat. The next minute he gave the word to charge, and down came the whole line, through a tremendous fire of cannon and musketry — and dreadful was the slaughter as they rushed onwards. As they came up with us, we sprang to our feet, gave one hearty cheer, and charged along with them, treading over our own dead and wounded, who lay in the front. The 50th were next us as we went, and I recollect, as I said, the firmness of that regiment in the charge. They appeared like a wall of iron. The enemy turned and fled, the cavalry dashing upon them as they went off.

"It was just at the close of the battle of Vimiero; the dreadful turmoil and noise of the engagement had hardly subsided, and I began to look into the faces of the men close around me, to see who had escaped the dangers of the hour. Four or five days back I had done the same thing at Roliça. One feels, indeed, a sort of curiosity to know, after such a scene, who is remaining alive amongst the companions endeared by good conduct, or disliked for bad character, during the hardships of the campaign. I saw that the ranks of the Riflemen looked very thin; it seemed to me one-half had gone down. We had four companies of the 95th, and were commanded that day by Major Travers. He was a tight hand, but a soldier likes that better than a slovenly officer; and indeed, he was deservedly beloved by all who knew him.

"I had observed him more than once during this day, spurring here and there, keeping the men well up, and apparently in the highest spirits. He could not have enjoyed himself more, I am sure, if he had been at a horse-race, or following a good pack of hounds. The battle was just over; a flag of truce had come over from the French; General Kellerman, I think, brought it. We threw ourselves down where we were standing when the fire ceased. A Frenchman lay close beside me; he was dying, and called to me for water, which I understood him to require more from his manner than his words (he pointed to his mouth). I need not say that I got up and gave it him. Whilst I did so, down galloped the major in front, just in the same good spirits he had been all day; plunging along, avoiding, with some little difficulty, the dead and dying which were strewed about. He was never a very good-looking man, being hard-featured and thin — a hatchet-faced man, as we used to say. But he was a regular good 'un — a real English soldier, and that's better than if he had been the handsomest ladies' man in the army.

"The major just now disclosed what none of us, I believe, knew before, namely, that his head was bald as a coot's, and that he covered the nakedness of his nob, up to the present time, by a flowing Caxon, which, during the neat of the action, had somehow been dislodged, and was lost; yet was the major riding hither and thither, digging the spurs into his horse's flanks, and just as busy as before the firing had ceased. 'A guinea,' he kept crying as he rode, 'to any man who will find my wig!' The men, I remember, notwithstanding the sight of the wounded and dead around them, burst into shouts of laughter at him as he went; and, 'a guinea to any man who will find my wig,' was the saying amongst us long after that affair."

Chapter Ten – When the Fight is Over

Harris sees with characteristic clearness of vision, and describes, with almost appalling resemblance, the grim scenes of the battle-field after the fiery tide of battle has ebbed from it. He says:

"After the day's work was over, whilst strolling about the field, just upon the spot where this charge had taken place, I remarked a soldier of the 43rd and a French grenadier both dead, and lying close together. They had apparently killed each other at the same moment, for both weapons remained in the bodies of the slam. Brotherwood was lying next me during a part of this day; he was a Leicestershire man, and was killed afterwards by a cannon ball at Vittoria. I remember his death more particularly from the circumstance of that very ball killing three of the company at the same moment, viz., Lieutenant Hopwood, Patrick Mahone, and himself. Brotherwood was amongst the skirmishers with me on this day. He was always a lively fellow, but rather irritable in disposition. Just as the French went to the right-about, I remember he d—d them furiously, and all his bullets being gone, he grabbed a razor from his haversack, rammed it down, and fired it after them.

"During this day I myself narrowly escaped being killed by our own dragoons, for somehow or other in the confusion I fell whilst they were charging, and the whole squadron thundering past just missed me as I lay amongst the dead and wounded. Tired and over-weighted with my knapsack and all my shoemaking implements, I lay where I had fallen for a short time and watched the cavalry as they gained the enemy. I observed a fine gallant-looking officer leading them on in that charge. He was a brave fellow, and bore himself like a hero; with his sword waving in the air he cheered the men on, as he went dashing upon the enemy and hewing and slashing at them in tremendous style. I watched for him as the dragoons came off after that charge, but saw him no more; he had fallen. Fine fellow, his conduct indeed made an impression upon me that I shall never forget, and I was told afterwards that he was a brother of Sir John Eustace.

"A French soldier was lying beside me at this time; he was badly wounded, and hearing him moan as he lay, after I had done looking at the cavalry I turned my attention to him, and getting up lifted his head and poured some water into his mouth. He was dying fast; but he thanked me in a foreign language, which, although I did not exactly understand, I could easily make out by the look he gave me. Mullins, of the Rifles, who stepped up whilst I supported his head, d—d me for a fool for my pains. 'Better knock out his brains, Harris,' said he, 'he has done us mischief enough, I'll be bound for it, today.'"

Harris, it will be noticed, has no reserves. He relates incidents which can hardly be regarded as creditable to the character of the British private, and does it with an amusing unconsciousness as to the impression his stories will produce on readers of a more sensitive age. The British soldier of that day had a rough chivalry of his own. He faced his foe gallantly on the battle-field. He would maintain a friendly barter of spirits and rations with him when night had fallen on contiguous bivouacs.

But when his enemy was dead, and no more fighting remained to be done, and no exchange of clandestine brandy was possible, then the British private would empty his foeman's pockets or take a pair of serviceable boots from his feet with the easiest nonchalance. The transaction, he considered, did not injure the dead, and it contributed to the comfort of the living. So Harris's tale of the plundering and the night scenes of a battle-field resemble those to be found in Smollett's *Count Fathom* with this superiority on the side of Harris, that his tales are transcripts of actual facts:

"After the battle I strolled about the field, in order to see if there was anything to be found worth picking up amongst the dead. The first thing I saw was a three-pronged silver fork, which, as it lay by itself, had most likely been dropped by some person who had been on the lookout before me. A little farther on I saw a French soldier sitting against a small rise in the ground or bank. He was wounded in the throat and appeared very faint, the bosom of his coat being saturated with the blood which had flowed down. By his side lay his cap, and close to that was a bundle containing a quantity of gold and silver crosses, which I concluded he had plundered from some convent or church. He looked the picture of a sacrilegious thief, dying hopelessly, and overtaken by Divine wrath. I kicked over his cap, which was also full of plunder, but I declined taking anything from him. I felt fearful of incurring the wrath of Heaven for the like offence, so I left him, and passed on.

"A little farther off lay an officer of the 50th Regiment. I knew him by sight, and recognised him as he lay. He was quite dead, and lying on his back. He had been plundered, and his clothes were torn open. Three bullet-holes were close together in the pit of his stomach. Beside him lay an empty pocket-book, and his epaulette had been pulled from his shoulder.

"I had moved on but a few paces, when I recollected that perhaps the officer's shoes might serve me, my own being considerably the worse for wear, so I returned again, went back, pulled one of his shoes off, and knelt down on one knee to try it on. It was not much better than my own; however, I determined on the exchange, and proceeded to take off its fellow. As I did so I was startled by the sharp report of a firelock, and at the same moment a bullet whistled close by my head. Instantly starting up I turned and looked in the direction whence the shot had come. There was no person near me in this part of the field. The dead and the dying lay thickly all around, but nothing else could I see. I looked to the priming of my rifle, and again turned to the dead officer of the 50th. It was evident that some plundering scoundrel had taken a shot at me, and the fact of his doing so proclaimed him one of the enemy. To distinguish him amongst the bodies strewn about was impossible; perhaps he might himself be one of the wounded. Hardly had I effected the exchange, put on the dead officer's shoes, and resumed my rifle, when another shot took place, and a second ball whistled past me. This time I was ready, and turning quickly I saw my man; he was just about to squat down behind a small mound about twenty paces from me. I took a haphazard shot at him, and instantly knocked him over. I immediately ran up to him; he had fallen on his face, and I heaved him over on his back, bestrode his body, and drew my sword-bayonet. There was, however, no occasion for the precaution, as he was even then in the agonies of death.

"It was a relief to me to find I had not been mistaken. He was a French light infantry man, and I therefore took it quite in the way of business — he had attempted my life, and lost his own. It was the fortune of war; so stooping down with my sword I cut the green string that sustained his calabash, and took a hearty pull to quench my thirst.

"After I had shot the French light infantry man, and quenched my thirst from his calabash, finding he was quite dead, I proceeded to search him. Whilst I turned him about in the endeavour at finding the booty I felt pretty certain he had gathered from the slain, an officer of the 60th approached and accosted me.

"'What, looking for money, my lad,' said he, 'eh?'

"'I am, sir,' I answered; 'but I cannot discover where this fellow has hid his hoard.'

"'You knocked him over, my man,' he said, 'in good style, and deserve something for the shot. Here,' he continued, stooping down, and feeling in the lining of the Frenchman's coat, 'this is the place where these rascals generally carry their coin. Rip up the lining of his coat, and then search in his stock. I know them better than you seem to do.'

"Thanking the officer for his courtesy, I proceeded to cut open the lining of his jacket with my sword-bayonet, and was quickly rewarded for my labour by finding a yellow silk purse, wrapped up in an old black silk handkerchief. The purse contained several doubloons, three or four Napoleons, and a few dollars. Whilst I was counting the money, the value of which, except the dollars, I did not then know, I heard the bugle of the Rifles sound out the assembly, so I touched my cap to the officer and returned towards them.

"The men were standing at ease, with the officers in front. As I approached them, Major Travers, who was in command of the four companies, called me to him.

"'What have you got there, sir?' he said. 'Show me.'

"I handed him the purse, expecting a reprimand for my pains. He, however, only laughed as he examined it, and turning showed it to his brother officers.

"'You did that well, Harris,' he said, 'and I am sorry the purse is not better filled. Fall in.' In saying this, he handed me back the purse, and I joined my company. Soon afterwards, the roll being called, we were all ordered to lie down and gain a little rest after our day's work.

"We lay as we had stood enranked upon the field, and in a few minutes, I dare say, one-half of that green line, overwearied with their exertions, were asleep upon the ground they had so short a time before been fighting on. After we had lain for some little time I saw several men strolling about the fields, so I again quietly rose, with one or two others of the Rifles, and once more looked about me to see what I could pick up amongst the slain.

"I had rambled some distance when I saw a French officer running towards me with all his might, pursued by at least half-a-dozen horsemen. The Frenchman was a tall, handsome-looking man, dressed in a blue uniform; he ran as swiftly as a wild Indian, turning and doubling like a hare. I held up my hand, and called to his pursuers not to hurt him. One of the horsemen, however, cut him down with a desperate blow when close beside me, and the next, wheeling round as he leaned from his saddle, passed his sword through the body.

"I am sorry to say there was an English dragoon amongst these scoundrels; the rest, by their dress, I judged to be Portuguese cavalry. Whether the Frenchman thus slaughtered was a prisoner trying to escape, or what was the cause of this cold-blooded piece of cruelty, I know not, as the horsemen immediately galloped off without a word of explanation; and, feeling quite disgusted with the scene I had witnessed, I returned to my comrades, and again throwing myself down, was soon as fast asleep as any there."

The plundering exploits of the British private were not always confined to his foes, living or dead. His own officers sometimes suffered. Says Harris:

"I remember there was an officer, named, I think, Cardo, with the Rifles. He was a great beau; but although rather effeminate and ladylike in manners, so much so as to be remarked by the whole regiment at that time, yet he was found to be a most gallant officer when we were engaged with the enemy in the field. He was killed whilst fighting bravely in the Pyrenees; and amongst other jewellery he wore, he had a ring on his finger worth 150 guineas.

"As he lay dead on the field, one of our Riflemen, named Orr, observed the sparkling gem, and immediately resolved to make prize of it. The ring, however, was so firmly fixed that Orr could not draw it from the finger, and, whipping out his knife, cut the finger off by the joint. After the battle Orr offered the ring for sale amongst the officers, and on inquiry the manner in which he had obtained it transpired. Orr was in consequence tried by court-martial, and sentenced to receive five hundred lashes, which sentence was carried into execution."

Chapter Eleven – A Memorable Retreat

Harris found a new commander-in-chief in Sir John Moore, and it was his fortune to share in the sufferings and glory of the immortal retreat to Corunna. Moore has never yet come to his true inheritance of fame as a commander. The great figure of Wellington hides him almost from human memory. Yet no British general, perhaps, ever conceived and executed a more audacious stroke of soldiership than did Moore when he made his famous stroke at Napoleon's communication, and spoiled the whole plans of that master-spirit in war for the conquest of Southern Spain, and brought him and his far-scattered columns hurrying up to the north-west angle of the Peninsula.

Napoleon had assumed in person the command of the French armies in Spain, and had 300,000 veterans under his eagles. He had shattered the Spanish armies, was in possession of the Spanish capital, and was on the point of marching to overwhelm the rich provinces as yet unravaged by war to the south. Moore, with 24,000 men under his command, resolved to strike boldly at Napoleon's communications, and so arrest the southward march of all the French columns. When, in this manner, he had paralysed the strategy of the French, Moore calculated he could outmarch all the converging columns rushing to destroy him, and escape. But he was accepting a terrific risk.

Moore's generalship, though it was followed by the tragedy of the retreat to Corunna, and his own death in the battle at that place, was perfectly successful. He wrecked Napoleon's strategy, and yet escaped his counter-stroke. He secured a breathing-space for the Spanish nation. He arrested and brought to a close Napoleon's personal career in that country. He made possible Wellington's great Peninsular campaigns. It is one of the examples of the irony of history that to Moore, one of the greatest soldiers England has produced, success brought no adequate fame, and it cost him his own life.

The second battalion of the Rifles, to which Harris belonged, joined Moore's forces at Sahagun, and the great retreat began almost immediately afterwards. On December 24 Moore turned his columns westward for their march to his sea-base at Corunna. It was a march of some 220 miles, through rugged mountainous country, with the French hanging on his rear or pushing past his flank, while the bitter tempests of the winter in Northern Spain blackened the skies above the toiling troops, and scourged them almost incessantly with snow and sleet and rain. At Astorga, Moore divided his army, and part, under Craufurd, took the road to Vigo. The Rifles formed part of Craufurd's force, and Harris's account thus sheds light on what is the least known branch of the famous retreat.

The retreat lasted in all eighteen days, and some 4000 men fell from the ranks, slain by mere hardship and exposure, during that comparatively brief period; yet the retreating British did not lose a flag or a gun in the retreat, and when they turned to bay at Corunna they proved that neither their discipline nor their fighting power had been in the least impaired by their sufferings. Harris's account is really a bit of very fine descriptive writing, though its charm lies in its simplicity and its unconscious realism. It must be remembered that when the second battalion of the Rifles joined Moore's forces at Sahagun they were worn out with long marches, and the fame of Roliça and Vimiero lay upon them. Moore's forces had up to that time seen no fighting, and still carried in face and uniform something of the freshness of barrack life:

"At Sahagun we fell in with the army under command of Sir John Moore. I forget how many thousand men there were; but they were lying in and around the town when we arrived. The Rifles marched to an old convent, some two miles from Sahagun, where we were quartered, together with a part of the 15th Hussars, some of the Welsh Fusiliers, and straggling bodies of men belonging to various other regiments, all seeming on the *qui vive*, and expecting the French to fall in with them every hour. As our small and wayworn party came to a halt before the walls of the convent, the men from these different regiments came swarming out to greet us, loudly cheering us as they rushed up and seized our hands. The difference in appearance between ourselves and these new-comers was indeed (just then) very great. They looked fresh from good quarters and good rations. Their clothes and accoutrements were comparatively new and clean, and their cheeks ruddy with the glow of health and strength; whilst our men, on the contrary, were gaunt-looking, wayworn, and ragged; our faces burnt almost to the hue of an Asiatic's by the sun, our accoutrements rent and torn, and many without even shoes to their feet. However, we had some work in us yet, and perhaps were in better condition for it than our more fresh-looking comrades."

Harris describes how, just before the retreat began, he was summoned at midnight to undertake, on somewhat alarming conditions, a very practical bit of preparation for the march:

"In the middle of the night I remember, as well as if the sounds were at this moment in my ear, that my name was called out many times without my being completely awakened by the summons. From weariness and the weight of my knapsack and the quantity of implements I carried, I was at first quite unable to gain my legs; but when I did so I found that Quarter-master Surtees was the person who was thus disturbing my rest.

"'Come, be quick there, Harris!' he said, as I picked my way by the light of the candle he held in his hand; 'look amongst the men, and rouse up all the shoemakers you have in the four companies. I have a job for them which must be done instantly.'

"With some little trouble, and not a few curses from them as I stirred them up with the butt of my rifle, I succeeded in waking several of our snoring handicrafts; and the quarter-master bidding us instantly follow him, led the way to the very top of the convent stairs. Passing then into a ruinous-looking apartment, along which we walked upon the rafters, there being no flooring, he stopped when he arrived at its farther extremity. Here he proceeded to call our attention to a quantity of barrels of gunpowder lying beside a large heap of raw bullocks' hides. 'Now, Harris,' said he, 'keep your eyes open, and mind what you are about here. General Craufurd orders you instantly to set to work and sew up every one of these barrels in the hides lying before you. You are to sew the skins with the hair outwards, and be quick about it, for the general swears that if the job is not finished in half-an-hour he will hang you.'

"The latter part of this order was anything but pleasant, and whether the general ever really gave it I never had an opportunity of ascertaining. Well knowing the stuff Craufurd was made of, I received the candle from the hands of Surtees, and bidding the men get needles and waxed thread from their knapsacks, as the quarter-master withdrew, I instantly prepared to set about the job.

"I often think of that night's work as I sit strapping away in my little shop in Richmond Street, Soho. It was a curious scene to look at, and the task neither very easy nor safe. The Riflemen were wearied, unwilling, and out of temper; and it was as much as I could do to get them to assist me. Moreover, they were so reckless that they seemed rather to wish to blow the convent into the air than to get on with their work. One moment the candle was dropped and nearly extinguished; the next they lost their implements between the rafters of the floor, flaring the light about amongst the barrels, and wishing, as I remonstrated with them, that the powder might ignite and blow me, themselves, and the general to. Such were the Riflemen of the Peninsular War — daring, gallant, reckless fellows. I had a hard task to get the work safely finished; but at length between coaxing and bullying these dare-devils I managed to do so, and together we returned down the convent stairs; and, finding Surtees awaiting us in the passage below, he reported to General Craufurd that his order had been obeyed. After which we were permitted again to lie down and sleep till the bugle awoke us next morning."

The exact moment when the advance for the purpose of falling on Soult was exchanged for retreat at speed before Napoleon's fiercely converging columns to the sea-coast is dramatically marked in Harris's *Recollections*. From the first, it will be noted, the retreat was pushed with the utmost sternness and energy, and at the cost of great suffering to the men. Moore had daringly advanced till his scanty columns were almost caught by the overwhelming forces of the French closing upon him; and to escape destruction the British had to tax their own strength and energy to the utmost:

"General Craufurd was in command of the brigade, and riding in front, when I observed a dragoon come spurring furiously along the road to meet us. He delivered a letter to the general, who turned round in his saddle the moment he had read a few lines, and thundered out the word 'to halt!' A few minutes more and we were all turned to the right-about, and retracing our steps of the night before — the contents of that epistle serving to furnish our men with many a surmise during the retrograde movement. When we again neared Sahagun, I remember seeing the wives and children of the men come rushing into the ranks, and embracing the husbands and fathers they expected never to see again.

"The entire Rifle corps entered the same convent we had before been quartered in; but this time we remained enranked in its apartments and passages, no man being allowed to quit his arms or lie down. We stood leaning upon the muzzles of our rifles, and dozed as we stood. After remaining thus for about an hour, we were then ordered out of the convent, and the word was again given to march. There was a sort of thaw on this day, and the rain fell fast. As we passed the walls of the convent, I observed our general (Craufurd) as he sat upon his horse, looking at us on the march, and remarked the peculiar sternness of his features; he did not like to see us going rearwards at all, and many of us judged there must be something wrong, by his severe look and scowling eye.

"'Keep your ranks there, men!' he said, spurring his horse towards some Riflemen who were avoiding a small rivulet. 'Keep your ranks and move on no straggling from the main body.'

"We pushed on all that day without halting; and I recollect the first thing that struck us as somewhat odd was our passing one of the commissariat waggons, overturned and stuck fast in the mud, and which was abandoned without an effort to save any of its contents. A sergeant of the 92nd Highlanders, just about this time, fell dead with fatigue, and no one stopped as we passed to offer him any assistance. Night came down upon us, without our having tasted food or halted I speak for myself and those around me and all night long we continued this dreadful march. Men began to look into each other's faces, and ask the question, 'Are we ever to be halted again?' and many of the weaker sort were now seen to stagger, make a few desperate efforts, and then fall, perhaps to rise no more. Most of us had devoured all we carried in our haversacks, and endeavoured to catch up anything we could snatch from hut or cottage in our route. Many, even at this period, would have straggled from the ranks and perished had not Craufurd held them together with a firm rein. One such bold and stern commander in the East, during a memorable disaster, and that devoted army had reached its refuge unbroken! Thus we staggered on night and day for about four days, before we discovered the reason of this continued forced march. The discovery was made to our company by a good-tempered, jolly fellow, named Patrick McLauchlan. He inquired of an officer marching directly in his front, the destination intended.

"'By J—s! Musther Hills,' I heard him say, 'where the devil is this you're taking us to?'

"'To England, McLauchlan,' returned the officer, with a melancholy smile upon his face as he gave the answer — 'if we can get there.'"

The Rifles formed part of the rear-guard, and to the hardships and sufferings common to the whole retreating force was added, in their case, the strain of constant engagement with the enemy. As a matter of fact, this served as a tonic to the men. It preserved their discipline. It gave them what they felt to be a delightful distraction from the monotony of splashing wet, hungry and faint, along muddy roads. They forgot the blinding rain, the eddying snowflakes, the pinch of hunger, as they turned a score of times in the day at bay and drove back with the roll of their volleys the pursuing French cavalry. Here are some pictures of how a British rear-guard bears itself in adverse circumstances:

"The information McLauchlan obtained from Lieutenant Hill quickly spread amongst us, and we now began to see more clearly the horrors of our situation, and the men to murmur at not being permitted to turn and stand at bay, cursing the French, and swearing they would rather die ten thousand deaths, with their rifles in their hands in opposition, than endure the present toil. We were in the rear at this time, and following that part of the army which made for Vigo, whilst the other portion of the British, being on the main road to Corunna, were at this moment closely pursued and harassed by the enemy, as I should judge from the continued thunder of their cannon and rattle of their musketry. Craufurd seemed to sniff the sound of battle from afar with peculiar feelings. He halted us for a few minutes occasionally, when the distant clamour became more distinct, and his face turned towards the sound, and seemed to light up and become less stern. It was then, indeed, that every poor fellow clutched his weapon more firmly and wished for a sight of the enemy.

"Before long they had their wish: the enemy's cavalry were on our skirts that night; and as *we* rushed out of a small village, the name of which I cannot now recollect, we turned to bay. Behind broken-down carts and tumbrils, huge trunks of trees, and everything we could scrape together, the Rifles lay and blazed away at the advancing cavalry.

"We passed the night thus engaged, holding our own as well as we could. Towards morning we moved down towards a small bridge, still followed by the enemy, whom, however, we had sharply galled, and obliged to be more wary in their efforts. The rain was pouring down in torrents on this morning, I recollect, and we remained many hours with our arms ported, standing in this manner, and staring the French cavalry in the face, the water actually running out of the muzzles of our rifles. I do not recollect seeing a single regiment of infantry amongst the French force on this day; it seemed to me a tremendous body of cavalry — some said nine or ten thousand strong — commanded, as I heard, by General Lefèbvre.

"Whilst we stood thus, face to face, I remember the horsemen of the enemy sat watching us very intently, as if waiting for a favourable moment to dash upon us like beasts of prey; and every now and then their trumpets would ring out a lively strain of music as if to encourage them. As the night drew on, our cavalry moved a little to the front, together with several fieldpieces, and succeeded in crossing the bridge; after which we also advanced and threw ourselves into some hilly ground on either side the road; whilst the 43rd and 52nd lay behind some carts, trunks of trees, and other materials with which they had formed a barrier.

"General Craufurd was standing behind this barricade, when he ordered the Rifles to push still farther in front, and conceal themselves amongst the hills on either side. A man named Higgins was my front-rank man at this moment. 'Harris,' he said, 'let you and I gain the very top of the mountain, and look out what those French thieves are at on the other side.'

"My feet were sore and bleeding, and the sinews of my logs ached as if they would burst, but I resolved to accompany him. In our wearied state the task was not easy, but, by the aid of Higgins, a tall and powerful fellow, I managed to reach the top of the mountain, where we placed ourselves in a sort of gully or ditch, and looked over to the enemy's side, concealing ourselves by lying flat in the ditch as we did so. Thus, in favourable situations, like cats watching for their prey, were the rest of the Rifles lying *perdu* upon the mils that night. The mountain we found was neither so steep nor so precipitous on the enemy's side. The ascent, on the contrary, was so easy that one or two of the videttes of the French cavalry were prowling about very near where we lay. As we had received orders not to make more noise than we could help, not even to speak to each other, except in whispers, although one of these horsemen approached close to where I lay, I forbore to fire upon him.

"At length he stopped so near me that I saw it was almost impossible he could avoid discovering that the Rifles were in such close proximity to his person. He gazed cautiously along the ridge, took off his helmet, and wiped his face, as he appeared to meditate upon the propriety of crossing the ditch in which we lay, when suddenly our eyes met, and in an instant he plucked a pistol from his holster, fired it in my face, and, wheeling his horse, plunged down the hillside. For the moment I thought I was hit, as the ball grazed my neck, and stuck fast in my knapsack, where I found it, when, many days afterwards, I unpacked my kit on shipboard. About a quarter of an hour after this, as we still lay in the gully, I heard some person clambering up behind us, and, upon turning quickly round, I found it was General Craufurd. The general was wrapped in his greatcoat, and, like ourselves, had been for many hours drenched to the skin, for the rain was coming down furiously. He carried in his hand a canteen full of rum and a small cup, with which he was occasionally endeavouring to refresh some of the men. He offered me a drink as he passed, and then proceeded onwards along the ridge. After he had emptied his canteen, he came past us again, and himself gave us instructions as to our future proceedings.

"'When all is ready, Riflemen,' said he, 'you will immediately get the word, and pass over the bridge. Be careful, and mind what you are about.'

"Accordingly, a short time after he had left us, we were ordered to descend the mountain side in single file, and having gained the road, were quickly upon the bridge. Meanwhile the Staff Corps had been hard at work mining the very centre of the structure, which was filled with gunpowder, a narrow plank being all the aid we had by which to pass over. For my own part, I was now so utterly helpless that I felt as if all was nearly up with me, and that, if I could steady myself so as to reach the farther end of the plank, it would be all I should be able to accomplish. However, we managed all of us to reach the other side in safety, when, almost immediately afterwards, the bridge blew up with a tremendous report, and a house at its extremity burst into flames. What with the concussion of the explosion and the tremulous state of my limbs, I was thrown to the ground, and lay flat upon my face for some time, almost in a state of insensibility. After a while I somewhat recovered; but it was not without extreme difficulty, and many times falling again, that I succeeded in regaining the column.

"Soon after I had done so, we reached Benevento, and immediately took refuge in a convent. Already three parts of it were filled with other troops, among which were mingled the loth Hussars, the Germ an Legion, and the 15th Dragoons; the horses of these regiments standing as close as they could stand, with the men dismounted between each horse, the animals' heads to the walls of the building, and all in readiness to turn out on the instant. Liquor was handed to us by the Dragoons, but having had nothing for some time to eat, many of our men became sick instead of receiving any benefit from it.

"Before we had been in the convent as long a time as I have been describing our arrival, every man of us was down on the floor, and well nigh asleep; and before we had slept half-an-hour, we were again aroused from our slumbers by the clatter of the horses, the clash of the men's sabres, and their shouts for us to clear the way.

"'The enemy! The enemy!' I heard shouted out.

"'Clear the way, Rifles! Up, boys, and clear the way!'

"In short, the Dragoons hardly gave us time to rise before they were leading their horses amongst us, and getting out of the convent as fast as they could scamper, whilst we ourselves were not long in following their example. As we did so, we discovered that the French cavalry, having found the bridge blown up, had dashed into the stream and succeeded in crossing. Our cavalry, however, quickly formed, and charged them in gallant style.

"The shock of that encounter was tremendous to look upon, and we stood for some time enranked watching the combatants. The horsemen had it all to themselves; our Dragoons fought like tigers, and, although greatly overmatched, drove the enemy back like a torrent, and forced them again into the river. A private of the 10th Hussars — his name, I think, was Franklin — dashed into the stream after their general (Lefebvre), assailed him, sword in hand, in the water, captured, and brought him a prisoner on shore again. If I remember rightly, Franklin, or whatever else was his name, was made a sergeant on the spot. The French general was delivered into our custody on that occasion, and we cheered the men heartily as we received him.

"After the enemy had received this check from our cavalry, and which considerably damped their ardour, making them a trifle more shy of us for a while, we pushed onwards on our painful march. I remember marching close beside the French general during some part of this day, and observing his chapfallen and dejected look as he rode along in the midst of the green jackets."

In spite of all his own sufferings, Harris was still able to note, with an unconsciously artistic eye, the scenes — wild, tragic, and picturesque — which the retreat afforded:

"Being constantly in rear of the main body, the scenes of distress and misery I witnessed were dreadful to contemplate, particularly amongst the women and children, who were lagging and falling behind, their husbands and fathers being in the main body in our front. We came to the edge of a deep ravine, the descent so steep and precipitous, that it was impossible to keep our feet in getting down, and we were sometimes obliged to sit and slide along on our backs; whilst before us rose a ridge of mountains quite as steep and difficult of ascent. There was, however, no pause in our exertion, but, slinging our rifles round our necks, down the hill we went; whilst mules with the baggage on their backs, wearied and urged beyond their strength, were seen rolling from top to bottom, many of them breaking their necks with the fall, and the baggage crushed, smashed, and abandoned.

"I remember as I descended this hill remarking the extraordinary sight afforded by the thousands of our red-coats, who were creeping like snails, and toiling up the ascent before us, their muskets slung round their necks, and clambering with both hands as they hauled themselves up. As soon as we ourselves had gained the ascent we were halted for a few minutes, in order to give us breath for another effort, and then onwards we moved again.

"It is impossible for me to keep any account of time in this description, as I never exactly knew how many days and nights we marched; but I well know we kept on for many successive days and nights without rest, or much in the way of food. The long day found us still pushing on, and the night caused us no halt.

"We pushed on still cursing the enemy for not again showing themselves, that we might revenge some of our present miseries upon their heads.

"'Why don't they come on like men,' they cried, 'whilst we've strength left in us to fight them?'

"We were now upon the mountains; the night was bitter cold, and the snow falling fast. As day broke, I remember hearing Lieutenant Hill say to another officer (who, by the way, afterwards sank down and died), 'This is New Year's Day; and I think if we live to see another we shall not easily forget it.'

"The mountains were now becoming more wild-looking and steep as we proceeded, whilst those few huts we occasionally passed seemed so utterly forlorn and wretched-looking, it appeared quite a wonder how human beings could live in so desolate a home. After the snow commenced the hills became so slippery (being in many parts covered with ice), that several of our men frequently slipped and fell, and being unable to rise, gave themselves up to despair and died. There was now no endeavour to assist one another after a fall; it was every one for himself, and God for us all!

"The enemy, I should think, were at this time frequently close upon our trail; and I thought at times I heard their trumpets come down the wind as we marched. Towards the dusk of the evening of this day I remember passing a man and woman lying clasped in each other's arms, and dying in the snow. I knew them both, but it was impossible to help them. They belonged to the Rifles and were man and wife. The man's name was Joseph Sitdown. During this retreat, as he had not been in good health previously, himself and wife had been allowed to get on in the best way they could in the front. They had, however, now given in, and the last we ever saw of poor Sitdown and his wife was on that night lying perishing in each other's arms in the snow.

"Many trivial things which happened during the retreat to Corunna, and which on any other occasion might have entirely passed from my memory, have been, as it were, branded into my remembrance, and I recollect the most trifling incidents which occurred from day to day during that march. I remember, amongst other matters, that we were joined, if I may so term it, by a young recruit, when such an addition was anything but wished for during the disasters of the hour. One of the men's wives (who was struggling forward in the ranks with us, presenting a ghastly picture of illness, misery, and fatigue), being very large in the family way, towards evening stepped from amongst the crowd and laid herself down amidst the snow, a little out of the main road. Her husband remained with her; and I heard one or two hasty observations amongst our men that they had taken possession of their last resting-place. The enemy were, indeed, not far behind at this time, the night was coming down, and their chance seemed in truth but a bad one.

"To remain behind the column of march in such weather was to perish, and we accordingly soon forgot all about them. To my surprise, however, I some little time afterwards (being myself then in the rear of our party) again saw the woman. She was hurrying with her husband after us, and in her arms she carried the babe she had just given birth to. Her husband and herself between them managed to carry that infant to the end of the retreat, where we embarked. God tempers the wind, it is said, to the shorn lamb, and many years afterwards I saw that boy a strong and healthy lad. The woman's name was M'Guire, a sturdy and hardy Irishwoman; and lucky was it for herself and babe that she was so, as that night of cold and sleet was in itself sufficient to try the constitution of most females. I lost sight of her, I recollect, on this night when the darkness came upon us, but with the dawn, to my surprise she was still amongst us."

Chapter Twelve – Stern Scenes

The sufferings of the retreat steadily increased. The weather grew more bitter, the country more difficult, the supply of food scantier. Under the strain of incessant marching, the strength of the men gave way. All were ragged and hungry; many were barefooted; many were sick, racked with coughs, shaken with ague, or burning with fever. Their discipline seemed to go to pieces. Nothing survived but a spirit of dogged, sullen courage that seized, with a thrill of something like fierce delight, every opportunity of turning on their relentless pursuers:

"The shoes and boots of our party were now mostly either destroyed or useless to us, from foul roads and long miles, and many of the men were entirely barefooted, with knapsacks and accoutrements altogether in a dilapidated state. The officers were also, for the most part, in as miserable a plight. They were pallid, wayworn, their feet bleeding, and their faces overgrown with beards of many days' growth. What a contrast did our corps display, even at this period of the retreat, to my remembrance of them on the morning their dashing appearance captivated my fancy in Ireland! Many of the poor fellows, now near sinking with fatigue, reeled as if in a state of drunkenness, and altogether I thought we looked the ghosts of our former selves; still we held on resolutely. Our officers behaved nobly, and Craufurd was not to be daunted by long miles, fatigue, or foul weather. Many a man in that retreat caught courage from his stern eye and gallant bearing. Indeed, I do not think the world ever saw a more perfect soldier than General Craufurd.

"As the day began to dawn, we passed through another village — a long, straggling place. The houses were all closed at this early hour, and the inhabitants mostly buried in sleep, and, I dare say, unconscious of the armed thousands who were pouring through their silent streets. When about a couple of miles from this village, Craufurd again halted us for about a quarter of an hour. It appeared to me that, with returning daylight, he wished to have a good look at us this morning, for he mingled amongst the men as we stood leaning upon our rifles, gazing earnestly in our faces as he passed, in order to judge of our plight by our countenances. He himself appeared anxious, but full of fire and spirit, occasionally giving directions to the different officers, and then speaking words of encouragement to the men. It is my pride now to remember that General Craufurd seldom omitted a word in passing to myself. On this occasion, he stopped in the midst and addressed a few words to me, and, glancing down at my feet, observed —

"'What! no shoes, Harris, I see, eh?'

"'None, sir,' I replied; 'they have been gone many days back.' He smiled, and passing on spoke to another man, and so on through the whole body.

"Craufurd was, I remember, terribly severe during this retreat, if he caught anything like pilfering amongst the men. As we stood, however, during tins short halt, a very tempting turnip field was close on the side of us, and several of the men were so ravenous, that although he was in our very ranks, they stepped into the field and helped themselves to the turnips, devouring them like famishing wolves. He either did not or would not observe the delinquency this time, and soon afterwards gave the word and we moved on once more.

"About this period I remember another sight, which I shall not to my dying day forget; and it causes me a sore heart even now as I remember it. Soon after our halt beside the turnip field the screams of a child near me caught my ear, and drew my attention to one of our women, who was endeavouring to drag along a little boy of about seven or eight years of age. The poor child was apparently completely exhausted, and his legs falling under him. The mother had occasionally, up to this time, been assisted by some of the men, taking it in turn to help the little fellow on; but now all further appeal was in vain. No man had more strength than was necessary for the support of his own carcass, and the mother could no longer raise the child in her arms, as her reeling pace too plainly showed. Still, however, she continued to drag the child along with her. It was a pitiable sight, and wonderful to behold the efforts the poor woman made to keep the boy amongst us. At last the little fellow had not even strength to cry, but, with mouth wide open, stumbled onwards, until both sank down to rise no more. The poor woman herself had, for some time, looked a moving corpse, and when the shades of evening came down, they were far behind amongst the dead or dying in the road."

Hunger and desperation sometimes tempted even the veterans of the Rifles to leave the ranks in the hope of discovering, in some fold of the lonely Asturian hills, a shepherd's hut, or a little farmhouse, where food might be got at and an hour's shelter enjoyed. Harris describes one such adventure undertaken by himself:

"Towards evening we came to a part of the country of a yet wilder and more desolate appearance even than that we had already traversed; a dreary wilderness it appeared at this inclement season, and our men, spite of the vigilance of the general, seemed many of them resolved to stray into the open country rather than traverse the road before them. The coming night favoured their designs, and many were before morning lost to us through their own wilfulness. Amongst others I found myself completely bewildered and lost upon the heath, and should doubtless have perished had I not fallen in with another of our corps in the same situation. As soon as we recognised each other I found my companion in adversity was a strapping resolute fellow named James Brooks, a north of Ireland man. He was afterwards killed at Toulouse. He was delighted at having met with me, and we resolved not to desert each other during the night. Brooks, as I have said, was a strong, active, and resolute fellow, as indeed I had on more occasions than one witnessed in Portugal At the present time his strength was useful to both of us.

"'Catch hold of my jacket, Harris,' said he; 'the ground here is soft, and we must help each other tonight or we shall be lost in the bogs.'

"Before long that which Brooks feared happened, and he found himself stuck so fast in the morass that although I used my best efforts to draw him out I only shared in the same disaster, so that, leaving him, I turned and endeavoured to save my own life if possible, calling to him to follow before he sank over head and ears. This was an unlucky chance in our wearied state, as the more we floundered in the dark, not knowing which way to gain a firmer foundation, the faster we fixed ourselves. Poor Brooks was so disheartened that he actually blubbered like a child. At length, during a pause in our exertions, I thought I heard something like the bark of a dog come down the wind. I bade Brooks listen, and we both distinctly heard it — the sound gave us new hope just as we were about to abandon ourselves to our fate. I advised Brooks to lay himself as flat as he could and drag himself out of the slough, as I had found some hard tufts of grass in the direction I tried; and so, by degrees, we gained a firmer footing, and eventually succeeded in extricating ourselves, though in such an exhausted state that for some time we lay helplessly upon the ground unable to proceed.

"At length, with great caution, we ventured to move forwards in the direction of the sounds we had just heard. We found, however, that our situation was still very perilous, for in the darkness we hardly dared to move a step in any direction without probing the ground with our rifles, lest we should again sink and be eventually smothered in the morasses we had strayed amongst. On a sudden, however, as we carefully felt our way, we heard voices shouting in the distance, and calling out 'Men lost, men lost!' which we immediately concluded were the cries of some of our own people who were situated like ourselves.

"After a while I thought I saw, far away, something like a dancing light, which seemed to flicker about, vanish, and reappear, similar to a Jack-o'-lantern. I pointed it out to Brooks, and we agreed to alter our course and move towards it. As we did so the light seemed to approach us and grow larger. Presently another and another appeared, like small twinkling stars, till they looked something like the lamps upon one of our London bridges as seen from afar. The sight revived our spirits, more especially as we could now distinctly hear the shouts of people who appeared in search of the stragglers, and as they approached us we perceived that such was indeed the case. The lights, we now discovered, were furnished by bundles of straw and dried twigs tied on the ends of long poles and dipped in tar. They were borne in the hands of several Spanish peasants, from a village near at hand, whom Craufurd had thus sent to our rescue.

"To return to my own adventures on this night. When Brooks and myself reached the village I have mentioned we found it filled with soldiers, standing and lying huddled together like cattle in a fair. A most extraordinary sight it appeared as the torches of the peasants flashed upon the wayworn and gaunt figures of our army. The rain was coming down, too, on this night, I remember; and soon after I reached our corps I fell helplessly to the ground in a miserable plight. Brooks was himself greatly exhausted, but he behaved nobly, and remained beside me, trying to persuade some of our men to assist him in lifting me up, and gaining shelter in one of the houses at hand. 'May I be!' I heard him say, 'if I leave Harris to be butchered in the streets by the cowardly Spaniards the moment our division leaves the town.'

"At length Brooks succeeded in getting a man to help him, and together they supported me into the passage of a house, where I lay upon the floor for some time. After a while, by the help of some wine they procured, I rallied and sat up, till eventually I got once more upon my legs, and, arm in arm, we proceeded again into the streets and joined our corps. Poor Brooks certainly saved my life that night. He was one of the many good fellows whom I have seen out, and I often think of mm with feelings of gratitude as I sit at my work in Richmond Street, Soho."

There were certainly not many men, even in Craufurd's rear-guard, stronger in body or hardier in temper than Harris, yet at last even his iron strength and dauntless energy failed him. He began to lag behind, making occasional and desperate rallies to keep up with his battalion. He says:

"I remember Sir Dudley Hill passing me on a mule this day. He wore a Spanish straw hat and had his cloak on. He looked back when he had passed, and addressed me: 'Harris,' said he, 'I see you cannot keep up.' He appeared sorry for me, for he knew me well. 'You must do your best,' he said, 'my man, and keep with us, or you will fall into the hands of the enemy.' As the day wore on I grew weaker and weaker, and at last, in spite of all my efforts, I saw the main body leave me hopelessly in the lurch. Brooks himself was getting weaker too; he saw it was of little use to urge me on, and at length, assenting to my repeated request to be left behind, he hurried on as well as he was able without a word of farewell. I now soon sank down in the road and lay beside another man who had also fallen and was apparently dead, and whom I recognised as one of our sergeants.

"Whilst we lay exhausted in the road the rear-guard, which was now endeavouring to drive on the stragglers, approached, and a sergeant of the Rifles came up and stopped to look at us. He addressed himself to me, and ordered me to rise; but I told him it was useless for him to trouble himself about me as I was unable to move a step farther. Whilst he was urging me to endeavour to rise up, the officer in command of the rear-guard also stepped up. The name of this officer was Lieutenant Cox; he was a brave and good man, and observing that the sergeant was rough in his language and manner towards me, he silenced him and bade the guard proceed and leave me. 'Let him die quietly, Hicks,' he said to the sergeant. 'I know him well; he's not the man to lie here if he could get on. I am sorry, Harris,' he said, 'to see you reduced to this, for I fear there is no help to be had now.' He then moved on after his men, and left me to my fate.

"After lying still for a while, I felt somewhat restored and sat up to look about me. The sight was by no means cheering. On the road behind me I saw men, women, mules, and horses lying at intervals, both dead and dying; whilst far away in front I could just discern the enfeebled army crawling out of sight, the women[4] huddled together in its rear, trying their best to get forward amongst those of the sick soldiery, who were now unable to keep up with the main body. After a while I found that my companion, the sergeant, who lay beside me, had also recovered a little, and I tried to cheer him up. I told him that opposite to where we were lying there was a lane, down which we might possibly find some place of shelter if we could muster strength to explore it. The sergeant consented to make the effort, but after two or three attempts to rise, gave it up. I myself was more fortunate; with the aid of my rifle I got upon my legs, and seeing death in my companion's face, I resolved to try and save myself, since it was quite evident to me that I could render him no assistance.

"After hobbling some distance down the lane, to my great joy I espied a small hut or cabin with a little garden in its front; I therefore opened the small door of the hovel, and was about to enter when I considered that most likely I should be immediately knocked on the head by the inmates if I did so. The rain, I remember, was coming down in torrents at this time, and, reflecting that to remain outside was but to die, I resolved at all events to try my luck within. I had not much strength left, but I resolved to sell myself as dearly as I could. I therefore brought up my rule and stepped across the threshold. As soon as I had done so I observed an old woman seated beside a small fire upon the hearth. She turned her head as I entered, and immediately upon seeing a strange soldier, she arose and filled the hovel with her screams. As I drew back

[4] Some of these poor wretches cut a ludicrous figure, having the men's greatcoats buttoned over their heads, whilst their clothing, being extremely ragged and scanty, their naked legs were very conspicuous. They looked a tribe of travelling beggars.

within the doorway an elderly man, followed by two, who were apparently his sons, rushed from a room in the interior. They immediately approached me; but I brought up my rifle again and cocked it, bidding them keep their distance.

"After I had thus brought them to a parley I got together what little Spanish I was master 01, and begged for shelter for the night and a morsel of food, at the same time lifting my feet and displaying them a mass of bleeding sores. It was not, however, till they had held a tolerably long conversation among themselves that they consented to afford me shelter, and then only upon the condition that I left by daylight on the following morning. I accepted the conditions with joy. Had they refused me I should indeed not have been here to tell the tale. Knowing the treachery of the Spanish character, I however refused to relinquish possession of my rifle, and my right hand was ready in an instant to unsheath my bayonet, as they sat and stared at me whilst I devoured the food they offered.

"All they gave me was some coarse black bread, and a pitcher of sour wine. It was, however, acceptable to a half-famished man; and I felt greatly revived by it. Whilst I supped, the old hag, who sat close beside the hearth, stirred up the embers, that they might have a better view of their guest, and the party meanwhile overwhelmed me with questions, which I could neither comprehend nor had strength to answer. I soon made signs to them that I was unable to maintain the conversation, and begged of them, as well as I could, to show me some place where I might lay my wearied limbs till dawn.

"Notwithstanding the weariness which pervaded my whole body, I was unable for some time to sleep except by fitful snatches, such was the fear I entertained of having my throat cut by the savage-looking wretches still seated before the fire. Besides which, the place they had permitted me to crawl into was more like an oven than anything else, and being merely a sort of berth scooped out of the wall, was so filled with fleas and other vermin, that I was stung and tormented most miserably all night long.

"Bad as they had been, however, I felt somewhat restored by my lodging and supper, and with the dawn I crawled out of my lair, left the hut; retraced my steps along the lane, and once more emerged upon the highroad, where I found my companion, the sergeant, dead, and lying where I had left him the night before.

"I now made the best of my way along the road in the direction in which I had last seen our army retreating the night before. A solitary individual, I seemed left behind amongst those who had perished. It was still raining, I remember, on this morning, and the very dead looked comfortless in their last sleep as I passed them occasionally lying on the line of march. It had pleased Heaven to give me an iron constitution, or I must have failed, I think, on this day, for the solitary journey and the miserable spectacles I beheld rather damped my spirits.

"After progressing some miles, I came up with a cluster of poor devils who were still alive, but apparently, both men and women, unable to proceed. They were sitting huddled together in the road, their heads drooping forward, and apparently patiently awaiting their end.

"Soon after passing these unfortunates, I overtook a party who were being urged forward under charge of an officer of the 42nd Highlanders. He was pushing them along pretty much as a drover would keep together a tired flock of sheep. They presented a curious example of a retreating force. Many of them had thrown away their weapons, and were linked together arm-in-arm, in order to support each other, like a party of drunkards. They were, I saw, composed of various regiments; many were bareheaded and without shoes, and some with their heads tied up in old rags and fragments of handkerchiefs. I marched in company with this party for some time, but as I felt after my night's lodging and refreshment in better condition, I ventured to push forward, in the hope of rejoining the main body, and which I once more came up with in the street of a village.

"On falling in with the Rifles, I again found Brooks, who was surprised at seeing me still alive, and we both entered a house, and begged for something to drink. I remember that I had a shirt upon my back at this time, which I had purchased off a drummer of the 9th Regiment before the commencement of the retreat. It was the only good one I had. I stripped, with the assistance of Brooks, and took it off, and exchanged it with a Spanish woman for a loaf of bread, which Brooks, myself, and two other men, shared amongst us.

"I remember to have again remarked Craufurd at this period of the retreat. He was in no whit altered in his desire to keep the force together, I thought; but, still active and vigilant as ever, he seemed to keep his eye upon those who were now most likely to hold out. I myself marched during many hours close beside him this day. He looked stern and pale, but the very picture of a warrior. I shall never forget Craufurd if I live to a hundred years, I think. He was in everything a soldier.

"Slowly and dejectedly crawled our army along. Their spirit of endurance was now considerably worn out, and, judging from my own sensations, I felt confident that, if the sea was much farther from us, we must be content to come to a halt at last without gaining it. I felt something like the approach of death as I proceeded a sort of horror, mixed up with my sense of illness; a reeling I have never experienced before or since. Still I held on; but with all my efforts, the main body again left me behind. Had the enemy's cavalry come up at this time I think they would have had little else to do but ride us down without striking a blow."

At last the great retreat, with its horrors and sufferings, drew to a close. The sea was reached, and not even Xenophon's Ten Thousand, as they caught from some hill summit the purple gleam of the far-off sea, knew a keener delight than did Craufurd's barefooted, famine-wasted veterans. Says Harris:

"It is astonishing how man clings to life. I am certain that had I lain down at this period, I should have found my last billet on the spot I sank upon. Suddenly I heard a shout in front, which was prolonged in a sort of hubbub. Even the stragglers whom I saw dotting the road in front of me seemed to have caught at something like hope; and as the poor fellows now reached the top of a hill we were ascending, I heard an occasional exclamation of joy — the first note of the sort I had heard for many days. When I reached the top of the hill the thing spoke for itself. There, far away in our front, the English shipping lay in sight.

"Its view had indeed acted like a restorative to our force, and the men, at the prospect of a termination to the march, had plucked up spirit for a last effort. Fellows who, like myself, seemed to have hardly strength in their legs to creep up the ascent, seemed now to have picked up a fresh pair to get down with. Such is hope to us poor mortals!

"As we proceeded down the hill we now met with the first symptoms of the good feeling from the inhabitants it was our fortune to experience during our retreat. A number of old women stood on either side of the road, and occasionally handed us fragments of bread as we passed them. It was on this day, and whilst I looked anxiously upon the English shipping in the distance, that I first began to find my eyesight failing, and it appeared to me that I was fast growing blind. The thought was alarming, and I made desperate efforts to get on. Bell, however, won the race this time. He was a very athletic and strong-built fellow, and left me far behind, so that I believe at that time I was the very last of the retreating force that reached the beach, though, doubtless, many stragglers came dropping up after the ships had sailed, and were left behind.

"As it was, when I did manage to gain the seashore, it was only by the aid of my rifle that I could stand, and my eyes were now so dim and heavy that with difficulty I made out a boat, which seemed the last that had put off.

"Fearful of being left half blind in the lurch, I took off my cap, and placed it on the muzzle of my rifle as a signal, for I was totally unable to call out. Luckily, Lieutenant Cox, who was aboard the boat, saw me and ordered the men to return, and making one more effort I walked into the water, and a sailor, stretching his body over the gunwale, seized me as if I had been an infant and hauled me on board. His words were characteristic of the English sailor, I thought.

"'Hullo, there, you lazy lubber!' he said, as he grasped hold of me, 'who the — do you think is to stay humbugging all day for such a fellow as you?'"

Here is Harris's description of how, after a stormy passage, the transports reached the English coast, and the wrecks of Moore's gallant battalions were allowed to land:

"After remaining off Spithead for about five or six days, one fine morning we received orders to disembark, and our poor bare feet once more touched English ground. The inhabitants flocked down to the beach to see us as we did so, and they must have been a good deal surprised at the spectacle we presented. Our beards were long and ragged; almost all were without shoes and stockings; many had their clothes and accoutrements in fragments, with their heads swathed in old rags, and our weapons were covered with rust; whilst not a few had now from toil and fatigue become quite blind.

"Let not the reader, however, think that even now we were to be despised as soldiers. Long marches, inclement weather, and want of food had done their work upon us; but we were perhaps better than we appeared, as the sequel showed, tinder the gallant Craufurd we had made some tremendous marches, and even galled our enemies severely, making good our retreat by the way of Vigo. But our comrades in adversity, and who had retired by the other road to Corunna, under General Moore, turned to bay there, and showed the enemy that the English soldier is not to be beaten even under the most adverse circumstances.

"The field of death and slaughter, the march, the bivouac, and the retreat, are no bad places in which to judge of men. I have had some opportunities of judging them in all these situations, and I should say that the British are amongst the most splendid soldiers in the world. Give them fair-play, and they are unconquerable. For my own part, I can only say that I enjoyed life more whilst on active service than I have ever done since; and as I sit at my work in my shop in Richmond Street, Soho, I look back upon that portion of my time spent in the fields of the Peninsula as the only part worthy of remembrance. It is at such times that scenes long past come back upon my mind as if they had taken place but yesterday. I remember even the very appearance of some of the regiments engaged; and comrades, long mouldered to dust, I see again performing the acts of heroes."

Harris gives a bit of dreadful arithmetic, which shows the losses sustained in the retreat:

"After the disastrous retreat to Corunna, the Rifles were reduced to a sickly skeleton, if I may so term it. Out of perhaps nine hundred of as active and fine fellows as ever held a weapon in the field of an enemy's country, we paraded some three hundred weak and crestfallen invalids.

"I myself stood the third man in my own company, which was reduced from near a hundred men to but three. Indeed, I think we had scarce a company on parade stronger than ten or twelve men at the first parade. After a few parades, however, our companies gradually were augmented by those of the sick who recovered, but many of those who did not sink in hospital were never more of much service as soldiers."

Chapter Thirteen – Some Famous Soldiers

Harris's *Recollections* abound in what may be called thumb-nail sketches of his comrades and his officers. He had a quick eye for character as well as for incident; and his descriptions are always interesting and often very amusing. Harris was naturally more interested, perhaps, in his comrades than in his officers and his generals. He was closer to them and understood them better. Yet he gives some sharply-drawn pictures of famous British battle-leaders as they were seen by the eyes of the men whom they led. Here, for example, is a picture of General — afterwards Lord-Hill, just before the battle of Roliça. "Farmer" Hill was his sobriquet amongst the men, and he owed that title as much to his homely and kindly spirit as to his red, broad, and farmer-like face. Says Harris:

"We were pelting along through the streets of a village, the name of which I do not think I ever knew, so I cannot name it. I was in the front and had just cleared the village when I recollect observing General Hill (afterwards Lord Hill) and another officer ride up to a house, and give their horses to some of the soldiery to hold. Our bugles at that moment sounded the halt, and I stood leaning upon my rifle near the door of the mansion which General Hill had entered; there was a little garden before the house, and I stood by the gate. Whilst I remained there the officer who had entered with General Hill came to the door and called to me. 'Rifleman,' said he, 'come here.' I entered the gate and approached him. 'Go,' he continued, handing me a dollar, 'and try if you can get some wine! for we are devilish thirsty here.' Taking the dollar I made my way back to the village. At a wine-house, where the men were crowding around the door, and clamouring for drink (for the day was intensely hot), I succeeded, after some little difficulty, in getting a small pipkin full of wine, but the crowd was so great that I found as much trouble in paying for it as in getting it; so I returned back as fast as I was able, fearing that the general would be impatient, and move off before I reached him.

"I remember Lord Hill was loosening his sword-belt as I handed him the wine. 'Drink first, Rifleman,' said he, and I took a good pull at the pipkin and held it to him again. He looked at it as I did so, and told me I might drink it all up, for it appeared greasy; so I swallowed the remainder, and handed him back the dollar which I had received from the officer. 'Keep the money,' he said, 'my man. Go back to the village once more and try if you cannot get me another draught.' Saying this, he handed me a second dollar, and told me to be quick. I made my way back to the village, got another pipkin full, and returned as fast as I could. The general was pleased with my promptness, and drank with great satisfaction, handing the remainder to the officer who attended him; and I dare say, if he ever recollected the circumstance afterwards, that was as sweet a draught, after the toil of the morning march, as he has drunk at many a nobleman's board in old England since."

Of Beresford, again — who, if he was not a great general, was at least a terrible fighter — Harris gives an amusing sketch:

"I remember a great many of the leaders and heroes of the wars of my own time. Alas! they have been cleared off of late pretty handsomely! A few years more and the world will be without another living remembrancer of either them or their deeds. The ranks are getting thin, too, amongst those who, like myself, were the tools with which the great men of former days won their renown. I don't know a single living man now who was a comrade during the time I served. Very nearly fifteen years back, I remember, however, meeting with Robert Liston, and that meeting brings Marshal Beresford to my mind.

"Robert Liston was a corporal in the second battalion of the Rifles, when we lay for a few days in the passages of a convent in Portugal. We were then making for the frontiers of Spain, when we were swept into that disastrous retreat to Corunna. There was a punishment parade in the square of this convent. A soldier of the 92nd or 79th was the culprit, and the kilts were formed to witness the performance. Some of the Rifles were looking from the windows of the convent at the punishment of the Highlander, when a brickbat was hurled from one of the casements and fell at the very toe of the lieutenant-colonel, who was standing in the midst, and in command of the regiment. The lieutenant-colonel (whose name I never knew) was, of course, indignant at such an act; he gazed up at the window from which the brick had been thrown, and caused an inquiry instantly to be made. It was between the lights when this happened, and it was impossible to discover who had done it; however, two or three men of the Rifles were confined on suspicion. A man named Baker flatly accused Corporal Liston of the act; upon which Liston was marched a prisoner to Salamanca (a distance, I should think, of some hundred miles); and often did he complain of his hard fate in being a prisoner so long. When we got to Salamanca we halted there for eight days; and Liston, being tried by general court-martial, was sentenced to receive eight hundred lashes. The whole brigade turned out on the occasion, and I remember that the drummers of the 9th Regiment were the inflicters of the lash. Liston received the whole sentence without a murmur. He had, indeed, been a good soldier, and we were all truly sorry for him; in fact, he always declared solemnly that he had no more to do with the brickbat than Marshal Beresford who commanded the brigade. Whoever committed the act, in my opinion, well deserved what Liston got.

"Marshal Beresford was in command of the brigade at this time; and I well remember what a fine-looking soldier he was. He was equal to his business, too, I should say; and he, amongst others of our generals, often made me think that the French army had nothing to show in the shape of officers who could at all compare with ours. There was a noble bearing in our leaders, which they on the French side (as far as I was capable of observing) had not; and I am convinced that the English soldier is even better pleased to be commanded by some men of rank in his own country than by one who has risen from his own station.

"They are a strange set, the English! and so determined and unconquerable, that they will have their way if they can. Indeed, it requires one who has authority in his face, as well as at his back, to make them respect and obey him.

"I never saw Liston after that punishment whilst in Spain; and I suppose he remained behind, and got on in the best manner he was able in the rear; but, about ten years afterwards, as I was passing down Sloane Street, Chelsea, I observed a watchman calling the hour. It struck me that I knew his face, and, turning back, I stopped him, asking if he was not Robert Liston, formerly a corporal in the 95th Rifles? After answering in the affirmative, the first words he spoke were, 'Oh, Harris! do you remember what happened to me at Salamanca?'

"'I do well,' I said.

"'I was never guilty,' he continued. 'There is no occasion for me to deny it now; but I tell you that I was never guilty of the crime for which I suffered. Baker was a villain, and I believe that he was himself the culprit.'

"I recollect Marshal Beresford making a speech on the subject of the buttons of our greatcoats; and, however such a subject may appear trifling for a general officer to speak on, I can tell you it was a discourse which our men (some of them) much needed; for they had been in the habit of tearing off the buttons from their coats, and after hammering them flat, passing them as English coin, in exchange for the good wines of Spain. So that, at last, the Spaniards, finding they got nothing by the exchange but trumpery bits of battered lead, and the children in that country not being in the habit of playing at dumps as ours are, they made complaints to the Marshal. Halting the brigade, therefore, one day, he gave them a speech upon this fraud, and ended by promising a handsome flogging to the first man he found thereafter whose greatcoat would not keep buttoned in windy weather."

Of another yet more famous soldier, Napier, we get an interesting glimpse in Harris's pages:

"I remember meeting with General Napier before the battle of Vimiero. He was then, I think, a major; and the meeting made so great an impression on me that I have never forgotten him. I was posted in a wood the night before the battle, in front of our army, where two roads crossed each other. The night was gloomy, and I was the very out-sentry of the British army. As I stood on my post, peering into the thick wood around me, I was aware of footsteps approaching, and challenged in a low voice. Receiving no answer, I brought my rifle to the port, and bade the strangers come forward. They were Major Napier (then of the 50th Foot, I think), and an officer of the Rifles. The major advanced close up to me, and looked hard in my face.

"'Be alert here, sentry,' said he, 'for I expect the enemy upon us to-night, and I know not how soon.'

"I was a young soldier then, and the lonely situation I was in, together with the impressive manner in which Major Napier delivered his caution, made a great impression on me, and from that hour I have never forgotten him. Indeed, I kept careful watch all night, listening to the slightest breeze amongst the foliage, in expectation of the sudden approach of the French."

Of Wellington himself — then Sir Arthur Wellesley — we have a brief sketch at Vimiero:

"I remember seeing the Duke of Wellington during the battle of Vimiero; and in these days, when so much anxiety is displayed to catch even a glance of that great man's figure as he gallops along the streets of London, it seems gratifying to me to recollect seeing him in his proper element, 'the raging and bloody field,' and I have frequently taxed my mind to remember each action and look I caught of him at that time.

"I remember seeing the great Duke take his hat off in the field of Vimiero, and methinks it is something to have seen that wonderful man even do so commonplace a thing as lift his hat to another officer in the battlefield. We were generally enveloped in smoke and fire, and sometimes unable to distinguish or make remarks upon what was going on around, whilst we blazed away at our opponents; but occasionally we found time to make our comments upon the game we were playing. Two or three fellows near me were observing what was going on just in the rear, and I heard one man remark, 'Here comes Sir Arthur and his staff;' upon which I also looked back, and caught sight of him just meeting two other officers of high rank. They all uncovered as they met, and I saw the Duke, as I said (then Sir Arthur Wellesley), take off his hat and bow to the other two. The names of the new-comers, however they were learnt, whether from some of the men who had before seen them, or picked up on the instant from an officer, seemed to be well known, as well as the business they were engaged in talking of; for it ran along the line from one to the other that Sir Hew Dalrymple and Sir Harry Burrard were about to take the command, instead of Sir Arthur Wellesley, a circumstance which, of course, could only be a random guess amongst these fellows at the moment."

The real hero of Harris's pages, however, is Craufurd, the stern and even rashly heroic leader of the Light Division, who ended his career on the great breach at Badajos. Harris came into close contact with Craufurd, studied him with a curious vividness of insight, and felt for him an admiring loyalty almost too great for words. His account of Craufurd gives us what is very rare in literature — a description of a great commander by one of the privates who trudged in the battalions he commanded. Harris, in the retreat to Vigo, saw Craufurd under conditions which might well tax to the uttermost the resources and temper of a general.

"I do not think I ever admired any man who wore the British uniform more than I did General Craufurd. I could till a book with descriptions of him, for I frequently had my eye upon him in the hurry of action. It was gratifying to me, too, to think he did not altogether think ill of me, since he has often addressed me kindly when, from adverse circumstances, you might have thought that he had scarcely spirits to cheer up the men under him. The Rifles liked him, but they also feared him, for he could be terrible when insubordination showed itself in the ranks. 'You think, because you are Riflemen, you may do whatever you think proper,' said he one day to the miserable and savage-looking crew around him in the retreat to Corunna; 'but I'll teach you the difference before I have done with you.' I remember one evening during the retreat he detected two men straying away from the main body; it was in the early stage of that disastrous flight, and Craufurd knew well that he must do his utmost to keep the division together. He halted the brigade with a voice of thunder, ordered a drum-head court-martial on the instant, and they were sentenced to a hundred apiece. Whilst this hasty trial was taking place, Craufurd dismounting from his horse stood in the midst, looking stern and angry as a worried bulldog. He did not like retreating at all, that man.

"The three men nearest him as he stood, were Jagger, Dan Howans, and myself. All were worn, dejected, and savage, though nothing to what we were after a few days more of the retreat. The whole brigade were in a grumbling and discontented mood, and Craufurd, doubtless, felt ill-pleased with the aspect of affairs altogether.

"'D—n his eyes!' muttered Howans, 'he had much better try to get us something to eat and drink than harass us in this way.'

"No sooner had Howans disburdened his conscience of this growl than Craufurd, who had overheard it, turning sharply round, seized the rifle out of Jagger's hand, and felled him to the earth with the butt-end.

"'It was not I who spoke,' said Jagger, getting up and shaking his head. 'You shouldn't knock me about.'

"'I heard you, sir,' said Craufurd, 'and I will bring you also to a court-martial.'

"'I am the man who spoke,' said Howans. 'Ben Jagger never said a word.'

"'Very well,' returned Craufurd, 'then I'll try you, sir.'

"And, accordingly, when the other affair was disposed of, Howans's case came on. By the time the three men were tried it was too dark to inflict the punishment. Howans, however, had got the complement of three hundred promised to him; so Crauford gave the word to the brigade to move on. He marched all that night on foot, and when the morning dawned I remember that, like the rest of us, his hair, beard, and eyebrows were covered with the frost, as if he had grown white with age. We were, indeed, all of us in the same condition. Scarcely had I time to notice the appearance of morning before the general once more called a halt we were then on the hills. Ordering a square to be formed, he spoke to the brigade, as well as I can remember, in these words, after having ordered the three before-named men of the 95th to be brought into the square.'

"'Although,' said he, 'I should obtain the goodwill neither of the officers nor the men of the brigade here by so doing, I am resolved to punish these three men according to the sentence awarded, even though the French are at our heels. Begin with Daniel Howans.'

"This was indeed no time to be lax in discipline, and the general knew it. The men, as I said, were some of them becoming careless and ruffianly in their demeanour, whilst others again I saw with the tears falling down their cheeks from the agony of their bleeding feet, and many were ill with dysentery from the effects of the bad food they had got hold of and devoured on the road. Our knapsacks, too, were a bitter enemy on this prolonged march. Many a man died, I am convinced, who would have borne up well to the end of the retreat, but for the infernal load we carried on our backs. My own knapsack was my bitterest enemy; I felt it press me to the earth almost at times, and more than once felt as if I should die under its deadly embrace. The knapsacks, in my opinion, should have been abandoned at the very commencement of the retrograde movement, as it would have been better to have lost them altogether, if, by such loss, we could have saved the poor fellows who, as it was, died strapped to them on the road.

"There was some difficulty in finding a place to tie Howans up, as the light brigade carried no halberts. However, they led him to a slender ash tree which grew near at hand.

"'Don't trouble yourself about tying me up,' said Howans, folding his arms, 'I'll take my punishment like a man!'

"He did so without a murmur, receiving the whole three hundred. His wife, who was present with us, I remember, was a strong, hardy Irishwoman. When it was over, she stepped up and covered Howans with his grey greatcoat. The general then gave the word to move on. I rather think he knew the enemy was too near to punish the other two delinquents just then; so we proceeded out of the corn-field in which we had been halted, and toiled away upon the hills once more, Howans's wife carrying the jacket, knapsack, and pouch, which the lacerated state of the man's back would not permit him to bear.

"It could not have been, I should think, more than an hour after the punishment had been inflicted upon Howans, when the general again gave the word for the brigade to halt, and once more formed them into a square. We had begun to suppose that he intended to allow the other two delinquents to escape, under the present difficulties and hardships of the retreat. He was not, however, one of the forgetful sort, when the discipline of the army under him made severity necessary.

"'Bring out the other two men of the 95th,' said he, 'who were tried last night.'

"The men were brought forth accordingly, and their lieutenant-colonel, Hamilton Wade, at the same time stepped forth. He walked up to the general, and lowering his sword, requested that he would forgive these men, as they were both of them good soldiers, and had fought in all the battles of Portugal.

"'I order you, sir,' said the general, 'to do your duty. These men shall be punished.'

"The lieutenant-colonel, therefore, recovering his sword, turned about, and fell back to the front of the Rifles. One of the men, upon this (I think it was Armstrong), immediately began to unstrap his knapsack, and prepare for the lash. Craufurd had turned about meanwhile, and walked up to one side of the square. Apparently he suddenly relented a little, and, again turning sharply around, returned towards the two prisoners. 'Stop,' said he. 'In consequence of the intercession of your lieutenant-colonel, I will allow you thus much: you shall draw lots and the wanner shall escape; but one of the two I am determined to make an example of.'

"The square was formed in a stubble-field, and the sergeant-major of the Rifles, immediately stooping down, plucked up two straws, and the men coming forward, drew. I cannot be quite certain, but I think it was Armstrong who drew the longest straw, and won the safety of his hide; and his fellow-gamester was in quick time tied to a tree, and the punishment commenced. A hundred was the sentence; but when the bugler had counted seventy-five, the general granted him a further indulgence, and ordered him to be taken down and to join his company. The general calling for his horse, now mounted for the first time for many hours; for he had not ridden all night, not indeed since the drum-head court-martial had taken place. Before he put the brigade in motion again, he gave us another short specimen of his eloquence, pretty much, I remember, after this style.'

"'I give you all notice,' said he, 'that I will halt the brigade again the very first moment I perceive any man disobeying my orders, and try him by court-martial on the spot.' He then gave us the word, and we resumed our march.

"Many who read this, especially in these peaceful times, may suppose this was a cruel and unnecessary severity under the dreadful and harassing circumstances of that retreat; but I, who was there, and was, besides, a common soldier of the very regiment to which these men belonged, say it was quite necessary. No man but one formed of stuff like General Craufurd could have saved the brigade from perishing altogether; and if he flogged two, he saved hundreds from death by his management.

"It was perhaps a couple of days after this had taken place that we came to a river. It was tolerably wide, but not very deep, which was just as well for us; for, had it been deep as the dark regions, we must have somehow or other got through. The avenger was behind us, and Craufurd was along with us, and the two together kept us moving, whatever was in the road. Accordingly, into the stream went the light brigade, and Craufurd, as busy as a shepherd with his flock, riding in and out of the water, to keep his wearied band from being drowned as they crossed over. Presently he spied an officer who, to save himself from being wet through, I suppose, and wearing a damp pair of breeches for the remainder of the day, had mounted on the back of one of his men. The sight of such a piece of effeminacy was enough to raise the choler of the general, and in a very short time he was plunging and splashing through the water after them both.

"'Put him down, sir! put him down! I desire you to put that officer down instantly!' And the soldier, in an instant, I dare say nothing loath, dropping his burden like a hot potato into the stream, continued his progress through. 'Return back, sir,' said Crauford to the officer, 'and go through the water like the others. I will not allow my officers to ride upon the men's backs through the rivers; all must take their share alike here.'

"Wearied as we were, this affair caused all who saw it to shout almost with laughter, and was never forgotten by those who survived the retreat.

"General Craufurd was indeed one of the few men who was apparently created for command during such dreadful scenes as we were familiar with in this retreat. He seemed an iron man; nothing daunted him nothing turned him from his purpose. War was his very element, and toil and danger seemed to call forth only an increasing determination to surmount them. I was sometimes amused with his appearance, and that of the men around us; for, the Rifles being always at his heels, he seemed to think them his familiars. If he stopped his horse, and halted to deliver one of his stern reprimands, you would see half-a-dozen lean, unshaven, shoeless, and savage Riflemen, standing for the moment leaning upon their weapons, and scowling up in his face as he scolded; and when he dashed the spurs into his reeking horse, they would throw up their rifles upon their shoulders and hobble after him again. He was sometimes to be seen in the front, then in the rear, and then you would fall in with him again in the midst, dismounted, and marching on foot, that the men might see he took an equal share in the toils which they were enduring. He had a mortal dislike, I remember, to a commissary. Many a time have I heard him storming at the neglect of those gentry, when the men were starving for rations, and nothing but excuses forthcoming.

"Twice I remember he was in command of the light brigade. The second time he joined them he made, I heard, something like these remarks, after they had been some little time in Spain.

"'When I commanded you before,' he said, 'I know full well that you disliked me, for you thought me severe. This time I am glad to find there is a change in yourselves.'"

Chapter Fourteen – The "Tommy Atkins" of a Century Ago

Harris's descriptions of his comrades are always kindly, but they are keen. There is a touch of barrack freedom about them, and they have a Dutch realism which sometimes makes them unquotable. They give an excellent idea of the British soldier of a bygone generation, the men who constituted the rank and file of the most famous army that ever marched beneath the British flag — the men of the Peninsula. Perhaps nowhere else in literature can be found descriptions so homely and real of the soldier as seen — on the march, in the firing line, and by the campfire — by his own comrade. Harris's attention is naturally most arrested by the human oddities amongst his comrades, or by such of them as had in their appearance, or in their fate, a gleam of the picturesque. Here are some of the portraits in his picture gallery:

"A youth joined the Rifles soon after I myself put on the green jacket, whose name was Medley. He was but a small chap, being under the standard by one inch;[5] but our officers thought he promised fair to become a tall fellow, and he was, accordingly, not rejected. Medley did not deceive them, for, on the day he first joined the Rifles, he was five feet one inch in height, and on the day he was killed, at Barossa, he was exactly six feet one. He was celebrated for being the greatest grumbler, the greatest eater, and the most quarrelsome fellow in the whole corps. I remember he cut a most desperate figure in the retreat to Corunna; for there he had enough to bear both of fatigue and hunger; and a very little of either of these disagreeables would make him extremely bad company at any time. It was dangerous, too, to bid him hold his tongue sometimes; for he had picked up so amongst us since he was only five feet one, and grown so bony as well as tall, that he would challenge and thrash any man in the corps. Corunna, however, though it could not stop his growling, took the desire of boxing quite out of him, and he sprawled, scrambled, and swore, till he somehow got through that business. If General Craufurd could have heard but the twentieth part of what I heard

[5] The standard at that time, when men were quickly used up, was five feet two with us.

him utter about him on that retreat, I think he would have cut Medley in half. He was, as I said, a capital feeder, and his own allowance was not half enough to satisfy his cravings, so that he often got some of his comrades to help him out with a portion of theirs. He was killed at Barossa, as I said, and he carried his ill-humour with him to the very last hour of his life; for, being knocked over by a musket-ball in the thigh, he was spoken to as he lay by some of his comrades, who, asking if they should assist him, and carry him to the rear, he told them to 'Go and be d—d!' and bidding them mind their own business, abused them till they passed on and left him. I was told this last anecdote of him by the very men who had spoken to him and got his blessing as he lay.

"We had another tall fellow in the four companies of Rifles who were in that retreat. His name was Thomas Higgins; he was six feet one and a half, and quite as lank and bony as Medley. He also was an ill-tempered fellow, but nothing to compare with him either in eating or grumbling. The tall men, I have often observed, bore fatigue much worse than the short ones; and Higgins amongst others of the big 'uns was dreadfully put to it to keep on. We lost him entirely when about half through this business, I remember; for, during a short halt of about ten minutes, he was reprimanded by one of our officers for the slovenly state of his clothing and accoutrements; his dress almost dropping from his lower limbs, and his knapsack hanging by a strap or two down about his waist. Higgins did not take it at all kind being quarrelled with at such a time, and, uttering sundry impertinences, desired to know if they were ever to be allowed to halt any more, adding that he did not see very well how he was to be very smart after what he had already gone through. The officer spoke to one of the sergeants upon this, and bid him remember, if they got to their journey's end, to give Higgins an extra guard for his behaviour. 'Oh! then, d—n me,' says Higgins, 'if ever I take it!' and turning about, as we all moved on at the word to march, he marched off in the contrary direction, and we never either saw or heard of him from that hour; and it was supposed afterwards, amongst us, that he had either perished alone in the night, or joined the French, who were at our heels. These were the two tallest men in the four companies of Rifles; and both were in the company I belonged to. Higgins was the right-hand, and Medley the left-hand man.

"Thomas Mayberry was a man well known at that time in the Rifles. He was a sergeant in my day, and was much thought of by our officers as a very active and useful non-commissioned officer, being considered, up to the time of his committing the slight mistake I shall have to tell of, one of the most honest men in the army. With the men he was not altogether so well-liked, as he was considered rather too blusterous and tyrannical. Whilst in the town of Hythe, he got the fingering of about two hundred pounds for the purpose of paying for necessaries purchased for the men of his company, and which two hundred pounds he had, in a very short space of time, managed to make away with, and lose in the society of a party of gamblers, who at that time infested the town of Hythe. He was brought to court-martial, together with two other men, whom he had seduced to become partners in his gambling transactions; and, on the inquiry, it was further discovered that he had been in the habit of cheating the men of his company out of a farthing a week each for the last ten months. That was, perhaps, the worst thing against him. He was sentenced to receive seven hundred lashes.

"When Mayberry was tied up, he was offered, as was then customary, the option of banishment; but he refused it, notwithstanding considerable entreaty was made to him by his two comrades to accept it, as, by so doing, they thought they all would escape the lash. However, Mayberry decided to take the seven hundred, and bore the sentence without a murmur. Not so the two others; Morrisson screamed and struggled so much that he capsized the triangle, and all came sprawling together, so that he was obliged to be held by a man at each side. Devine came last. He was rather an effeminate-looking man, and the colonel rode round and told him he lamented being obliged to break so fair a skin, but he must do his duty. However, as he had borne a good character, and was not so much to blame as the other two, he let him down after five-and-twenty.

"Mayberry after this was much scouted by his fellow-soldiers, and also ill-thought-of by the officers; and, on a detachment being sent to Portugal, he volunteered for the expedition. Captain Hart, however, would fain have declined taking him, as he had so bad an opinion of him after this affair; but Mayberry showed himself so desirous of going, that at last he consented, and took him. At the siege of Badajos, Mayberry wiped off, in a measure, all his former ill-conduct. He was seen by

Captain Hart to behave so bravely in the breach, that he commended him on the spot.

"'Well done, Mayberry!' said he; 'you have this day done enough to obliterate your disgrace; and, if we live, I will endeavour to restore you to your former rank. Go now to the rear; you have done enough for one day.' Mayberry, however, refused to retire, although covered with wounds; for he was known to have killed seven with his own hand, with his rifle-sword-bayonet.

"'No going to the rear for me,' he said. 'I'll restore myself to my comrades' opinion, or make a finish of myself altogether.'

"He accordingly continued in the front of all, till at last he was seen to be cut down, in the clear light of the fire-balls, by a tremendous sword-cut, which cleft his skull almost in twain. Morrisson, I heard, also died at that siege. Devine returned safe home, and died of fatigue at Fermoy.

"The intelligence of these men was indeed very great, and I could relate instances of their recklessness and management which would amuse the reader much. I remember a fellow, named Jackman, getting close up to the walls at Flushing, and working a hole in the earth with his sword, into which he laid himself, and remained there alone, in spite of all the efforts of the enemy and their various missiles to dislodge him. He was known, thus earthed, to have killed, with the utmost coolness and deliberation, eleven of the French artillerymen as they worked at their guns. As fast as they relieved each fallen comrade did Jackman pick them off; after which he took to his heels, and got safe back to his comrades.

"There were three brothers in the Rifles named Hart — John, Mike, and Peter — and three more perfectly reckless fellows, perhaps, never existed. Nothing ever escaped their notice; and they would create the greatest fun and laughter, even when advancing under the hottest fire of the enemy, and their comrades being shot down beside them. I remember Lieutenant Molly, who was himself 'as fine a soldier as ever stepped, and as full of life in the midst of death' as these Harts, being obliged to check them at Vimiero. 'D—n you!' he said to them, 'keep back, and get under cover. Do you think you are fighting here with your fists that you are running into the teeth of the French?'

"I never saw those three men, to appearance, in the least degree worse for hard work during the time we remained in Portugal. They could run like deer, and were, indeed, formed by nature and disposition for the hardships, difficulties, and privations of the sort of life we then led. They were, however, all three pretty well done up during the retreat to Corunna; though, even in that dreadful business, their light-heartedness and attempts at fun served to keep up the spirits of many a man who would else have been broken-hearted before the English shipping appeared in sight. They even carried their pleasantry on that occasion so far as to make a jest of their own appearance, and the miserable plight of the whole turn-out, as we disembarked upon the beach at Portsmouth. One of them even went so far as to observe, 'that we looked more like the rakings of h— than the fragments of an army!'

"Nothing, indeed, but that grave of battalions, that unwholesome fen, Flushing, could have broken the spirits of three such soldiers as John, Mike, and Peter Hart. A few weeks, however, of that country sufficed to quiet them for evermore. One, I remember, died; and the other two, although they lived to return, were never worth a rush afterwards, but, like myself, remained living examples of what climate can bring even a constitution and body framed as if of iron to.

"Nothing I suppose could exceed the dreadful appearance we cut on the occasion of the disembarkation from Corunna; and the inhabitants of Portsmouth, who had assembled in some numbers to see us land, were horror-stricken with the sight of their countrymen and relatives returning to England in such a ghastly state; whilst the three Harts, with feet swathed in bloody rags, clothing that hardly covered their nakedness, accoutrements in shreds, beards covering their faces, eyes dimmed with toil (for some were even blind), arms nearly useless to those who had them left, the rifles being encrusted with rust, and the swords glued to the scabbard — these three brothers, I say (for I heard them myself), as they hobbled up the beach, were making all sorts of remarks, and cracking their jokes upon the misery of our situation and the appearance they themselves cut.

"Whilst we lay near Cork we were joined by one Richard Pullen, amongst others; he had exchanged from the English militia into the Irish, and volunteered to us Rifles from the North Mayo. He brought with him little else to boast of but his wife and his two children, Charles and Susan. Charles was a mischievous boy of about twelve, and Susan was a pretty little lass of about fourteen years of age. I remember they all went with us to Copenhagen, and got through that expedition pretty well. That affair suited a man of Pullen's description, for he didn't like too much service; and we soon found he was rather a shy cock. I remember remarking that Pullen (even on the first day of the retreat to Corunna) looked very chapfallen and seedy; and he was beginning even then to complain that he could not stand much more. The wife and children, too, were dropping behind. They all thought, poor souls, that when night came on they were, of course, to be billeted; but the open world was now their only refuge, and no allowance to stop or lie down, even on the bare heath, at that time. I saw Pullen again on the third or fourth day; neither the wife nor children were then with him, nor could he tell where they were; he could only answer for himself, and expected to drop dead, he said, every step. That's all I saw of Pullen and his wife and children on the retreat, or even thought of them; for I had enough to do to keep my own strength up. When we landed at Portsmouth, both myself and others (to our no small surprise) saw Pullen once more; and much we wondered at the sight of him, when so many better and stronger soldiers had died before half of that retreat was accomplished. We found that he had left behind him, and knew nothing of the fate of either his wife or his children, Charles and Susan. As the men continued to disembark, however, there was Pullen inquiring anxiously of every one for some tidings of them. None, however, could he get. At last he saw his wife coming up the beach, and hobbled off to meet her, each at the same moment inquiring for the children, Charles and Susan. He trusted they were with the wife; and she hoped they were with the husband; and both sat down upon the beach and cried in concert. All our men thought it useless of them to continue their inquiries; but they never failed to ask after their offspring of every fresh face they fell in with who had been in that retreat. In about a fortnight's time, not satisfied, they advertised Charles and Susan in the public newspapers; and we all. laughed at the very idea of their ever finding them again, and told them they might have spared the money. To our no small surprise, however, the artillery at Plymouth answered their advertisement, stating that a little girl had been heard screaming upon the mountains in Spain by them in the night, and that they had taken care of her as well as they could, and had her then with them. The description answering, the girl was forwarded to Hythe; and Pullen and his wife once more embraced their daughter Susan.

"There was, I recollect, a man of the name of Bell, of the Rifles, who had been during this day holding a sort of creeping race with me — we had passed and repassed each other as our strength served. Bell was rather a discontented fellow at the best of times; but during this retreat he had given full scope to his ill-temper, cursing the hour he was born, and wishing his mother had strangled him when he came into the world, in order to have saved him from his present toil. He had not now spoken for some time, and the sight of the English shipping had apparently a very beneficial effect upon him. He burst into tears as he stood and looked at it.

"'Harris,' he said, 'if it pleases God to let me reach those ships, I swear never to utter a bad or discontented word again.'

"The history of Sergeant-Major Adams is somewhat singular. I was his great friend at this time, and he confided some part of it to me. He had been a croppy (a rebel) and had fought at Vinegar Hill. When the rebels were defeated he escaped, and lived some time in the wilds of Connemara. He afterwards thought it best to enlist in the Donegal militia, and then volunteered to the Rifles. Here he soon rose (whilst in Spain) to the rank of sergeant. During the retreat to Corunna, Sergeant-Major Crosby failed, and Craufurd promoted Adams in his place. At St. Sebastian he was noticed by General Graham for his bravery with the forlorn hope; a commission was given him, and he afterwards joined a regiment in Gibraltar, where he was made adjutant. He then went to America, where he served with credit till he died. I believe I was the only man in the regiment who knew of his having been a rebel, and I kept the secret faithfully till his death.

"The story of Demon, whom I myself enlisted from the Leicester militia, is not a little curious. Demon was a smart and very active man, and serving as corporal in the light company of the Leicestershire, when I persuaded him to join our corps, where he was immediately made a sergeant in the third battalion then just forming, and from which he eventually rose to be a commissioned officer in one of our line regiments. The cause which led to Demon's merits being first noticed was not a little curious, being neither more nor less than a race.

"It happened that at Shoreham Cliff, soon after he joined, a race was got up among some Kentish men who were noted for their swiftness, and one of them, who had beaten his companions, challenged any soldier in the Rifles to run against him for two hundred pounds. The sum was large, and the runner was of so much celebrity that, although we had some active young fellows amongst us, no one seemed inclined to take the chance, either officers or men, till at length Demon stepped forth and said he would run against this Kentish boaster or any man on the face of the earth, and fight him afterwards into the bargain, if any one could be found to make up the money. Upon this an officer subscribed the money, and the race was arranged.

"The affair made quite a sensation, and the inhabitants of the different villages from miles around flocked to see the sport; besides which the men from different regiments in the neighbourhood, infantry, cavalry, and artillery, also were much interested, and managed to be present, which caused the scene to be a very gay one. In short the race commenced, and the odds were much against the soldier at starting, as he was a much less man than the other, and did not at all look like the winner. He, however, kept well up with his antagonist, and the affair seemed likely to end in a dead heat, which would undoubtedly have been the case, but Demon, when close upon the winning-post, gave one tremendous spring forward, and won it by his body's length.

"This race, in short, led on to notice and promotion. General Mackenzie was in command of the garrison at Hythe. He was present, and was highly delighted at the Rifleman beating the bumpkin, and saw that the winner was the very cut of a soldier, and, in short, that Demon was a very smart fellow, so that eventually the news of the race reached the first battalion then fighting in Spain. Sir Andrew Barnard at the time was then in command of the Rifles in Spain; upon being told of the circumstance, remarked that, as Demon was such a smart runner in England, there was very good ground for a Rifleman to use his legs in Spain, he was accordingly ordered out with the next draft to that country, where he so much distinguished himself that he obtained his commission, as already mentioned."

One gleam of the more tender sentiments which shines in Harris's *Recollections* — almost the solitary love affair he records — was of a very amusing kind. He was the shoemaker of the company, and when in Lisbon he was detailed, with three other men, to discover a shoemaker's shop, where all the worn-out shoes of the battalion might be mended. Says Harris:

"We carried with us three small sacks filled with old boots and shoes, and entering Lisbon went into the first shoemaker's shop we saw. Here I endeavoured in vain to make myself understood for some time. There was a master shoemaker at work and three men. They did not seem to like our intrusion, and looked very sulky, asking us various questions which I could not understand, the only words I could at all comprehend being, 'Bonos Irelandos, brutu Englisa.' I thought, considering we had come so far to fight their battles for them, that this was the north side of civil; so I signed to the men, and, by way of explanation of our wishes, and in order to cut the matter short, they emptied the three sackful of boots and shoes upon the floor. We now explained what we would be at; the boots and shoes of the Rifles spoke for themselves, and, seating ourselves, we commenced work forthwith. In this way we continued employed whilst the army lay near Lisbon, every morning coming in to work and returning to the camp every night to sleep.

"After we had been there several days, our landlord's family had the curiosity to come occasionally and take a peep at us. My companions were noisy, good-tempered, jolly fellows, and usually sang all the time they hammered and strapped. The mistress of the house, seeing I was the head-man, occasionally came and sat down beside me as I worked, bringing her daughter, a very handsome dark-eyed Spanish girl, and as a matter of course I fell in love.

"We soon became better acquainted, and the mother one evening, after having sat and chatted to me, serving me with wine and other good things, on my rising to leave the shop, made a signal for me to follow her. She had managed to pick up a little English, and I knew a few words of the Spanish language, so that we could pretty well comprehend each other's meaning; and after leading me into their sitting-room, she brought her handsome daughter, and, without more circumstance, offered her to me for a wife. The offer was a tempting one, but the conditions of the marriage made it impossible for me to comply, since I was to change my religion and desert my colours. The old dame proposed to conceal me effectually when the army marched, after which I was to live like a gentleman, with the handsome Maria for a wife.

"It was hard to refuse so tempting an offer, with the pretty Maria endeavouring to back her mother's proposal. I, however, made them understand that nothing would tempt me to desert, and, promising to try and get my discharge when I returned to England, protested would then return and marry Maria.

"Soon after this the army marched for Spain; the Rifles paraded in the very street where the shop I had so long worked at was situated, and I saw Maria at the window. As our bugles struck up she waved her handkerchief; I returned the salute, and in half-an-hour had forgotten all about her. So much for a soldier's love!"

Part Three – A Royal Highlander

Chapter Fifteen – About Soldiers' Wives

James Anton, who rose to be quarter-master-sergeant of the 42nd, or Royal Highlanders, and wrote a *Retrospect of Military Life*, published in 1841, was a typical Scottish soldier of the ranks. His memoir gives, quite unconsciously, an amusing picture of the writer. He was but an infant when his father died. His mother, a Scottish peasant woman, hardy and frugal like all her class, reared her child with an even greater economy of oatmeal and a more plentiful allowance of the Shorter Catechism than is common in the poorest Scottish homes.

Anton is fond of describing his experiences in large literary terms. Of his mother he says, "Sparta never had her equal in respect to what may be called self-denial. She ceased not by precept, as well as example, to impress on me the same contempt for ease and luxury she herself entertained." Probably Anton's mother had the vaguest notion of what such words as "ease and luxury" meant. She worked like a slave, fared like a Trappist monk, and trained her child to thin diet, long lessons, and hard work from his tenderest years.

Like most Scottish mothers, she was a God-fearing woman, rich in the homely wisdom of peasant life. A love of education burns in Scottish blood of all ranks, and young Anton was drilled in grammar and the multiplication table, plentifully flavoured with the Shorter Catechism, the proverbs of Solomon, the Psalms of David, and Scripture history generally.

He emerged from the process lean and stunted physically — he was rejected at first for the militia as being under the standard, and only succeeded in striking the gauge on a second test by standing on half tip-toe. But he had some of the qualities which go to make a good soldier. He was cool, shrewd, tough, rich, after the fashion of Scottish youth, in hard-headed common-sense, with a stomach that could extract nutriment from the sternest diet, and a frugality which could accumulate savings from the very scantiest pay. He records with true Scottish complacency that when he entered the militia he had saved the magnificent sum of £15; and before he left that corps for the line this had grown to £60. That was a very remarkable record for a private soldier; and, characteristically enough, he adds that during this whole process he sent a, £1 note at regular intervals to his mother — a form of domestic piety in which a Scottish lad, peasant or soldier, does not often fail.

It may be asked what impulse sent a youth of this type — undersized, lean, frugal, canny — to a soldier's life? But a fighting impulse is native to Scottish blood, whether Lowland or Highland; and Anton, in addition, had wit enough to see that a soldier's career for the sober, frugal, order-obeying, pence-accumulating Scottish peasant had many advantages. Certainly, Anton himself did not do badly as a private of the 42nd.

Anton joined the militia in 1802. While serving in Aberdeen the militiamen were allowed to sell their labour, when drill was over, to the contractors then occupied in building a bridge over the Denburn; and Anton, of course, worked hard and long, and so the pence in his pouch grew fast. He records, quaintly, his joy in the very frugality of the rations served out to him and his fellow-militiamen. They received half a pound of beef or mutton per man daily; and this was a quarter of a pound less than the orthodox allowance. But, Anton argues, "if we did not get it, we did not pay for it. Indeed, small allowances of provisions are always best. Why force upon us," he asks indignantly, "more than is barely necessary for subsistence, when — when, in brief, more meal in the platter means fewer pence in the pocket?" It was not for nothing that Anton had been brought up with something more than Spartan rigour!

Anton entered the army just in time to see one ridiculous custom disappear. The long, elaborate, flour-besprinkled and grease-besmeared queue of Marlborough's days still dangled down the unfortunate soldier's back. Anton records the deliverance of the army from this barbaric ornament with a touch of unusual feeling:

"During the time that the regiment was quartered in Musselburgh, a general order was issued for the army to discontinue the tying of the hair, and to have it cropped. Never was an order received with more heartfelt satisfaction than this, or obeyed with more alacrity, notwithstanding the foolish predictions of some old superannuated gentlemen that it would cause a mutiny in the army. The tying was a daily penance, and a severe one, to which every man had to submit; and there is little doubt but this practice had been introduced by some foreign fops, and enforced by antiquated prigs as necessary to the cleanly appearance of the soldier. It had been very injurious in its effects on the general comforts of those who were obliged to submit to it, and the soldier looks back to the task with the painful remembrance of the punishment he suffered every morning, daubing the side of his head with dirty grease, soap, and flour, until every hair stood like the burr of a thistle, and the back was padded and pulled so that every hair had to keep its due place; if one less subordinate than the rest chanced to start up in spite of grease, soap lather, and flour, the poor man had to sit down and submit his head to another dressing, and afterwards parade for inspection among the defaulters of the regiment.

"A certain latitude and longitude was assigned for the breadth and length of the queue, to which a gauge was frequently applied, in the same manner as some modern sticklers for uniformity at this day use a measure to ascertain the dimensions of the soldiers' folded greatcoats at guard mounting; but with this difference, the coat receives no bad impression from the stickler's gauge, whereas the greased and powdered hair retained the mark, and the poor fellow who had the misfortune to have the powder brushed aside by his awkward inspector, stood a chance of being turned off parade to have his hair dressed afresh, just as if the unlucky mark rendered him unfit for any military movement, or divested him of all the requisites of a soldier. Indeed, it was no uncommon circumstance for us, when on the guard-bench and asleep, to have the rats and mice scrambling about our heads, eating the filthy stuff with which our hair was bedaubed."

In 1805 Anton joined the 42nd, and his professional life as a soldier began.

Anton's officers were quick to discover his steadiness, his frugality, his methodical loyalty to every duty of a soldier. He was first put on recruiting service, and then had his reward in the form which most delighted him. He was allowed to marry. Only to a certain proportion of soldiers in each regiment was granted this privilege; and Anton, who was an odd combination of soft domestic instincts and hard soldierly pluck, welcomed with a joy which he takes no pains to conceal the permission to impose on the object of his affections the hardships and the perils which must befall the wife of a soldier who accompanies her husband on active service.

Anton plainly showed all his usual Scottish sense in his choice of a helpmate. She was a hardy peasant girl, plain-featured and strong-bodied, as frugal, as uncomplaining, and as canny as Anton himself; and one chief merit of Anton's memoirs is the picture it offers of a woman's experiences, caught in the rush and whirl of the great history-making campaigns of the Peninsula.

Anton was still happier when, on his regiment being ordered on active service, he was allowed to take his wife with him. This was a very rare privilege indeed. Only four women were permitted to follow each company of the regiment; and Anton tells how, when the regiment had reached Ostend, at the beginning of the Waterloo campaign, even this privilege was suddenly narrowed, and instructions were received that only two women could be allowed to go with each company. Half the women of the regiment were thus left stranded, penniless and friendless, in a foreign port, and saw their red-coated husbands march off into space with many a backward look at their weeping wives.

But the hardy women of the barracks are not easily defeated. "We had been only two days in Ghent," says Anton, "when the women left at Ostend found their way to the regiment." They had marched on their own account in the regiment's track, and presented themselves bedraggled and footsore at its quarters in Ghent. The authorities were inexorable, and the weeping women were again conveyed back to the same place from which they escaped, and there closely watched. But woman's wit and wiles proved too much for the sentinels. In a week or two the forsaken but enterprising wives eluded the vigilance of the sentries, and joined their husbands once more; and as no official reports were made to their prejudice, they were allowed to follow the fortunes of their husbands during the campaign.

Anton, somewhat ungratefully — considering the devotion and sufferings of his own wife — says that, in his judgment, women ought not to be allowed to accompany the soldiers through a campaign. He writes:

"On all occasions of troops being despatched to the scene of expected hostilities women should not be permitted to accompany them. If any exception is made in one single instance it only gives room for pressing and almost irresistible applications from others, and throws the performance of a very painful duty, namely, refusing permission, on the officers commanding companies. Every private soldier conceives that he has as good a right to this indulgence for his wife as the first non-commissioned officer in the regiment, and certainly he is right; she will prove much more useful than one who, instead of being serviceable, considers herself entitled to be served, assumes the consequence of a lady without any of the good qualifications or accomplishments of one, and helps to embitter the domestic enjoyments of others by exciting petty jealousies that otherwise would never exist."

Anton gives very sensibly, and from the private soldier's point of view, his opinion of how the soldier's wife should be treated:

"It is generally the case in selecting women to follow the army to a foreign station, that choice is made of those without children, as they are considered more capable of performing the services that may be required of them than those encumbered with a family. This, though just as regards our wants, is not so with respect to many a well-deserving woman, who is thus cast on the public or left to her own exertions, which too often fail her in the endeavour to support herself and children, while the childless woman is selected to profit from that circumstance.

"A woman who is permitted to accompany her husband receives a half ration free; a child above seven years, one-third; and one under seven years, a quarter of a ration; and although this is but a very trifling allowance, would it not be much better to give it to those of good character who are not permitted to accompany their husbands? I must also remark that, on foreign stations where this allowance is made to the women and children, it will be found that the least necessitous are the first to apply and the first-to be placed on this benevolent list. I have seen privates' waves, with three or more children, without rations; while the wives and children of sergeant-majors and quartermaster-sergeants were getting them."

Anton gives — quite incidentally, and without betraying any consciousness that he is adding a very exceptional chapter to military records — an account of his own experiences as a married soldier, which is very amusing and sometimes very touching. Here is his story of an early Spanish bivouac, and one cannot but pity the feelings of a modest Scottish girl in such an environment:

"After having seen the provisions distributed I set about looking out for some accommodation for my wife, for we had not as yet been accustomed to lie on the open field, as in bivouac, nor even seen the like, and the tent was far from comfortable for a poor, wearied, young woman; I shall not mention delicacy, for that would be out of place — we must submit to circumstances. The names of seventeen men were on the roll of the tent besides myself, so it may be easily guessed how crowded it must have been had the whole been off duty, but this was seldom the case. However, as no other shelter was to be had we took a berth under it.

"Eleven soldiers lay in it that night along with us, all stretched with their feet to the centre and their heads to the curtain of the tent, every man's knapsack below his head, and his clothes and accoutrements on his body.; the one-half of the blankets under, and the other spread over the whole, so that we all lay in one bed. Often did my poor wife look up to the thin canvas that screened her face from the night-dew and wish for the approaching morn, it was announced at last, before daybreak, by an exclamation of 'Rouse!' which passed from tent to tent along the lines, when every man started up, folded his blanket, and strapped it on the back of his knapsack, ready for a march, and soon afterwards the sound of bugle and drum echoed from hill to hill; meanwhile, the army stood to arms, each regiment at its alarm post, until about sunrise."

The regiment was in camp here for a short time, and Anton resolved on securing better accommodation for his wife. He says:

"I now set about erecting a hut for myself and wife, resolving, if possible, not to mix blankets with so many bedfellows again. This I was the more anxious to do, because at that time the whole of the men were affected with an eruption on their skin similar to the itch, and their clothing was in a very filthy state, owing to its being seldom shifted, and always kept on during the night.

"With the assistance of a few willing hands I finished the hut in the course of the day, so that it served for a temporary shelter, and prevented myself and wife from depriving the men of their very limited accommodation in the tent. When I stretched myself down at night in my new habitation, my head rested against the one end, while my feet touched the other, at which was the entrance; my wife's apron being hung up as a substitute for a door, a couple of pins on each side served for lock and hinges, and feeble as that barrier was, none of the men entered when that was suspended, and we might have left it to its own keeping from morning till night without an article being abstracted.

Thieving, indeed, was unknown in the regiment; but, in fact, there was little of worth to steal amongst us."

Later — in October, when the bitter winds were beginning to awake on the cold summits of the Pyrenees — the division encamped on the heights above Urdach. Anton then tried his fortunes once more with a hut. But disaster followed. He writes:

"Here I erected a hut, larger than my former one and more substantial. Having occupied that which I had left nearly four weeks, I considered that, if I were to occupy this the half of that time, I should be satisfied in bestowing more labour on it, and making my accommodation more complete; but rain continued to fall for two days in succession, and placed us in a very unpleasant situation. I had cut a trench round the outside of my hut so as to carry off the torrents which rushed against it from the declivities above, and my poor wife was no less busily employed in securing the few articles within.

"When the weather cleared I set about re-thatching my new habitation, but the first night after I had finished my work a violent gale struck every tent in the camp, and swept my little hut completely off. I had thrown my blanket over it and fixed it down with cords and pegs, on purpose to secure the thatch; having thus secured the roof, or I may rather say my hut, for it was all roof and ends, we stretched ourselves down, and the roaring of the wind in a few minutes lulled us to sleep, for we felt confident of having made all secure.

"Our repose, however, was short; we were awakened by the feeble branches which composed the rafters falling on our heads, and, on looking up, no roof sheltered us from the blast. The stars shone brightly between the flying clouds, and the busy hum of a thousand voices rose on the wind as the men strove to re-pitch the fallen tents. We started to secure the few loose articles around us; we looked for our blanket, but it was gone with the thatch and several minor articles that were no more to be seen. The men lay close under the fallen, fluttering tents, whilst I and my trembling companion found shelter in the lee of a rock, until morning roused every soldier to arms.

"My wife in the meantime hastily collected a few of the scattered branches of the hut, and huddled them together, so as to cover an umbrella, which served as a celling to the thatchless roof, until I should return from duty and construct a more substantial dwelling. Our loss, trifling as it may seem, was the more severely felt as there was no opportunity of replacing it by any fair means of purchase. Our day's provisions were among the articles missing, and this was far from being a comfortable lookout for the day, as I had to mount the advance picket that morning: however, we had a little money, and, scarce as bread was, it was to be had for a good price.

"The advance picket was more than two miles from the camp, and as I had not taken any provisions with me for the day, my wife bought a small loaf and a little wine; this last she mulled and mixed with some of the bread, and was bringing it to me, but in her too great anxiety to reach me soon, by short roads, she slipped on one of the steep banks and rolled down a considerable declivity. Fortunately, she was not hurt, but heartily vexed at her own mishap, returned to the camp, made a fresh purchase, and again hastened to me. The tear was in her eye as she related the misfortunes of the day, but she returned to camp gratified at having provided me with an unexpected and comfortable refreshment.

"I speak not of these casualties as sufferings on my part, for there were many worse off than I; but I point them out as some of the privations to which the poor women following the army had to submit, and which many of them were ill able to endure, and received but little sympathy from their husbands while patiently bearing them."

Perseverance is a Scottish virtue, and Anton, with the industry of a Robinson Crusoe in kilts, set to work to invent a third hut. It represented a gallant but melancholy attempt to secure the comforts of domestic life amid the severities of war:

"I set about constructing a hut that should be proof against wind and rain. One of my officers (Lieutenant D. Farquharson) very kindly made an offer of any pecuniary assistance I might require, and gave me a blanket to replace that which was lost. The latter I accepted gratefully, it was more than money could purchase; the former I declined, as I was far from being in want.

"I now became a complete Robinson Crusoe in my daily labour, when regimental duties permitted; and much I owe in gratitude to the memory of those who then superintended those duties for the indulgent manner m which I was treated, and not being troubled with vexatious interruptions to draw me oft' from my domestic avocations. They are now no more; they have fallen on the battle-field of a foreign land. A few men willingly afforded me every assistance; their only recompense being a small drop of spirits, which my wife had carefully reserved from my daily allowance. The wood was at no great distance, and the face of the hills was covered with broad ferns, which served for thatch.

"I now laboured hard for three days, and every spare hour, when off duty, was dedicated to the rendering of my hut proof against the weather. My friend Fraser gave me the use of the intrenching tools, and I dug an ample space within, three feet deep, and a trench around the outside, four feet deep; this was to carry off the water from the roof, and the latter I secured more substantially than many of our Highland bothies are in the north of Scotland, or than the cabins in the remote districts of Ireland. We were enjoying the comfort of its nightly shelter, and I was adding something daily towards its stability for upwards of two weeks; at last I constructed a fireplace under the roof, and one of the men had brought a bundle of sticks for fuel, and the fire was lighted for the first time.

"'I was sitting on my knapsack taking a late dinner, quite at home, with the dish on my knee, for I had no table, when the drum beat 'Orders.' I set down my dish (a wooden canteen, the one end of which was taken out) unfinished, attended the call, and with no small regret heard that the camp was to be struck, and everything ready to be moved off that night (November 9, 1813). I cannot express how vexed I was to leave my little habitation, my sole property, which I held by military right; but I was bound to follow my feudal superior. I had reared it at the expense of a blister on every finger, and I exulted as much over it, in secret, as the rich man in the Gospel did over his extensive possessions and his plentiful stores. On leaving the camp that night, many of the married people set fire to their huts, but I left mine with too much regret to become its incendiary; and my poor Mary shed tears as she looked back upon it, as a bower of happiness which she was leaving behind."

What the poor soldier's wife felt as she hung in the rear of the fighting line and watched the drifting smoke, pierced with gleams of red flame, where her husband stood to shoot and to be shot at; or with what emotion she scrutinised the figure of each wounded soldier limping, or being carried, to the rear cannot be guessed; and Anton does not stop to tell. Perhaps he had not imagination enough to understand any such emotions in his wife's bosom. Nothing, indeed, is more wonderful than the unconquerable cheerfulness Anton shows, as a husband, under all conditions; and if his wife ever grumbled, Anton does not allow her complaints to become audible to us. After the passage of the Nivelle the regiment encamped on the actual scene of the fighting. Says Anton:

"We bivouacked on the field until morning, and fortunately for us the night was fair, though cold and frosty. This was the first night on which my wife and I had to lie down with no other covering than a blanket between us and the sky, but we had many worse nights than this afterwards, and worse fields before us; however, on looking around, we generally saw many worse off than ourselves; and, doubtless, were we always to look into others' misfortunes or sufferings, when we suffer ourselves, we would find some cause for self-congratulation amidst the most distressing hardships."

It would be interesting to know whether Mrs. Anton shared her husband's stubborn Scottish philosophy. But she is the inarticulate figure of the two. Her notes on her husband's memoirs would be very interesting; but, unfortunately, they are not handed down to us. Occasional glimpses are afforded us of the experience of other wives whose husbands probably had less of resource and address than Anton. Here is another picture of a woman's experiences in a campaign:

"In the neighbourhood of our bivouac were a few straggling houses, in which some staff officers took up their quarters, and our guard was posted under the leafless branches of a chestnut tree in the close vicinity. The sergeant of our guard, being a married man, considered himself very fortunate in having secured a small pigsty near his post for his wife's accommodation, and the poor woman felt happy in the possession, small as it was; for its roof was a shelter from the wintry blasts, and its contiguity to the guard left no room to fear danger, were she permitted to keep possession; however, this was not to be the case.

"Our adjutant's clerk, who had never occasion to approach the field in time of danger, had taken up his quarters in one of the adjoining houses, after the action ceased, but, being dispossessed by some superiors, and every other place preoccupied by soldiers who would not suffer his intrusion, he meanly invaded the miserable shelter selected for the poor woman. In vain she remonstrated with him, in vain she requested him with tears to allow her the sole possession of a place so unfit for his accommodation, and which she had laboured hard to clean out for her own; but to no purpose, she might remain if she pleased, but he should not depart. It is doubtful whether we had a woman in the regiment so regardless of her character as to have taken a night's shelter, in the absence of her husband, otherwise than with the crowd, where no advantage could be taken of her situation or weakness; but every man acted towards a modest woman with that kindness which he would towards a sister. Indeed, we had women in the regiment that, if they had been in possession, would have kept him out and put him at defiance to enter, but this one was not possessed of that masculine boldness; she therefore bundled up her few articles, and, hastening across the road, the only distance by which she had been separated from her husband, threw herself in his arms and burst into tears.

"Three months only had elapsed since this couple joined the regiment. She was a comely, modest, interesting young woman, and always unassumingly but cleanly and decently dressed. But allowing that she had had but few or no accomplishments or amiable qualifications to recommend her to sympathy, it is but natural to think that whatever distressed her affected the husband. They had as yet seen or experienced but little of the petulant intrusions or consequential presumptuous ill-manners to which soldiers and their wives are sometimes obliged to submit without remonstrance. 'What is the matter with you, dear?' the sergeant asked, somewhat astonished at her unexpected appearance. 'Oh!' she exclaimed, 'I've been turned out o' yon bit placey that I was in, an' I'm come to stop wi' you a' night." 'Who turned you out?' the sergeant nastily inquired. 'Oh, say naething about it, I'll be as well here wi' you as I would ha'e been yonder by mysel'; let us mak' no disagreement about the matter wi' them that we canna shake oursel's free o'; let the proud little creature keep it to himsel' in quietness; we are strangers as yet, so dinna let angry words be heard.' 'But what creature turned you out? surely it was not a roan.' 'Ay, he thinks himsel' ane;' she whispered,' It was G—t.' 'Is it possible,' said the sergeant, 'that a married man can be possessed of so little feeling as to turn you out to the inclemency of the night, and neither his wife nor child accompanying him to plead for the accommodation?' 'I am happier with you,' she replied, 'than if I had lain all night in yon hole; but, dear, oh, dear, how hard it rains; the fire will be drowned out, an' we'll be starved to death before mornin'.'

"'Poor body!' the sergeant ejaculated, as he wrapped the blanket round her shoulders, 'I'll soon make a good fire; sit you under that branch of the tree, the reek will annoy you less, and the drops will not fall so thick nor so heavy.' 'I'm well enough,' she returned, 'and I care na' for the reek or the rain when wi' you; but dinna min' the fire till this heavy dag's o'er, ye'll get yoursel' a' wet.' The sergeant threw a faggot of wood on the fire, and in a short time nothing was heard but the rattling of rain and hailstones, the braying of mules, and the tinkling of their bells.

"This was a severe night, the rain poured down in torrents until midnight, when it was succeeded by snow, which covered the face of the country before daybreak."

It may be suspected that Anton, who is much given to literary excursions and alarums, has infused a little of what he regarded as appropriate pathos into this scene. Nevertheless, it is a picture with real human interest.

Here are some additional examples of what the soldiers' wives in Wellington's campaign suffered. The troops had to ford the Adour, whose ice-fed and ice-cold waters were swollen with winter rams. Says Anton:

"In passing through, the men supported each other as well as they could, so as to prevent them falling, for the stones in the bottom were very slippery. The wife of a sergeant of one of the regiments attempted to pass on a donkey with a child in her arms, and owing to some sudden stumble or slip of the animal, the child gave a start and dropped into the stream; the distracted mother gave a shriek, leaped after the infant, and both were swept off by the rapid current in the presence of the husband, who plunged into the water in hopes to recover them, but they were gone for ever, and he himself was with difficulty rescued. After this accident, the women who were following the army remained until the bridge was so far repaired as to enable them to pass over."

Anton's own wife had an unfortunate experience on the Adour:

"After having crossed the river, we marched a few miles up the right bank, or contiguous thereto, on the main road, and took up our camp-ground for the night in a newly ploughed field, rendered a complete mire by the rain and hail which fell upon us with dreadful fury as we were piling our arms on the broken ridges. Yet, notwithstanding the severity of this headlong torrent, a hundred fires were blazing in a few minutes along the side of the fences that bordered the fields. Fortunately for us, General Pack had taken up his quarters in the farmhouse adjoining, and allowed straw, of which there was abundance, to be taken for the bottom of the tents; this was an unexpected indulgence, even although the straw was rather wet.

"I was General Pack's orderly this night, and had a good roof over my head, and the dry floor of a cart-shed, with plenty of dry straw for a bed; but my poor wife was absent, for the first time since we left home. She was detained, along with several other women, on the right bank of the Adour, until the bridge was repaired. While this was doing, one of the women belonging to the regiment begged her to take charge of a little ass-colt with a couple of bundles, until she should go back to St. Severe to make some purchases; she complied, and before the other returned, the bridge was repaired. One regiment had passed, and she followed, driving the colt before her; but before she got to the farther end, the stubborn animal stood still and would not move a foot. Another regiment was advancing, the passage was impeded, and what to do she knew not.

"She was in the act of removing the woman's bundles from the beast's back, and struggling to get out of the way, determined to leave the animal, when a grenadier of the advancing regiment, casting his eye on a finely-polished horn with the masonic arms cut on it, and slung over her shoulder, stepped aside, saying, 'Poor creature, I shall not see you left struggling there, for the sake of what is slung by your side.' At the same time, handing his musket to one of his comrades, he lifted the colt in his arms and carried it to the end of the bridge. My poor wife thanked him with the tear in her eye, the only acknowledgment she could make for his kindness."

In the fighting at Toulouse, one of the married men in the regiment was killed, and Anton gives a somewhat laboured, but touching, account of the grief of the soldier's widow:

"Here fell Cunningham, a corporal in the grenadier company, a man much esteemed in the regiment; he was a married man, but young, and was interred before his wife entered the dear-bought field; but she had heard of his fate, and flew, in spite of every opposition, to the field; she looked around among the yet unburied soldiers to find her own, but she found him not. She flew to the place where the wreck of the regiment lay on the field. 'Tell me,' she asked, 'where Cunningham is laid, that I may see him and lay him in the grave with my own hand!' A tear rose in the soldier's eye as he pointed towards the place, and twenty men started up to accompany her to the spot, for they respected the man and esteemed the woman.

"They lifted the corpse; the wounds were in his breast; she washed them, and pressing his cold lips to hers, wept over him, wrapped the body in a blanket, and the soldiers consigned it to the grave. Mournful she stood over the spot where her husband was laid, the earth was again closed over him, and she now stood a lonely, unprotected being, far from her country or the home of her childhood. I should not, perhaps, say unprotected, for, however callous our feelings may occasionally be, amidst a thousand distressing objects that surround us, any one of which, if individually presented to our consideration at any other time or place than the battle-field, would excite our sympathy, yet amidst all these neither the widow nor the orphan is left unregarded, or in some measure unprovided for. In this instance, the officer who commanded the company to which Cunningham belonged, having been severely wounded, sent for the widow; she became his sick-nurse, and under his protection was restored in decent respectability to her home.

"The only protection a poor soldier can offer to a woman, suddenly bereft of her husband, far from her kinsfolk, and without a residence or home, would, under more favourable circumstances, be considered as an insult, and perhaps under these, from the pressure of grief that actually weighs her down, be extremely indelicate.

"I make free to offer this remark, in justification of many a good woman, who, in a few months, perhaps weeks, after her sudden bereavement, becomes the wife of a second husband; and, although slightingly spoken of by some of little feeling, in and out of the army, yet this is, perhaps, the only alternative to save a lone, innocent woman's reputation; and the soldier who offers himself may be as little inclined to the connection through any selfish motive as the woman may be from any desire of his love, but the peculiar situation in which she is placed renders it necessary, without consulting false feelings, or regarding the idle remarks that may be made, to feel grateful for a protector, and in a soldier, the most binding is the surest."

Chapter Sixteen – Fighting in the Pyrenees

Anton's own adventures in the Peninsula were brief, but of a stern and exciting quality. His regiment embarked on August 17, 1813, and thus reached Spain when the war had come to its latest stage — on the rough and hilly floor of the Pyrenees. The 42nd landed at Passages on September 7. The first sound of war which reached its ears was the sullen and distant boom of the guns thundering on San Sebastian. Anton had an eye for the picturesque, and he gives some interesting pictures of the scenery of the Pyrenees. Here is his description of a scene which met his eyes one daybreak shortly after landing:

"The view from the summits of these mountains at that early hour, when the sun began to gild their tops, and to throw his cheering rays on the white canvas which speckled their sides, was grand beyond description. The valleys below were hidden under an ocean of white, wreathing mist, over which the hills, like a thousand islands, raised their rocky summits amidst the pure serenity of a cloudless atmosphere; the white tents of a British army spotted their sides, while ten thousand bayonets glittered around. The drums, fifes, bugles, and wild, warlike strains of the Highland bagpipe, drowned the notes of a hundred useless instruments that offered their softer sounds to the soldiers' ears. Flocks of vultures hovered around to feed on the bodies of men who had fallen in sequestered spots by the hostile bullet, and were left to wolves and birds of prey, along with the carcasses of the exhausted animals that had failed in bearing their oppressive burdens to the expectant camp.

"As the sun rose over the mountains, the misty vapours rolled away, and all the vales, woods, streams, and distant cottages appeared to view. What a lovely prospect this must have been to the once happy native of the soil!"

On October 6 the 42nd had its first near glimpse of mountain fighting, though the regiment took no actual part in the combat:

"On October 6 we advanced towards the heights of Urdach, and descended a few paces on the brow of that part of the mountain which overlooks the valley of that name and the distant course of the Nivelle. A thick cloud hovered beneath us, and hid the country from our view. The loud report of guns in the valley shook the hills and echoed throughout the dark woody ravines below, while the quick rounds of musketry prepared us to expect an order to descend to the scene of action. The division stood in columns of brigade, or in lines along the mountain paths, as the position could be taken up.

"We remained upwards of two hours enveloped in the misty clouds, every man full of anxiety to view the contest below. At last our wishes were gratified; the curtain arose, and the interesting scene burst all at once on our view. A far-discerning eye might see the skirmishers of both armies approaching close to each other, each man with well-directed aim looking along the deadly tube that sent the intended messenger of death to the opposing adversary. Vineyards, orchards, straggling bushy fences, and streamlets with steep banks intersected the country, and afforded occasional cover to both sides, as well as a rest to the marksman's musket in taking a deliberate aim. The ascent of the cloud, which had hovered beneath us and over the combatants, afforded them a view of our columns and lines ready to descend, a prospect no less discouraging to the enemy than animating to our friends."

Anton's first personal experience in the stirring business of war was at the passage of the Nivelle. The river, it will be remembered, was approached by a night march. Anton's account is interesting, though marred by a laborious attempt at fine writing:

"The moon shone in the cloudless vault of heaven as we descended the narrow paths of the mountains; behind us were our camp-fires and blazing huts, while the ill-clothed and worse-disciplined troops of Spain were hurrying up the mountain path to occupy the ground we had left. To our right appeared the enemy's watch-fires, blazing brightly on the distant brow of one of the diverging ridges that jut out from the main body of the Pyrenees, their pickets little dreaming that we were worming our way through the intricate windings so near their posts, in order to rouse them to work in the morning. On our left a deep, woody ravine, with its roaring stream, skirted our path; before us the narrow ridge jutted out between two of those ravines, in a peninsula form, until its extremity overlooked the valley where we had witnessed the contest on October 6. The path led us down by many a circuitous and steep descent to the vale of Urdach, which we reached by daybreak.

"We were now approaching the Nivelle, and all its woody margins were lined with light troops, our battalions forming in columns about two furlongs from the bank of the river: not a musket was yet fired. The guns were already posted on all the commanding eminences on the left of the river. The generals had given their orders regarding the attack about to be made, the movements likely to follow, and their aides-de-camp were flying from corps to corps with the preparatory directions. No voice was heard, save that of command, until the foot of the advanced skirmisher was dipped in the stream; the bullet arrests him in his advance, and, as if at the command of some necromancer, thick and obscuring clouds rise from bank to bank, from eminence to eminence, as the loud thunder of war bursts from ten thousand muskets.

"The river is passed, and the soldiers of France retire or fall before their stern invaders. We pass through a wood and come to the bottom of a steep hill (the heights of Ainhoe), the face of which presents long ridges of formidable breastworks, behind which the enemy keeps up a heavy fire of musketry, and fears no danger in the security of his cover. On the summit overlooking these works is a battery which commands that part of the river within its range.

"The 11th Regiment was now ordered to ascend and storm those breastworks, and never did a regiment perform a task so dangerous, so obstructed, and apparently impracticable, with better success or in better order. Its line was preserved without a break, not only in climbing the hill but in springing over the breast-works, bayoneting those that waited its approach, even until it cleared the battery on the western summit, where, justly proud of its conquest, it made the hills echo to its loud huzzahs.

"Meantime our regiment advanced more to the right, where, on a gentle slope of the hill, stood the huts (the recent camp or quarters) of the enemy. Some of those huts caught fire, and, owing to the combustible material of which they were constructed, the whole were nearly enveloped in one blaze. The position which the enemy had occupied in the morning was now in our possession, and the sixth division crowned the heights of Ainhoe.

"The regiment's loss this day did not exceed twenty-seven killed and wounded; among the latter were Captain Mungo M'Pherson and Lieutenant Kenneth M'Dougall.

"This was the first engagement I was in, and I considered myself no longer a recruit. I had now smelled the enemy's powder, as the old soldiers boastingly exclaimed; I had heard his bullets whistling past my ears, seen them dropping harmless at my feet, and burrowing in the ground. I had observed, during this contest, the men whom I knew to be the greatest boasters in the company, men who never ceased enlarging on the exploits they had accomplished, the actions they had witnessed, or the hardships they had endured, when they had such a one as myself to listen to their stories; I observed some of those boasters very closely, and I could not help remarking that the men who spoke less acted better.

"It is, perhaps, needless to observe that it is scarcely in the power of an individual foot-soldier to perform any enterprising feat in the field of action, unless he be on some detached duty in front, such as is frequently the case with the skirmishers. If he is with the battalion he must keep in his ranks; it is on the united movement of the whole body that general success depends; and he that rushes forward is equally blameable with him who lags behind, though certainly the former may do so with less chance of censure, and no dread of shame. A man may drop behind in the field but this is a dreadful risk to his reputation, and even attended with immediate personal danger, while within the range of shot and shells; and woe to the man that does it, whether through fatigue, sudden sickness, or fear — let him seek death, and welcome it from the hand of a foe, rather than give room for any surmise respecting his courage; for when others are boasting of what they have seen, suffered, or performed, he must remain in silent mortification.

"I have seen it frequently remarked, in the periodicals of the time, that the loss in killed and wounded was greater than was actually acknowledged on our side; that we overrated the enemy's loss, and underrated our own; but this is not the case. The loss of the enemy, of course, is a guess rather than a certainty, until we become possessed of their official returns; but that of our own is never underrated. Indeed, a soldier feels a greater pride in boasting of his wounds than in trying to conceal them; mere scratches are often magnified into wounds, and stated as such in the returns.

"I never yet, among the many I have seen wounded, knew but one individual who kept his wound from being placed on the list; his name was Stewart. We were evacuating a redoubt on the heights of Toulouse, when a bullet struck him behind, pierced through his cartridge-box, cut his clothes, and hit him smartly on the breech. 'I shall give that to the rascal again,' he said, as he recovered himself and picked up the bullet. 'I shall be ashamed,' he added, 'to let it be known that I was struck behind.' Had this bullet struck him on the breast or limbs, there would have been one more on our list of that day's casualties."

Late in November the army went into cantonments; but on the night of December 8, the troops were in motion again. Says Anton:

"On the night of December 8, our division was under arms in columns of brigades until nearly daybreak, the artificers being employed in placing a bridge of pontoons over the river, below the town. As soon as this was finished, the troops began to pass along, while the drummers, left behind, beat the reveille at the usual places. This circumstance induced the enemy to conclude that we still occupied our quarters, although we were forming our columns silently in their neighbourhood, concealed amidst a dense mist. As soon as objects were discernible, a signal gun announced our time of advance. A wooden bridge still remained over the river at Ustritz, but so far broken down by the enemy as to be impassable; the discharge of this gun, however, so alarmed the French conscript sentries posted at the end of the bridge, on the right bank, that they retired in great haste towards the picket to which they belonged, and our artificers lost no time in making the necessary repairs for the passage of the troops and stores.

"The greater part of this day's action consisted in skirmishing, in which the light infantry companies sustained the principal brunt. Towards the close of the day, the enemy retired upon a farmhouse situated on a commanding eminence, having some of the adjoining fields enclosed by low dry-stone walls and quickset hedges, behind which they appeared in considerable force, supported by some artillery. In dislodging these troops, Captain George Stewart and Lieutenant James Stewart, both of the light company, were killed on the spot, and Lieutenant Brander was severely wounded."

A sudden burst of tempestuous weather arrested the movements of the troops, and the men returned to their camps. Directly the rains ceased, however, Soult was once more in movement. Swiftly marching to his right, he threw the whole strength of his army on the British left, holding the Jean de Luz road. Failing here, he faced about, pushed on at speed to his left, and leaped on the British right. In the toilsome marches and bloody combats of these operations, the 42nd had a full share. Here is a picture by Anton of the fighting near Bayonne:

"On the sixth division's attaining the heights overlooking Bayonne, its movements were immediately directed to its right, so as to support more effectually the left of the second; and Sir Denis Pack ordered the 42nd to advance to the main road, by which a brigade of the enemy was retiring. Our colonel was as anxious to execute the order as the men were proud to have been selected to perform it, but he led us into such a brake of furze, thorns, and brambles that it would have been impossible to have taken our bare-thighed regiment through its impenetrable meshes. The general, observing our painful but ineffectual struggling, withdrew us from that spot, and pointed to another place by which we should have advanced, and which would have been practicable; but by this time the enemy had passed our mark, and were descending towards the valley of the Adour, where, joined by another brigade, they made a determined stand against the 92nd Highlanders, that were coming round on the other flank.

"The ground at that place was intersected with deep drains, loose stone walls, and thorn bushes. Here a contest ensued, which cannot be described with justice to both parties; perhaps the like seldom or never occurred during the war. The enemy, although on their retreat, were within a short distance of their own fortified position of Bayonne, and in view of their own army and people, from, whom praise or censure was to be expected; they were also in the animating discharge of an urgent duty, namely, that of opposing the invaders of their beloved country. Yet, notwithstanding all these stimulants, the gallant 92nd bore down every opposition. The guns ceased to play upon this spot, so closely were both parties intermixed. Muskets were broken, bayonets bent, and stones were thrown with deadly vengeance. Victory crowned our native band, but it was dearly bought. Fourteen officers, eight sergeants, and 163 rank and file lay killed and wounded on the spot, and thrice that number of the enemy were scattered in heaps around them.

"The sun sank over the blue waves of the Bay of Biscay, and darkness rested on the fields, before the fire of the skirmishers ceased. Both armies, wearied of the struggle, rested on the ground during the night, the pickets occupying the dilapidated remains of the houses m front; to these the wounded men crawled for shelter, or were carried thither if near the spot.

"The unfortunate men who had fallen in remote places were suffered to remain under the inclement sky, until morning brought them relief, or death ended their sufferings. The rain poured down heavily during the night, and those who had crawled for shelter to the dry ditches along the roads or fields breathed their last beneath the gathering floods."

The bitter, incessant rain now drove the army into permanent winter quarters, and the British troops shivered in their bleak camps from December 14, 1813, to February 21, 1814. On the latter date camps were broken up, and the campaign of 1814 began. Anton's account of the first great fight of that campaign — Orthez — is naturally concerned only in the doings of his own regiment:

"On the afternoon of the 25th we were ordered to halt, just as we were about to ford the Gave, below a large farmhouse, where the river is fordable, but was said to have been set with spikes, so as to form an obstruction to our passage, perhaps there was no truth in this report; however, we suddenly retrograded and passed on pontoons, not far from a small village, in which we were quartered for the night. On the following day we approached the neighbourhood of Orthez, where we pitched camp on the south side of the gently rising heights, the north side of which forms the left bank of the Pau and overlooks the handsome town beyond.

"An explosion, occasioned by the blowing up of a bridge, excited the curiosity of a few to steal up the height, notwithstanding that we had been charged against discovering ourselves to the enemy. Others followed the example, and as no measures were taken, or perhaps were necessary, to prevent it, the men indulged themselves with a view of Orthez, the beautiful valley, with the Pau stealing softly along its south side, while the long range of mountain heights bounding it on the north rose abruptly over the road leading from Bayonne and Peyrehorade. Many a man gazed on that mountain range who little thought that before tomorrow's sun should go down, he would be stretched upon it a lifeless corpse."

Orthez was, in many respects, a memorable fight. Soult was superior in numbers, held an almost impregnable position, fought with great skill, and for one delusive golden moment believed he had beaten Wellington!

As he saw the British columns which had attacked both his right and left flanks reeling back, broken and disordered, it is said that he smote his thigh and exclaimed with excitement, "At last I have them!" The battle was won by the obstinate valour of the British soldiers, especially of the immortal Light Division and the swiftness of Wellington's counter-stroke at Soult's centre. Soult's left was covered by the Pau, and his centre by what seemed to be an impassable marsh. Two diverging and hilly ridges, thrust out like the horns of a bull, constituted his right and left flanks.

Beresford's attack on the French right, though urged five times over, failed. Picton's assault on the horn which formed Soult's left, urged with equal fire, also failed. Wellington won by sending the Light Division across the marsh and breaking Soult's centre. The 42nd formed part of Picton's attacking force, and the onfall of such troops under such a leader is not easily arrested; but the position held by the French was practically impregnable. In a private letter Picton wrote: "We were for nearly two hours exposed to the most continued and severe cannonade I ever witnessed. One of our 9-pounders had every man killed by round shot." In Anton's account the fire of this fierce fight is somehow chilled:

"Early on the morning of Sunday, the 27th, we marched down the left bank of the Pau, passed over on a pontoon bridge, and directed our course upon the main road up the valley towards Orthez. Two divisions of the army were already on the road before us. The heights on our left appeared to be in the possession of the enemy, and as our movements were plainly to attack his centre or his left, which was posted in and above the town, corresponding movements became necessary on his part, and his ranks were seen advancing along the ridge parallel with ours. As the mountain approaches that place where the road to St. Severe passes over it from Orthez, there is a downward bend of about a mile; it rises, however, to a considerable height on the east side of that road, and commands the town and its approaches.

"On our coming near this bending, our brigade was ordered to move to its left; several enclosures were in our way, but this was no time to respect them, as the enemy was welcoming us with round shot and shell. The gardens and nurseries were trodden down in an instant, and a forest of bayonets glittered round a small farmhouse that overlooked a wooded ravine on the north side.

"The light companies which had preceded the brigade were keeping up a sharp fire upon the enemy's skirmishers, and our Grenadier company was ordered to take post along the bank overlooking the ravine, and commanding a narrow road below. No place seemed less practicable for cavalry to act, but the enemy were determined to make every effort to re-establish their lines on the heights from which they had been driven by the light troops, and some of their squadrons were seen approaching to drive back our advance, which by this time was reinforced by the Grenadiers, but the more effectually to repel an attack, two additional companies were despatched to reinforce those already sent, and these had scarcely been formed when the charge of cavalry was announced; it was met and repulsed; men and horses were tumbled over the steep bank on the narrow road below, skirting the ravine.

"The gallant young officer who led that charge passed through the ranks like a lion pouncing on his prey, and was made prisoner by M'Namara of the Grenadier company. This man, if my memory serve me well, gave the horse and sword to one of our captains, who was afterwards appointed brevet-major; but poor M'Namara, who was more of a soldier than a courtier, rose not to corporal. After this repulse of the cavalry, we passed through the ravine, and moved towards the road that passes over the bending of the hill. The light infantry companies of the brigade, under the command of Major Cowel, were skirmishing in front. The major was severely wounded, and carried to the rear.

"The hill rises rather abruptly on the east side of the road, and slopes gradually towards the north side, to which our advance was directed, in order to turn the enemy's right, which had fallen back as we advanced. There is a small village consisting of one street on that brow of the hill towards the north, upon which the enemy was driven back, and from this kept up a destructive fire of musketry from garden walls, windows, and loopholes. Our regiment was ordered to drive him from that annoying post, which I may say had now become the right of his position. The bearer of this order was Lieutenant Innes, who was then acting brigade-major to Sir D. Pack; he preceded the regiment, and may be said to have led it on. The word of command to advance at the charge was received with loud animating cheers.

"No movement in the field is made with greater confidence of success than that of the charge; it affords little time for thinking, while it creates a fearless excitement, and tends to give a fresh impulse to the blood of the advancing soldier, rouses his courage, strengthens every nerve, and drowns every fear of danger or of death; thus emboldened, amidst the deafening shouts that anticipate victory, he rushes on and mingles with the flying me.

"In an instant the village was in our possession, and the fugitives were partly intercepted by the advance of the second division of the army, under Lord Hill, which had passed the Pau above Orthez, and was now approaching round the east end of the heights.

"The enemy, thus dispossessed of his last position of any importance, commenced a hasty retreat through some enclosed fields and young plantations, through which his columns directed their course, until impeded by intersecting ditches which induced them to take the main road; there the ranks were broken, confusion ensued, and a complete rout was the consequence.

"Fortunately for them the sun was nearly set, and although the pursuit continued for several miles, they succeeded in keeping the lead, and having reassembled during the night, continued their retreat towards the Adour.

"The loss of the regiment in this battle was four officers, six sergeants, and eighty-eight rank and file. We left behind us our dead, our dying, and our wounded; the former careless who shut those eyes that looked up to heaven from their gory bed, or who should consign their naked limbs to a grave in the field of a strange land. Night suspended hostilities, and the army bivouacked in columns on the fields bordering the road leading to St. Severe.

"Night after a battle is always glorious to the undisputed victors; they draw close to one another to hear and tell of the hazards of the day, while some show the petty prizes snatched off the field, and curse some intermeddling satrap that would not let them linger behind to get a better. The batmen and baggage-guard join the jocund circles round the camp-fires, and exhibit some full canteens of wine, the hastily snatched spoil of the day, or the plunder of some poultry-house, baker's oven, or farmer's pantry, no less acceptable to men long used to mouldy ship biscuit and scanty fare than silver or gold would have been to those who experienced no want.

"Midnight shuts our eyes in welcome slumber, and nought is heard to break the awful stillness that prevails, save the tinkling of the mule-bells and the tread of a silent soldier round the expiring embers of a campfire."

The pursuit of the enemy after Orthez witnessed some wild and some amusing scenes:

"On the 28th we advanced on the road leading to St. Severe, our cavalry in front pursuing and harassing the enemy's rear, and making a number of his stragglers prisoners. Many of these were deeply gashed by sabre wounds, and, being unable to get on so fast as the escorts urged, they fell down by the roadside faint from loss of blood, or panting with thirst, frequently soliciting a little water to cool their parched tongues. It is but justice to say that the British soldier attended to their appeals and relieved them when in his power so to do, and sympathised as much for them as if they had never fired a shot at him.

"We halted this day about three leagues from St. Severe, where the road is crossed by a considerable stream. A considerable quantity of vine-supporters lay scattered in bundles contiguous to our regiment's camp ground, and dry wood being always a desirable article for those who had the culinary duties to perform, a general charge was made in order to secure a quantity before the other regiments came to the knowledge of it.

"Our colonel had just dismounted, and was about to proceed to a farmhouse adjoining to stable his horse, when the sudden rush of the men, after having piled their arms and thrown down their knapsacks, attracted his attention. He gazed upon them with astonishment, hesitated a moment, and asked one of the guard the cause of so sudden a movement. This soon discovered itself, for the men were loaded with armfuls of sticks, and rejoicing over their booty and good luck, anticipating the comfortable warmth it would afford during the drizzly night. Sir Denis Pack had taken up his quarters in the farmhouse, or was supposed to have done so, and nothing was more likely than that he would take an interest in protecting the owner's property. The colonel, whether in dread of the general, or a mistaken sense of justice, called out to the marauders, as he was pleased to call them, to carry back their burdens. Some obeyed, others dropped them at their feet, and a few less obedient persisted in bringing them along; but the whole seemed rather unwilling to comply. The colonel, dissatisfied at the apathy displayed in obeying his orders, darted among the offenders and personally chastised those who seemed the most reluctant to obey.

"Among the most refractory of those wood foragers were two men of singular dispositions; their names were Henderson and Doury. The former was a contradictory, obstinate, careless, awkward fellow. His visage was long, his lips thick, his mouth always open, and, to use a Scotch term, slavering. His feet were flat-soled, without any spring, and he marched like a wearied pedlar under a pack, jolting along the road. He had not seen much service, but, like many old soldiers, he had much to say — he was nicknamed 'the Gomeral.' Doury was a silly, good-natured simpleton, the butt of every man's jest, yet no jester himself; for, when excited, his utterance failed so far that it was little else than a breathless gibbering of inarticulate sounds. Such another couple was not in the regiment, or perhaps in the brigade, and would not be accepted of for the service in time of peace. Those two were bringing in their burdens notwithstanding the interdiction, and had entered the field on which the colonel was standing. The colonel, observing that Henderson led the other on, strode hastily forward to enforce obedience. Doury was the first to observe him, fled past his companion, dropped the sticks at his feet, and escaped. Not so Henderson: he fell over the bundle dropped at his feet, with his face pressed against the soft, miry field; the colonel overtook him as he recovered, seized him by the kilt, the pins of which yielded to the tug, and left his naked flesh to some merited chastisement. This excited bursts of laughter from all the men, and the poor fellow afterwards declared that he was more vexed at the laughter than hurt by the punishment."

War is a rough school, and under its hard experiences all the finery of an army quickly vanishes. Colours fade, feathers moult, bright metals turn rusty, uniforms grow ragged, and the once "smart" army becomes, from the tailor's point of view, a thing to weep over or to shudder at. Here is a picture of a gallant army in rags and sandals:

"At this time the clothing of the army at large, but the Highland brigade in particular, was in a very tattered state. The clothing of the 91st Regiment had been two years in wear; the men were thus under the necessity of repairing their old garments in the best manner they could: some had the elbows of their coats mended with grey cloth, others had the one-half of the sleeve of a different colour from the body; and their trousers were in equally as bad a condition as their coats.

"The 42nd, which was the only corps in the brigade that wore the kilt, was beginning to lose it by degrees; men falling sick and left in the rear frequently got the kilt made into trousers, and on joining the regiment again no plaid could be furnished to supply the loss. Thus a great want of uniformity prevailed; but this was of minor importance when compared to the want of shoes. As our march continued daily, no time was to be found to repair them until completely worn out; this left a number to march with bare feet or, as we termed it, to pad the hoof. These men being occasionally permitted to straggle out of the ranks to select the soft part of the roads or fields adjoining, others who had not the same reason to offer for this indulgence followed the example, until each regiment marched regardless of keeping in rank, and sometimes mixed with other corps in front and rear. To put a stop to this irregularity, the men without shoes were formed by themselves and marched, under the command of officers and non-commissioned officers, in rear of the brigade.

"It is impossible to describe the painful state that some of those shoeless men were in, crippling along the way, their feet cut or torn by sharp stones or brambles. To remedy the want of shoes, the raw hides of the newly-slaughtered bullocks were given to cut up, on purpose to form a sort of buskins for the barefooted soldiers. This served as a substitute for shoes, and enabled the wearers to march in the ranks of their respective companies.

"Our knapsacks were also by this time beginning to display, from their torn ends, their worthless contents; and as our line of march was in an opposite direction from our expected supplies, our exterior appearance was daily getting worse; but the real spirit of the soldier was improving, and I make little doubt but we would have followed our leaders to the extremity of Europe without grumbling. We were getting hardier and stronger every day in person; the more we suffered, the more confidence we felt in our strength; all in health, and no sickness. The man in patched clothes and a piece of untanned hide about his feet, when he looked around him, saw others in some respects as ill appointed as himself; and he almost felt a pride in despising any new-comer with dangling plumes, plaited or crimped frills, white gloves, and handsome shoes — all good-for-nothing frippery to the hardy, toil-worn soldier, the man of flint, powder, and steel, as he thought himself. His was the gloveless hand and the shoeless foot that braved alike the cold and the heat, the toil of the field and the fatigue of the march; nothing came wrong to him; he started in the morning from his hard pillow and harder bed, required no time to blacken his shoes, but braced up his knapsack, regardless of the state of the roads or weather, and was ready to march off.

"I have already mentioned that there was some skirmishing with the enemy this day, as we advanced. Here we had three men killed and several wounded. One of those who were killed had been doing the duty of pioneer previous to this day; doubtless he had considered this a degrading duty, and had pressingly requested to be permitted to join the ranks. His request was granted; this was his first entry on the field since he obtained that indulgence, and here he fell. He lay on the field adjoining the road; some one had rifled his knapsack, but had thrown the blanket over him. Having the general's baggage in charge I was following the brigade with the guard and the mules when I observed some soldiers examining to what regiment the killed belonged; one bore off the knapsack, but left the blanket carelessly cast on the corpse, a batman was making a prize of the blanket, and a Portuguese muleteer was about to take off the kilt.

"I could be at no loss to know to what regiment he belonged, as the 42nd was the only corps in the division that had that dress, and I desired one of the guard to recover the blanket, and to spread it over the body, for we had no time to inter it. He sprang on the spoilers in an instant, snatched the blanket from the batman, and seizing the muleteer rather roughly, tumbled him into the ditch that lined the road; then, spreading the blanket over the corpse, left it; but doubtless to be soon stripped again. Thus falls the poor soldier."

Chapter Seventeen – The Hillside at Toulouse

Anton attempts a more ambitious account of the battle of Toulouse than of any other fight in which he was engaged; and there is some reason for this. It was a cluster of Scottish regiments — the 42nd conspicuous amongst them — which, by mere invincible and all-enduring valour, saved Wellington from failure in that great fight. Soult, it will be remembered, knew Toulouse almost with the familiarity of a native. A strong place by nature, he had made it almost impregnable by the energy and skill with which he had multiplied its defences during the long pause before the British advanced.

Wellington delivered his attack at three points. Hill assailed the west front of the city; Picton the north; Beresford the east. The first two attacks were, perhaps, not seriously meant, and certainly failed. Freire, with his Spaniards, whose task it was to carry the northern shoulder of Mont Rave, fell on gallantly, but was smitten into utter rout, extorting from Wellington the grim comment, "Well, me, if ever I saw ten thousand men run a race before!" Beresford's task was perilous in the highest degree; to any other troops than those he led, it might well have proved impossible. He had to toil for two miles along a road which was little better than a strip of marsh, past the flank of Mont Rave, strongly held by the French. On his left was the river Ers. The road was so difficult that the guns were left behind. There was deadly peril at every step that the French might overwhelm the toiling column with a flank attack; or break through betwixt it and the main body of the British army.

But Beresford — who had fought Albuera — was exactly the man for a task which required blind and desperate valour. His men splashed doggedly on their way; on their right the foe, tormenting their flank with his fire; the fordless river to their left; their guns left behind them. When they had reached the southern extremity of the ridge, the regiments brought up their left shoulder, and proceeded to carry the hill. It was seamed with trenches, and bristled with guns. Soult, who saw that this was the one point of peril to his battle-line, had brought up two divisions to the threatened point, and the French, gallantly led, and confident in their numbers, in their advantage of position, and in their success at the other attacked points, came boldly down the hill to crush Beresford's slender and extended line.

Nothing, however — not the slippery hill-slope, the cruel fire of the French guns, nor the onfall of the solid French battalions — could stay Beresford's men. Soult's columns were smashed with rolling musketry volleys. The batteries were carried with the bayonet, and the hill was won. The 42nd played a most gallant part in this great fight, and endured dreadful losses. Anton came through it all untouched, and tells the whole story in a spirited fashion. He sees nothing, however, and describes nothing, but what takes place immediately about himself:

"We broke up camp a little after midnight, on the morning of Easter Sunday, April 10, and marched towards Toulouse. The moon shone bright in the unclouded heavens, and reflected a stream of light from the muskets of our advanced columns, for our arms had not then received the brown varnish that now 'dims their shine.'

"General Pack's brigade was formed in contiguous columns of regiments to the left of the road leading to Toulouse. At this time the Spaniards, who were in advance and ascending the heights, were attacked with such fury that they gave way in all directions. It was apprehended that the enemy would have borne down upon us in the impetuosity of the movement, and we deployed into lines. The 19th Regiment was at this time in front of the 42nd, and General Pack, anticipating a charge from the enemy's victorious and elated infantry, after thus scattering the Spaniards, gave orders to the 79th to receive them with a volley, immediately form four deep, face about, and pass through the ranks of the 42nd. The latter received orders to form four deep, as soon as the former had given its fire; let the line pass through, then form up, give a volley, and charge. This was providing against what might have taken place, but did not, for the enemy was recalled, and the Spaniards were afterwards rallied.

"We now moved off to our left, along a green embankment, a small lake or large pond [really a flooded river] on our left, and a wet ditch and marshy meadow on the right. The shot and shell were flying over our heads into the lake, but the range was too elevated to hurt us, and we ran along the bank until we came to a place where we could leap the ditch and form on the swampy ground beyond it. We had scarcely formed, when a strong column of the enemy, with drums beating a march, descended the hill in our front, and thinking from the nature of the ground that we should be neither able to advance nor retreat, rushed down confident of success. For us to retire would have been scarcely practicable; the bank from which we had leaped down and over the ditch was too high in several places for us to leap back from such uncertain footing, for we were sinking to the ankles, and sometimes deeper at every step; to advance was the only alternative, and it was taken.

"The light companies of the division were by this time in our front, and without any hesitation dashed forward; we followed fast, and the opposing column reascended the hill, and left us the undisputed masters of the valley. We now ascended at double quick time, and the whole of the division crowned the eastern summit of the heights. Here we were exposed to a destructive fire of round shot, shell, grape, and musketry, while we had not as yet got up one gun, owing to the numerous obstructions that lay in the way. The ground we occupied sloped towards one of the main roads that run over the hill to the city, and the fields on the opposite side of the road were in possession of the enemy, and extremely broken and intersected by deep cross-roads, breastworks, and redoubts, but could, from our present position, have been commanded by artillery, had it been practicable to bring a few guns forward; but this required some time, and indefatigable labour.

"The light companies of the division advanced beyond the road, and maintained a very unequal skirmish with the enemy, who lay securely posted behind their breast-works and batteries, and in their redoubts, from all of which they took the most deadly aim. The 6ist Regiment was ordered forward to support the skirmishers, and became the marked object of the enemy's batteries, from which incessant showers of grape cut down that corps by sections, while Soult was, perhaps, not losing a man, being so safely sheltered from our musketry; it was, therefore, seen necessary to withdraw the skeleton of that regiment to the road, on which we had taken post after its advance. It was now warmly welcomed back, for its retreat was no defeat, and its loss was scarcely equalled by any corps in the field. Not a subaltern left the field without a wound, and the honour of the colours was assigned to sergeants.

"The enemy, emboldened by this momentary success on his part, began to advance towards the road, and our regiment was ordered to advance by wings and storm one of the redoubts.

"Our colonel was a brave man, but there are moments when a well-timed manoeuvre is of more advantage than courage. The regiment stood on the road with its front exactly to the enemy, and if the left wing had been ordered forward, it could have sprung up the bank in line and dashed forward on the enemy at once. Instead of this, the colonel faced the right whig to its right, countermarched in rear of the left, and when the leading rank cleared the left flank it was made to file up the bank, and as soon as it made its appearance the shot, shell, and musketry poured in with deadly destruction; and in this exposed position we had to make a second countermarch, on purpose to bring our front to the enemy. These movements consumed much time, and by this unnecessary exposure exasperated the men to madness.

"The word 'Forward — double quick!' dispelled the gloom, and forward we drove, in the face of apparent destruction. The field had been lately rough ploughed or under fallow, and when a man fell he tripped the one behind, thus the ranks were opening as we approached the point whence all this hostile vengeance proceeded; but the rush forward had received an impulse from desperation, 'the spring of the men's patience had been strained until ready to snap, and when left to the freedom of its own extension, ceased not to act until the point to which it was directed was attained.' In a minute every obstacle was surmounted; the enemy fled as we leaped over the trenches and mounds like a pack of noisy hounds in pursuit, frightening them more by our wild hurrahs than actually hurting them by ball or bayonet.

"The redoubt thus obtained consisted of an old country farm cottage, the lower part of its walls stone, the upper part mud or clay. It stood in the corner of what had been a garden, having one door to a road or broad lane, and another to the garden; the whole forming a square which had been lately fortified on three sides by a deep but dry trench, from which the earth had been cast inwards, and formed a considerable bank, sloping inwards, but presenting a perpendicular face of layers of green turf outwards. The cottage served as a temporary magazine, and the mound or embankment as a cover to the enemy from the fire of our troops; and from this place our men had been dreadfully cut down.

"It cannot be for an instant supposed that all this could have been effected without very much deranging our ranks, and as the enemy had still a powerful force, and other works commanding this, time would not permit of particularity, and a brisk independent fire was kept up with more noise than good effect by our small groups upon our not yet defeated enemy. Our muskets were getting useless by the frequent discharges, and several of the men were having recourse to the French pieces that lay scattered about, but they had been as freely used as our own, and were equally unserviceable. Our number of effective hands was also decreasing, and that of the again approaching foe seemed irresistible.

"Two officers (Captain Campbell and Lieutenant Young) and about sixty of inferior rank were all that now remained without a wound of the right wing of the regiment that entered the field in the morning. The flag was hanging in tatters, and stained with the blood of those who had fallen over it. The standard cut in two, had been successively placed in the hands of three officers, who fell as we advanced; it was now borne by a sergeant, while the few remaining soldiers who rallied around it, denied with mire, sweat, smoke, and blood, stood ready to oppose with the bayonet the advancing column, the front tiles of which were pouring in destructive showers of musketry among our confused ranks. To have disputed the post with such overwhelming numbers, would have been the hazarding the loss of our colours, and could serve no general interest to our army, as we stood between the front of our advancing support and the enemy; we were therefore ordered to retire. The greater number passed through the cottage, now filled with wounded and dying, and leaped from the door that was over the road into the trench of the redoubt, among the killed and wounded.

"We were now between two fires of musketry, the enemy to our left and rear, the 79th and left wing of our own regiment in our front. Fortunately, the intermediate space did not exceed a hundred paces, and our safe retreat depended upon the speed with which we could perform it. We rushed along like a crowd of boys pursuing the bounding ball to its distant limit, and in an instant plunged into a trench that had been cut across the road; the balls were whistling amongst us and over us; while those in front were struggling to get out, those behind were holding them fast for assistance, and we became firmly wedged together, until a horse without a rider came plunging down on the heads and bayonets of those in his way; they on whom he fell were drowned or smothered, and the gap thus made gave way for the rest to get out.

"The right wing of the regiment, thus broken down and in disorder, was rallied by Captain Campbell (afterwards brevet lieutenant-colonel) and the adjutant (Lieutenant Young) on a narrow road, the steep banks of which served as a cover from the showers of grape that swept over our heads.

"In this contest, besides our colonel, who was wounded as he gave the word of command, 'Forward,' the regiment lost, in killed and wounded, twenty officers, one sergeant-major, and four hundred and thirty-six of inferior rank.

"Meantime the Portuguese brigade was ordered to take possession of the evacuated redoubt, which was accomplished with little loss, for the enemy had been backward of entering, lest we might have been drawing them into an ambush, or had an intention of blowing up the cottage, in which a considerable quantity of loose cartridges had been left near a large fire by themselves when they were driven out, and most likely intended for that purpose against us, but we had removed the whole to a place of less danger.

"Thus far the left flank of our army was secured; the Spaniards, farther to the right, were making good their advances, our artillery was about getting posted on commanding eminences, while only one battery remained on the western summit in the enemy's possession, and before sunset it was stormed also, and all the heights overlooking Toulouse remained in our possession."

As soon as the fight is over Anton proceeds to mount the pulpit and deliver himself of a homily on the night scene after a battle, which may be usefully abridged:

"Night after battle is always glorious to the undisputed victors, and whatever the loss may have been, the idea of it seems to be banished from our thoughtless minds. Here, however, by the first early dawning of the morning, let us more seriously cast our eye over this scene of slaughter, where the blood of the commander and the commanded mix indiscriminately together over the field.

"Here lies many a gallant soldier, whose name or fame wall never pass to another generation; yet the annals of our country will do justice to the general merit of the whole; from my feeble pen no lasting fame can be expected; time blots it out as I write; and even were I to attempt to pass an eulogy it might be considered contemptible from so humble an individual, by those who survive and witnessed the action.

"I trust I shall not be considered egotistical in saying that I had some narrow escapes this day; but what soldier entered the field and came safe out of it had not narrow escapes? A musket-ball struck my halberd in line with my cheek, another passed between my arm and my side, and lodged in my knapsack, another struck the handle of my sword, and a fourth passed through my bonnet and knocked it off my head; had the ball been two inches lower, or I that much higher, the reader would have been saved the trouble of perusing this narrative. The company in which I was doing duty lost four officers, three sergeants, and forty-seven rank and file, in killed and wounded. The officers were: Lieutenant D. M'Kenzie severely wounded, Lieutenants Farquharson and Watson mortally wounded, and Ensign Latta killed.

"There was one officer of the regiment taken prisoner this day: he had lately joined us from the 1st Royals, in which he had been cadet, and had not the uniform of the regiment; but his deficiency of the uniform betrayed no lack of personal courage; the charm of the bonnet and plume, though wanting, did not make him less the soldier; he fell, wounded, near to Lieutenant Farquharson, at the side of the redoubt, as we entered it, and when we fell back he was made prisoner.

"I have already mentioned that before the regiment advanced to storm the redoubt, we were posted on the main road that passes over the heights. During the short time we were in that position we had orders not to raise our heads above the bank, nor let the enemy see where we were posted. Notwithstanding this prohibition, our sergeant-major, as brave a man as ever entered a field, was despatched from the right flank to warn those on the left to comply with this order, for several were rising up occasionally and sending a bullet at the enemy, and thus, perhaps, defeating the intention of the order. He went, but though cautioned to stoop as he proceeded, he considered this unmanly, and never did he walk with a more upright dauntless carriage of the body or a firmer step: it was his last march; a bullet pierced his brain and stretched him lifeless, without a sigh.

"There was a man of the name of Wighton in the regiment, a grumbling, discontented, disaffected sort of a character. He was one of the men attached to the tent placed under my charge on joining the regiment. Some men take all for the best; not so with Wighton, he took everything for the worst; indeed, his very countenance indicated something malignant, misanthropic, and even sottish in his disposition. He was a low, thick, squat fellow, with a dark yellowish swarthy complexion, and his broad face bore a strong resemblance to that of a Calmuc Tartar. As he rushed along the field his front-rank man exclaimed, 'God Almighty preserve us, this is dreadful!' 'You be d—d,' Wighton replied, 'you have been importuning God Almighty this half-dozen of years, and it would be no wonder although He were to knock you down at last for troubling him so often; as for myself, I do not believe there is one; if there were, He would never have brought us here!' The last word hung unfinished on his tongue; the messenger of death sealed his lips in everlasting silence.

"The contest that raged upwards of an hour around the redoubt, of which we had gained possession, was maintained without much regard to order or strict discipline; in short, it was rather tumultuary. Every man was sensible of the necessity of having order restored, but thought himself the only orderly man of all the rest, and his voice was heard over that of his commander calling out 'Form up.' In the meantime, his own attention was more engaged in keeping in the crowd, to load his piece, and afterwards pushing forward, to send a bullet to the enemy as often as he possibly could load and discharge, than attending to formation.

"A Grenadier of the 79th Regiment, for both regiments (the 42nd and 79th) were somewhat intermixed, rushed forward, discharged his piece with effect, and suddenly turning the musket so as to grasp the muzzle, dealt deadly blows around him; he fell, grasping one of the enemy in one hand, and the broken firelock in the other. Another sprung up on the top of the bank, called on his comrades to follow, and with a loud cheer, in which many joined that did not follow, he rushed forward in the same manner as his brave companion had done, and like him shared a similar fate.

"It is only in this disorganised kind of conflict that individual courage may best act and best be seen. In united, orderly movements, the whole acquires the praise; and in this each individual is comprised, and proud of contributing his part to the honour of his corps, does his duty without attempting those feats of romantic daring which ancient historians record, but which modern tactics render nugatory or almost useless. Individual daring is lost in orderly movements."

Chapter Eighteen – The 42nd at Quatre Bras

The return of Napoleon from Elba found the 42nd on duty in Ireland. But when Great Britain was pouring her choicest troops into the Netherlands, in readiness for the last great struggle, so famous a regiment as the 42nd could not be left behind. The regiment embarked at Cork on May 4, 1815, for Ostend, and thence marched in leisurely fashion to Brussels.

Anton discovers quite a new justification for the Duchess of Richmond's famous ball, which will live in history longer than any other ball at which men and maidens ever danced. He says:

"On the night of June 15, we were roused from our peaceful slumbers by the sounding of bugles, the rolling of drums, and the loud notes of our Highland bagpipes, which threw their wild, warlike strains on the midnight breeze, to awaken the plaided sons of Caledonia to arms. Until daybreak of the 16th we stood to our arms on the streets of Brussels, and here we were served out with four days' provisions for each man. The grand ball was broken up, and our Highland dancers, who had been invited to display their active movements before the assembled lords, ladies, and military chieftains, were sent to their respective regiments to prepare for other sport — that of glorious battle.

"I have heard some passing animadversions upon our great commander, for thus passing away time upon the eve of so momentous an affair as that about to take place. I think, as a soldier, and one who was on the spot, I have as good a right to give my opinion concerning it as any of those croaking politicians who were hundreds of miles from the scene or operations; and in giving my opinion, I give it as that of every soldier who was in Brussels at the time, and I believe we are not the worst judges of what is most likely to forward a ready assembling, or a speedy concentration of the troops, in order to attain the end in view.

"Owing to this general assembly of all our principal officers, the Duke had not only all his personal staff about him, but that of the generals under his command. They, again, had around them all the commanding officers of corps, to whom they could personally communicate their orders. The unusually late hour at which the despatches from the scene of hostilities had arrived, and the information respecting the intended movements of our allies, in consequence of their having unexpectedly had to retreat from the bravely contested field, might have changed all our commander's plans. If this should have been the case, he had all those about him to whom he could communicate his designs, without passing hours at the desk, and sending orderlies off to the quarters of officers in a city, the language of whose inhabitants was foreign to us. All this trouble, happily for us and for Britain, was saved by this fortunate ball."

Quatre Bras was not the least perilous of Wellington's battles. Ney's onfall took the Iron Duke by surprise, and that Quatre Bras was not a British defeat was due as much to Ney's blunders in attack as to Wellington's fine skill in defence, and to the magnificent courage of his troops. Ney could, with ease, have thrown 40,000 men into the fight. Wellington, at the beginning of the battle, had in hand only 7000 Dutch-Belgian troops, with seventeen guns. Picton's division only reached the field in the afternoon, having started on their long march from Brussels at five o'clock in the morning. Later, reinforcements came trickling in, till, just as night was darkening, the Guards reached the scene of action.

But the British came up in fragments, and at remote intervals of time. Wellington had very inefficient artillery, and no horsemen; and a fight under such conditions might well have gone wrong. Fortunately, Ney left half his forces out of the fight, and attacked with 20,000 instead of overwhelming the British with 40,000.

The Highland regiments formed Pack's brigade. They came up almost exhausted with their long march, and were flung hurriedly into the strife. The 42nd, in particular, fared very badly. In the whirl and passion of the fight it changed commanders no less than four times in little more than as many minutes. But disaster itself could hardly shake the ranks of the veterans of the Peninsula. Here is Anton's description of Quatre Bras. It gives a most spirited account of the struggle betwixt horsemen and infantry:

"On the morning of June 16, before the sun rose over the dark forest of Soignes, our brigade, consisting of the 1st, 44th, and 92nd Regiments, stood in column, Sir Denis Pack at its head, waiting impatiently for the 42nd, the commanding officer of which was chidden severely by Sir

Denis for being so dilatory. We took our place in the column, and the whole marched off to the strains of martial music, and amidst the shouts of the surrounding multitude. We passed through the ancient gate of the city, and hundreds left it in health and high spirits who before night were lifeless corpses on the field to which they were hastening.

"As we entered the forest of Soignes, our stream of ranks following ranks, in successive sections, moved on in silent but speedy course, like some river confined between two equal banks. The forest is of immense extent, and we continued to move on under its welcome shade until we came to a small hamlet, or auberge, embosomed in the wood to the right of the road. Here we turned to our left, halted, and were in the act of lighting fires on purpose to set about cooking. We were nattering ourselves that we were to rest there until next day; for whatever reports had reached the ears of our commanders, no alarm had yet rung on ours. Some were stretched under the shade to rest; others sat in groups draining the cup, and we always loved a large one, and it was now almost emptied of three days' allowance of spirits, a greater quantity than was usually served out at once to us on a campaign; others were busily occupied in bringing water and preparing the camp-kettles, for we were of the opinion, as I have already said, that we were to halt there for the day.

"But, 'Hark! a gun!' one exclaims; every ear is set to catch the sound, and every mouth seems half opened, as if to supersede the faithless ear that doubts of hearing. Again another and another feebly floats through the forest. Every ear now catches the sound, and every man grasps his musket. The distant report of the guns becomes more loud, and our march is urged on with greater speed. Quatre Bras appears in view; the frightened peasantry come running breathless and panting along the way. We move off to the left of the road, behind a gently rising eminence, form column of companies, regardless of the growing crop, and ascend the rising ground; a beautiful plain appears in view, surrounded with belts of wood, and the main road from Brussels runs through it.

"We now descended to the plain by an echelon movement towards our right, halted on the road (from which we had lately diverged to the left), formed in line, fronting a bank on the right side, whilst the other regiments took up their position to right and left, as directed by our general. A luxuriant crop of grain hid from our view the contending skirmishers beyond, and presented a considerable obstacle to our advance. We were in the act of lying down by the side of the road, in our usual careless manner, as we were wont when enjoying a rest on the line of march, some throwing back their heads on their knapsacks, intending to take a sleep, when General Pack came galloping up, and chid the colonel for not having the bayonets fixed. This roused our attention, and the bayonets were instantly on the pieces.

"There is something animating to a soldier in the clash of the fixing bayonet; more particularly so when it is thought that the scabbard is not to receive it until it drinks the blood of its foe.

"Our pieces were loaded, and perhaps never did a regiment in the field seem so short taken. We were all ready and in line — 'Forward!' was the word of command, and forward we hastened, though we saw no enemy in front. The stalks of the rye, like the reeds that grow on the margin of some swamp, opposed our advance; the tops were up to our bonnets, and we strode and groped our way through as fast as we could. By the time we reached a field of clover on the other side we were very much straggled; however, we united in line as fast as time and our speedy advance would permit. The Belgic skirmishers retired through our ranks, and in an instant we were on their victorious pursuers.

"Our sudden appearance seemed to paralyse their advance. The singular appearance of our dress, combined, no doubt, with our sudden debut, tended to stagger their resolution: we were on them, our pieces were loaded, and our bayonets glittered, impatient to drink their blood. Those who had so proudly driven the Belgians before them, turned now to fly, whilst our loud cheers made the fields echo to our wild hurrahs.

"We drove on so fast that we almost appeared like a mob following the rout of some defeated faction. Marshal Ney, who commanded the enemy, observed our wild unguarded zeal, and ordered a regiment of lancers to bear down upon us. We saw their approach at a distance, as they issued from a wood, and took them for Brunswickers coming to cut up the flying infantry; and as cavalry on all occasions have the advantage of retreating foot, on a fair field, we were halted in order to let them take their way; they were approaching our right flank, from which our skirmishers were extended, and we were far from being in a formation fit to repel an attack, if intended, or to afford regular support to our friends if requiring our aid. I think we stood with too much confidence, gazing towards them as if they had been our friends, anticipating the gallant charge they would make on the flying foe, and we were making no preparative movement to receive them as enemies, further than the reloading of the muskets, until a German orderly-dragoon galloped up, exclaiming, 'Franchee! Franchee!' and, wheeling about, galloped off.

"We instantly formed a rallying square; no time for particularity; every man's piece was loaded, and our enemies approached at full charge; the feet of their horses seemed to tear up the ground. Our skirmishers having been impressed with the same opinion that these were Brunswick cavalry, fell beneath their lances, and few escaped death or wounds; our brave colonel fell at this time, pierced through the chin until the point of the lance reached the brain. Captain (now Major) Menzies fell, covered with wounds, and a momentary conflict took place over him; he was a powerful man, and, hand to hand, more than a match for six ordinary men. The Grenadiers, whom he commanded, pressed round to save or avenge him, but fell beneath the enemies' lances.

"Of all descriptions of cavalry, certainly the lancers seem the most formidable to infantry, as the lance can be projected with considerable precision, and with deadly effect, without bringing the horse to the point of the bayonet; and it was only by the rapid and well-directed fire of musketry that these formidable assailants were repulsed.

"Colonel Dick [who afterwards fell at Sobraon] assumed the command on the fall of Sir Robert Macara, and was severely-wounded. Brevet-Major Davidson succeeded, and was mortally wounded; to him succeeded Brevet-Major Campbell (now lieutenant-colonel on the unattached list). Thus, in a few minutes, we had been placed under four different commanding officers.

"An attempt was now made to form us in line; for we stood mixed in one irregular mass — grenadier, light, and battalion companies — a noisy group; such is the inevitable consequence of a rapid succession of commanders. Our covering sergeants were called out on purpose that each company might form on the right of its sergeant; an excellent plan had it been adopted, but a cry arose that another charge of cavalry was approaching, and this plan was abandoned. We now formed a line on the left of the Grenadiers, while the cavalry that had been announced were cutting through the ranks of the 69th Regiment. Meantime the other regiments to our right and left, suffered no less than we; the superiority of the enemy in cavalry afforded him a decided advantage on the open plain, for our British cavalry and artillery had not yet reached the field.

"We were at this time about two furlongs past the farm of Quatre Bras, as I suppose, and a line of French infantry was about the same distance from us in front, and we had commenced firing at that line, when we were ordered to form square to oppose cavalry. General Pack was at our head, and Major Campbell commanded the regiment. We formed square in an instant; in the centre were several wounded French soldiers witnessing our formation round them; they doubtless considered themselves devoted to certain death among us seeming barbarians, but they had no occasion to speak ill of us afterwards; for as they were already incapable of injuring us, we moved about them regardful of their wounds and suffering.

"Our last file had got into square, and into its proper place, so far as unequalised companies could form a square, when the cuirassiers dashed full on two of its faces; their heavy horses and steel armour seemed sufficient to bury us under them, had they been pushed forward on our bayonets.

"A moment's pause ensued; it was the pause of death. General Pack was on the right angle of the front face of the square, and he lifted his hat towards the French officer, as he was wont to do when returning a salute. I suppose our assailants construed our forbearance as an indication of surrendering; a false idea; not a blow had been struck nor a musket levelled, but when the general raised his hat, it served as a signal, though not a preconcerted one, but entirely accidental; for we were doubtful whether our officer commanding was protracting the order, waiting for the general's command, as he was present. Be this as it may, a most destructive fire was opened; riders cased in heavy armour, fell tumbling from their horses; the horses reared, plunged, and fell on the dismounted riders; steel helmets and cuirasses rang against unsheathed sabres as they fell to the ground; shrieks and groans of men, the neighing of horses, and the discharge of musketry, rent the air, as men and horses mixed together in one heap of indiscriminate slaughter. Those who were able to fly, fled towards a wood on our right, whence they had issued to the attack, and which seemed to afford an extensive cover to an immense reserve not yet brought into action.

"Once more clear of these formidable and daring assailants we formed line, examined our ammunition boxes, and found them getting empty. Our officer commanding pointed towards the pouches of our dead and dying comrades, and from them a sufficient supply was obtained. We lay down behind the gentle rise of a trodden-down field of grain, and enjoyed a few minutes' rest to our wearied limbs; but not in safety from the flying messengers of death, the whistling music of which was far from lulling us to sleep.

"Afternoon was now far spent, and we were resting in line, without having equalised the companies, for this would have been extremely dangerous in so exposed a position, for the field afforded no cover, and we were in advance of the other regiments. The enemy were at no great distance, and, I may add, firing very actively upon us. We had wasted a deal of ammunition this day, and surely to very little effect, otherwise every one of our adversaries must have bled before this time. Our commanding officer cautioned us against this useless expenditure, and we became a little more economical.

"Our position being, as I have already observed, without any cover from the fire of the enemy, we were commanded to retire to the rear of the farm, where we took up our bivouac on the field for the night. The day's contest at a close, our attention was directed to the casualties which had occurred in our ranks. We had lost, in killed, one colonel, one lieutenant, one ensign, one sergeant-major, two sergeants, and forty-eight rank and file. One brevet lieutenant-colonel, five captains, five lieutenants, two ensigns, fourteen sergeants, one drummer, and two hundred and fourteen rank and file composed our list of wounded. Six privates fell into the enemy's hands; among these was a little lad (Smith Fyfe) about five feet high. The French general, on seeing this diminutive-looking lad, is said to have lifted him up by the collar or breech and exclaimed to the soldiers who were near him, 'Behold the sample of the men of whom you seem afraid!' This lad returned a few days afterwards, dressed in the clothing of a French Grenadier, and was saluted by the name of Napoleon, which he retained until he was discharged.

"The night passed off in silence: no fires were lit, every man lay down in rear of his arms, and silence was enjoined for the night. Round us lay the dying and the dead, the latter not yet interred, and many of the former, wishing to breathe their last where they fell, slept to death with their heads on the same pillow on which those who had to toil through the future fortunes of the field reposed."

Chapter Nineteen – The Highlanders at Waterloo

Anton's account of the retreat from Quatre Bras to Waterloo, of the camp on the historic ridge through the falling rains and blackness of the night before the great battle, and of the tumult and passion, the perils and the triumph, of the memorable day, has many merits. But it is marred by a perfect paroxysm of apostrophes to posterity, to the spirits of the fallen, to freedom, to all sorts of more or less heroic and nonexistent abstractions. In describing the struggle in which he was a microscopic and almost nameless actor, Anton feels it necessary to mount on the tallest literary stilts available, and walking on stilts is not usually a very graceful performance. Anton's account of the battle, in a word, recalls the famous description of a Scotch haggis. It contains much good substance, but in a very confused and planless state. His story, indeed, only becomes intelligible by virtue of generous omissions. Here is Anton's tale of the march from Quatre Bras:

"On the morning of the 17th the unclouded heavens began to present the approach of day, our usual signal to rise from our sky-canopied bed. We started to arms and took up a new line on the field, facing our yet silent foe. Here, after arranging our ranks and equalising the companies, we piled our arms, and commenced to prepare our yesterday's dinner, which served us for an excellent breakfast.

"The men not thus engaged were now busily employed in burying the dead, and those who had been attending the wounded in the adjoining houses had not neglected the interest of their respective messes. Besides our own allowances of meat which we had brought from Brussels, there was not a mess without a turkey, goose, duck, or fowl floating in the seething kettle; and an abundance of vegetables from the neighbouring gardens helped to add to the richness of the soup which was preparing, and which we got good time to take, and for this we were truly thankful, for we were very hungry.

"A passing fog hung over the plain a short time, but soon disappeared, and left us with a cloudless sky. A general retrograde movement now took place, and we retired on the main road by which we had advanced from Brussels.

"It was with regret that many of us left that field, on which some of our men lay breathing their last. Among this number was a young man whose wound was in his forehead, from which the brain protruded. In this state he had lain on the field during the night; his eyes were open, with a death film over them; two of his comrades were watching the last throb of his expiring breath before they would consign his body to the grave, already opened to receive it, when the call to arms made us leave him on the field to the hands of strangers.

"The sun shone brightly on our arms as we left the fields of Quatre Bras, and passed the farms round which the remains of some thousands of brave men, British, Brunswick, Belgic, and French, were interred; and many yet lay scattered over the fields, and may have remained hidden amidst the grain which still continued standing, until the sickle or the scythe laid the fields bare.

"The enemy did not as yet seem to notice our movement, and we continued our march until we had passed the village, halfway to Waterloo. Here we turned off the road to our right, formed in columns, and halted; and, short as that halt was, it afforded time for one of our regiments to hold a drum-head court-martial and carry the sentence into effect on the spot. Examples of this kind are absolutely necessary, whatever philanthropists may say to the contrary. They tend to preserve regularity, order, and discipline; and although an individual may suffer a punishment which is debasing and cruel, yet it is better that this should be awarded and inflicted than to see hundreds fall victims to the rapacity that might ensue from not timely visiting the aggressor with punishment.

"We had now attained the undulating height of Mont St. Jean, and Wellington said, 'We shall retire no farther.' The thunder ceased to roll its awful peals through the heavens, the thick embodied clouds deployed, spread wide, and half dissolved in drizzly mist, but, as if doubtful of man's resolves, resumed again their threatening aspect, as if to secure our halt."

At Waterloo Sir Denis Pack's brigade — the 1st, 42nd, 44th, and 92nd — formed part of Picton's division, and held the line immediately to the left of the great Brussels road. It was on this part of Wellington's battle-front that Napoleon launched his first great infantry attack — D'Erlon's corps, four close-massed columns — over 13,000 bayonets in all — with the fire of seventy-four guns sweeping the path in their front as with a besom of flame.

The story of how Picton's slender lines met this mighty onfall, shook the French columns into retreat with actual bayonet push, and how the Life Guards, Inniskillings, and Greys swept down the slope and utterly wrecked D'Erlon's swaying battalions is one of the most dramatic passages in the story of the famous day.

Anton's account of the night before Waterloo is graphic:

"Our lines now formed behind the long-extended ridge of Mont St. Jean, having the village of Waterloo a mile or two in our rear, and at no less a distance the dark forest of Soignes, which extends to Brussels. The right of our front British line extended beyond Hougoumont as far as Merke Braine; the left is said to have extended to Wavre! Sir T. Picton's division consisted of the 28th, 32nd, 79th, and the 95th (rifle corps), under the command of Sir James Kempt; and the 1st, 42nd, 44th, and 92nd Regiments, under the command of Sir Denis Pack, extended from the left of the Brussels road to a copse on a rising ground which probably overlooked the whole field, The extensive farmhouses and offices of La Haye Sainte were to the right of the division, but in front and on the right side of the road.

"Before us was a line of Belgic and Dutch troops; a narrow road, lined with stunted quickset hedges, runs between this line of foreigners (or I may, with more justice, say natives) and us. This road commands a view of the enemy's position, and the side next to us is the artillery's post; the hedges in front form a feeble cover from the enemy's view, but no defence against his shot, shell, or musketry.

"Our line, being on the slope next to Waterloo, was hidden from the enemy, who took up his position on the heights of La Belle Alliance, parallel to those of St. Jean: a valley corresponding to those wavy heights on either side divides the two armies, a distance of about half a musket-shot intervening between the adverse fronts.

"We piled our arms, kindled fires, and stood round the welcome blaze to warm ourselves and dry our dripping clothes. Midnight approached, and all the fields towards the artillery's post were hid in darkness, save what the fitful gleams of our fires cast over them. Silence prevailed, and wet although we were, we were falling asleep sitting round the fires or stretched on scattered branches brought for fuel. At this time a very heavy shower poured down upon us, and occasioned some movement or noisy murmur in the French army or line of Belgians. This induced our sentries to give an alarm. In an instant each man of the brigade stood by his musket; the bayonets were already on the pieces, and these all loaded, notwithstanding the rain. We stood thus to our arms for nearly an hour, sinking to our ankles amongst the soft muddy soil of the field, when the alarm was found to be false, and we again sat or lay down to repose.

"Long-looked-for day at last began to break; we stood to our useless arms for a few minutes, and then began to examine their contents. The powder was moistened in the piece and completely washed out of the pan. The shots were drawn, muskets sponged out, locks oiled, and everything put to rights."

Anton's description of the actual on-coming of the French and of the charge of the Greys is in his worst style; turgid, windy, unreal. Yet it is the story of a man who actually plied 'Brown Bess' in the central passion of the fight, and ran in with levelled bayonet on D'Erlon's Grenadiers, and cheered the gallant Greys as they rode past on their famous charge. Had Anton told his tale with the prosaic simplicity of Defoe or the stern realism of Swift, we might have had a battle picture memorable in literature. As it is, we must be thankful for small mercies. The present reader at least shall be spared Anton's incessant apostrophes:

"Now, on our right, Napoleon urged on his heavy columns, while a like movement was made against our left. The guns opened their war-breathing mouths in thundering peals, and all along the ridge of Mont St. Jean arose one dense cloud of smoke.

"France now pushed forward on the line of our Belgic allies, drove them from their post, and rolled them in one promiscuous mass of confusion through the ranks of our brigade, which instantly advanced to repel the pursuers, who came pushing on in broken disorder, in the eagerness of pursuit, till obstructed by the hedge and narrow road, while a like obstruction presented itself to us on the other side. We might have forced ourselves through as the Belgians had done, but our bare thighs had no protection from the piercing thorns; and doubtless those runaways had more wisdom in shunning death, though at the hazard of laceration, than we would have shown in rushing forward upon it in disorder, with self-inflicted torture. The foe beheld our front and paused; a sudden terror seized his flushed ranks. We were in the act of breaking through the hedge, when our general gave orders to open our ranks. In an instant our cavalry passed through, leaped both hedges, and plunged on the panic-stricken foe. 'Scotland for ever!' burst from the mouth of each Highlander as the Scots Greys pass through our ranks.

"What pen can describe the scene? Horses' hoofs sinking in men's breasts. Eiders' swords streaming in blood, waving over their heads, and descending in deadly vengeance. Stroke follows stroke, like the turning of a flail in the hand of a dexterous thresher; the living stream gushes red from the ghastly wound. There the piercing shrieks and dying groans; here the loud cheering of an exulting army, animating the slayers to deeds of signal vengeance upon a daring foe. It was a scene of vehement destruction, yells and shrieks, wounds and death; and the bodies of the dead served as pillows for the dying.

"A thousand prisoners are driven in before our cavalry as they return over the corpse-strewn field, and the loud shouts of ten thousand soldiers welcome the victors back. But long and loud are the enthusiastic cheerings of the proud Highlanders as they greet the gallant Greys' approach. 'Glory of Scotland!' bursts spontaneously from the mouth of each Highlander, while rending shouts of 'England!' or 'Ireland!' welcome the 1st and Inniskilling Dragoons, and echo along the lines. This dreadful charge made by our cavalry in our immediate front gave an impulse bordering on enthusiasm to our spirits that nothing could depress. But the enemy, as if dreading more than common opposition at this spot, forbore to press upon it during the remaining part of the day.

"The right and left both sustained the impetuous onset of Napoleon's cavalry, and these on each occasion met with powerful opposition, and were driven back in wild confusion. But on the right and centre he seems to urge his greatest force throughout the whole day. La Have Sainte is one pool of blood; against it Napoleon's artillery incessantly play, and columns of infantry are urged on to drive the brave defenders out. But these meet them with fire and steel, and repel them with determined resolution. Here a never-ceasing combat rages throughout the day, and forms an interesting object in the general picture of the field. Hougoumont is no less a scene of slaughter; there, every effort is made to obtain possession and to break in upon our right wing. Sometimes in the heat of a charge they rush past its bounds, but meet with wounds or death as they fly back; for it is only when the enemy occasionally pursues his apparently victorious course beyond his lines and past our guns that he gets a view of our columns or lines of infantry, which immediately take advantage of his disordered front, and drive him back, with immense loss, beyond our guns and down the descent; they then retire to their well-chosen ground and send out a company or two of skirmishers from each regiment to keep up a never-ceasing fire, save when driven back on their respective columns in those repeated charges.

"The sun, as he hastens down, bursts through the hazy clouds and gleams in brightness over the long-contested field. It is the setting sun of Napoleon's greatness.

"The loss of the regiment this day was trifling, if compared with that which it sustained on the 16th at Quatre Bras: we had only six men killed; one captain, three lieutenants, and thirty-three rank and file wounded. Brussels, which had been kept in a state of excitement since the night of the 15th, heard the glad tidings of the result of the battle, and the doors were opened wide for the reception of the bleeding soldiers, who had been conveyed thither on waggons or had dragged their maimed limbs along the way without assistance. The poor women, who had been forced back to the rear of the army when the battle commenced, were hurried amidst the mingled mass of fugitives, panic-struck batmen, mules, horses, and cattle, back to the gates of Brussels; but on entering, found no friendly hand stretched out to take them off the streets.

"Night passes over the groaning field of Waterloo, and morning gives its early light to the survivors of the battle to return to the heights of St. Jean, on purpose to succour the wounded or bury the dead. Here may be seen the dismounted gun, the wheels of the carriage half sunk in the mire; the hand of the gunner rests on the nave, his body half-buried in a pool of blood, and his eyes open to heaven, whither his spirit has already fled. Here are spread, promiscuously, heaps of mangled bodies some without head, or arms, or legs: others lie stretched naked, their features betraying no mark of violent suffering.

"The population of Brussels, prompted by a justifiable curiosity, approach the field to see the remains of the strangers who fell to save their spoil-devoted city, and to pick up some fragment as a memorial of the battle, or as a relic for other days. Of these the field affords an abundant harvest; cuirasses, helmets, medals, swords, pistols, and all the various weapons of destruction in military use, besides the balls and bullets, which may be ploughed up a thousand years hence. Here also are hundreds of blankets, ripped-up knapsacks, torn shirts, stockings, and all the simple contents of the fallen soldiers kits. Letters and memoranda of the slain strew the field in every direction, which are picked up by the curious and carefully preserved."

Part Four – With the Guns at Waterloo

Chapter Twenty – Waiting for the Guns

Mercer, the author of the *Journal of the Waterloo Campaign*, came of a soldierly stock. His father belonged to the Royal Engineers, served on the staff of Sir Henry Clinton in the American War of Independence, and rose to the rank of general. Cavalie Mercer, with whose book we are concerned, was born in 1783, passed through the Military Academy at Woolwich, obtained a commission in the artillery at sixteen, and had not reached the retired list when he died at the age of eighty-five. But though his career as a soldier was long and honourable, it cannot — except for the three great days of Quatre Bras and Waterloo — be called very inspiring.

Mercer's first military service was in Ireland at the time of the rebellion. War is always hateful, but its blackest form is civil war. Mercer was next unfortunate enough to take part in the most ignoble expedition known to British arms — Whitelocke's shameful and unhappy performance at Buenos Aires. This was the worst school imaginable for a young soldier, but Mercer had fine military gifts, and though he was shut out from the Peninsular campaigns, when he made his appearance on the field of Waterloo he showed himself to be an artillery officer of very fine quality — cool, skillful, and gallant. He served after the peace in North America, and commanded the artillery in Nova Scotia in the troubled days of the Maine boundary-line dispute, when it seemed likely that England and the United States would drift into war.

Mercer's long military career found its climax in the three memorable days of June 16-18, 1815; and the splendours and terrors, the bloodshed and the triumph of those mighty battles are vividly reflected in his pages.

Mercer only held the rank of second captain in troop G, but Sir Alexander Dickson, whose troop it was, being employed on other duties, Mercer was in actual command. It was a fine troop, perfect in drill, and splendidly horsed. It owed this latter circumstance, perhaps, to a characteristic bit of War Office administration. The artillery was being reduced to the level of a peace establishment when Napoleon broke loose from Elba, and there came the sudden summons to war. A second troop of horse-artillery was at that moment in Colchester barracks. It was broken up, and troop G took the picked horses of both batteries — "thus," says Mercer proudly, "making it the finest troop in the service." One fine troop was in this way made out of two half-dismantled batteries.

The troop was made up of eighty gunners and eighty-four drivers, with the usual proportion of officers and non-commissioned officers. The horses numbered no less than 226. There were six guns — five of them being nine-pounders, and one a heavy five-and-a-half inch howitzer. Mercer has the wholesome pride of a good officer in his own men and guns. He tells with pardonable complacency the story of how his troop shone in a grand cavalry review held on May 29, near Gramont:

"About two o'clock the Duke of Wellington and Prince Blücher, followed by an immense cortège, in which were to be seen many of the most distinguished officers and almost every uniform in Europe, arrived on the ground. Need I say that the foreigners were loud in praise of the martial air, fine persons, and complete equipment of the men and horses, and of the strength and beauty of the latter? And my vanity on that occasion was most fully gratified, for on arriving where we stood, the Duke not only called old Blüchers attention to 'the beautiful battery,' but, instead of proceeding straight through the ranks, as they had done everywhere else, each subdivision — nay, each individual horse — was closely scrutinised, Blücher repeating continually that he had never seen anything so superb in his life, and concluding by exclaiming, 'Mein Gott, dere is not von orse in dies batterie wich is not goot for Veldt Marshal': and Wellington agreed with him. It certainly was a splendid collection of horses. However, except asking Sir George Wood whose troop it was, his Grace never even bestowed a regard on me as I followed from sub-division to sub-division."

The troop, as Mercer's story shows, was literally smashed up at Waterloo; but Mercer, with great energy and skill, quickly built it up again, and at a great review in Paris, where the allied sovereigns were present, the English guns were once more the admired of all observers. He writes:

"It seems that we have been the *rara avis* of the day ever since our review. The rapidity of our movements, close-wheeling, perfection of our equipment, &c., &c., excited universal astonishment and admiration. The consequence of this was an application to the Duke for a closer inspection, which he most magnanimously granted, and ordered Ross's troop out for that purpose. They paraded in the fields near Clichy. The reviewers, I understand, were *maréchaux de France*; but there was also a great concourse of officers of all nations. After the manoeuvres the troop was dismounted, and a most deliberate inspection or ammunition, and even of the men's kits, appointments, shoeing, construction of carriages, &c., &c., took place. I believe they were equally astonished and pleased with what they saw, and as there were several among them taking notes, have no doubt that we shall soon see improvements introduced into the Continental artillery."

Mercer, curiously enough, declares that the British artilleryman of his day had no affection for his horse, and in this respect compares very ill with the German artilleryman; the same thing, he says, applies to British and German cavalry:

"Affection for, and care of, his horse is the trait *par excellence* which distinguishes the German dragoon from the English. The former would sell everything to feed his horse; the latter would sell his horse itself for spirits, or the means of obtaining them. The one never thinks of himself until his horse is provided for; the other looks upon the animal as a curse and a source of perpetual drudgery to himself, and gives himself no concern about it when once away from under his officer's eye. The German accustoms his horse to partake of his own fare. I remember a beautiful mare, belonging to a sergeant of the 3rd Hussars, K.G.L., which would even eat onions. She was one of the very few that escaped after the disastrous retreat of Corunna, and had been saved and smuggled on board ship by the sergeant himself. In the Peninsula the only means of enforcing some attention to their horses amongst our English regiments was to make every man walk and carry his saddle-bags whose horse died or was ill."

All branches of the British army, it may be added, did not impress the allied sovereigns in the same favourable manner as the artillery. The British infantry seemed undersized as compared with Austrians, Prussians, &c. Mercer's account of the memorable review, held only five weeks after Waterloo, is interesting:

"At length the approach of the sovereigns was announced, and they came preceded and followed by a most numerous and brilliant cortège, in which figured, perhaps, some of almost every arm of every army in Europe. It was a splendid and most interesting sight. First came the Emperor Alexander and the King of Prussia, in their respective green and blue uniforms, riding together the former, as usual, all smiles; the latter taciturn and melancholy. A little in their rear followed the Austrian Emperor, in a white uniform, turned up with red, but quite plain — a thin, dried-up, thread-paper of a man, not of the most distinguished bearing; his lean, brown visage, however, bore an expression of kindness and *bonhomie*, which folk say his true character in no way belies. They passed along, scanning our people with evident interest and curiosity; and in passing me (as they did to every commanding officer), Bulled off their hats, and saluted me with most gracious smiles. I wonder if they do the same to their own. Until yesterday I had not seen any British infantry under arms since the evening the troops from America arrived at Garges, and, in the meantime, have constantly seen corps of foreign infantry.

"These are all uncommonly well dressed in new clothes, smartly made, setting the men off to the greatest advantage — add to which their coiffure of high broad-topped shakos, or enormous caps of bearskin. Our infantry — indeed our whole army — appeared at the review in the same clothes in which they had marched, slept, and fought for months. The colour had faded to a dusky brick-dust hue; their coats, originally not very smartly made, had acquired by constant wearing that loose, easy set so characteristic of old clothes, comfortable to the wearer, but not calculated to add grace to his appearance. *Pour surcroit de laideur*, their cap is perhaps the meanest, ugliest thing ever invented. From all these causes it arose that our infantry appeared to the utmost disadvantage — dirty, shabby, mean, and very small. Some such impression was, I fear, made on the sovereigns, for a report has reached us this morning that they remarked to the Duke what very small men the English were. 'Ay,' replied our noble chief, 'they are small; but your Majesties will find none who fight so well.' I wonder if this is true. However small our men and mean their appearance, yet it was evident that they were objects of intense interest from the immense time and close scrutiny of the inspection."

Mercer, with his troop, embarked at Harwich on April 9, and landed at Ostend on the 13th. Thence he marched, with frequent halts, to Brussels. His account of the marches and experiences of his troop is very interesting, if only as showing that even under a great commander like Wellington, amazing blunders and much distracted confusion were possible. Nothing more absurd can well be imagined than the fashion in which Mercer's fine troop was disembarked at Ostend; and nothing could be more planless and belated than the marching — or rather the loitering — of troop G towards Brussels. Wellington used to complain afterwards that in the Waterloo campaign he had the most villainous staff with which an unhappy general was ever afflicted; and the helpless quality of Wellington's staff is reflected in Mercer's account of the orders he received — or did not receive — directing his march to the front. Here is Mercer's account of how his troops started from their English barracks on the march which was to end on the smoky ridge at Waterloo:

"On the morning of the 9th, the troop paraded at half-past seven o'clock with as much regularity and as quietly as if only going to a field-day; not a man either absent or intoxicated, and every part of the guns and appointments in the most perfect order. At eight, the hour named in orders, we marched off the parade. The weather was fine, the scenery, as we skirted the beautiful banks of the Stour, charming, and the occasion exhilarating. Near Manningtree we halted a short time to feed our horses, and then, pursuing our route, arrived at Harwich about three o'clock in the afternoon. Here we found the transports — the *Adventure*, *Philarea*, and *Salus*, in which last I embarked.

"About 2 P.M. on the 11th, a light breeze from the N.W. induced our agent to get under way, and we repaired on board our respective ships with every prospect of a good and speedy passage. In this, however, we were disappointed, for the breeze dying away as the sun went down, we anchored, by signal, at the harbour's mouth, just as it got dark.

"The evening was splendid. A clear sky studded with myriads of stars overhead, and below a calm unruffled sea, reflecting on its glassy surface the lights of the distant town, the low murmuring sounds from which, and the rippling of the water under the ships' bows, were the only interruptions to the solemn stillness that prevailed after the people had retired to their berths. In our more immediate neighbourhood stretched out the long, low, sandy tract, on the seaward extremity of which the dark masses and Land-guard fort could just be distinguished.

"With daybreak on the morning of the 12th came a favourable wind, though light, and again we took up our anchors and proceeded to sea. For some distance after clearing the harbour our course lay along the Suffolk coast, and so near in that objects on shore were plainly discernible. To us who had long been stationed at Woodbridge, only a few miles inland, this was highly interesting. We knew every village, every copse, every knoll — nay, almost every tree. There were the houses in which we had so oft been hospitably entertained; there were the sheep-walks on which we had so often manoeuvred; and there in the distance, as we passed the mouth of the Deben, our glasses showed us the very barrack on the hill, with its tiled roofs illumined by the noontide sun. About Bawdsey we left the coast, and steered straight over with a light but favourable wind; the low, sandy shores of Suffolk soon sank beneath the horizon.

"During the night a light breeze right aft and smooth water enabled us to make good progress; but towards morning (13th) the wind had very considerably increased, and although the coast was not in sight, we were sensible of its neighbourhood from the number of curious heavy-looking boats plying round us in all directions, having the foremast with its huge lug-sail stuck right up in the bow or rather inclining over it.

"Nothing, certainly, could be more repulsive than the appearance of the coast — sandhills as far as the eye could reach, broken only by the grey and lugubrious works and buildings of Ostend, and further west by the spires of Mittelkerke and Nieuport peering above the sandhills. The day, too, was one little calculated to enliven the scene. A fresh breeze and cloudy sky; the sea black, rough, and chilly; the land all under one uniform cold grey tint, presenting scarcely any relief of light and shadow, consequently no feature. Upon reconnoitring it, however, closer, we found that this forbidding exterior was only an outer coating to a lovely gem. Through the openings between the sandhills could be seen a rich level country of the liveliest verdure, studded with villages and farms interspersed amongst avenues of trees and small patches of wood.

"A black-looking mass of timber rising from the waters off the entrance of the harbour, and which we understood to be a fort, now became the principal object of our attention. The harbour of Ostend is an artificial one, formed by *jetées* of piles projecting as far as low-water mark. The right on entering is merely a row of piles running along in front of the works of the town; but on the left is a long mole or *jetée* on the extremity of which is a small fort. Behind this mole to the north-east the shore curving inwards forms a bight, presenting an extent of flat sandy beach on which the water is never more than a few feet deep even at the highest tides. A tremendous surf breaks on this whenever it blows from the westward.

"Followed by a crowd of other craft of all sorts and sizes, we shot rapidly along towards that part of the harbour where a dense assemblage of shipping filled up its whole breadth and forbade further progress, so that one wondered what was to become of the numerous vessels in our wake. The mystery was soon explained, for each having attained the point, turning her prow to the town, ran bump on the sands and there stuck fast. Those immediately above us had just arrived, and from them a regiment of Light Dragoons was in the act of disembarking, by throwing their horses overboard and then hauling them ashore by a long rope attached to their head-collars. What a scene! What hallooing, shouting, vociferating, and plunging! The poor horses did not appear much gratified by their sudden transition from the warm hold to a cold bath.

"Our keel had scarcely touched the sand ere we were abruptly boarded by a naval officer (Captain Hill) with a gang of sailors, who, *sans ceremonie*, instantly commenced hoisting our horses out, and throwing them, as well as our saddlery, &c., overboard, without ever giving time for making any disposition to receive or secure the one or the other. To my remonstrance his answer was, 'I can't help it, sir; the Duke's orders are positive that no delay is to take place in landing the troops as they arrive, and the ships sent back again; so you must be out of her before dark.' It was then about 3 P.M., and I thought this a most uncomfortable arrangement.

"The scramble and confusion that ensued baffle all description. Bundles of harness went over the side in rapid succession as well as horses. In vain we urged the loss and damage that must accrue from such a proceeding. 'Can't help it no business of mine — Duke's orders are positive,' &c., &c., was our only answer. Meantime the ebb had begun to diminish the depth of water alongside, and enabled us to send parties overboard and to the beach to collect and carry our things ashore, as well as to haul and secure the horses. The same operation commenced from the other vessels as they arrived, and the bustle and noise were inconceivable. The dragoons and our men (some nearly, others quite, naked) were dashing in and out of the water, struggling with the affrighted horses, or securing their wet accoutrements as best they could. Some of the former were saddling their dripping horses, and others mounting and marching off in small parties. Disconsolate-looking groups of women and children were to be seen here and there sitting on their poor duds, or roaming about in search of their husbands, or mayhap of a stray child, all clamouring, lamenting, and materially increasing the babel-like confusion.

"It was not without difficulty that I succeeded at last in impressing upon Captain Hill the necessity of leaving our guns and ammunition-waggons, &c., on board for the night — otherwise his furious zeal would have turned all out to stand on the wet sand or be washed away. Meantime, although we were on shore, we were without orders what to do next. Not an officer, either of the staff, the garrison, or even of our own corps, came near us. Night approached, and with it bad weather evidently. Our poor shivering horses and heaps of wet harness could not remain on the sands much longer, when the flood began to make again; and it was necessary to look about and see what could be done. With this intent, therefore, leaving the officers to collect their divisions, I got one of my horses saddled and rode into the town. Here was the same bustle (although not the same confusion) as on the sands. The streets were thronged with British officers, and the quays with guns, waggons, horses, baggage, &c.

"One would hardly expect to meet with any delay in finding the commandant of a fortress, yet such was my case; and it was not until after long and repeated inquiry that I discovered Lieut.-Colonel Gregory, 44th Regiment, to be that personage, and found his residence. From him, however, I could obtain nothing. He seemed hardly to have expected the compliment of reporting our arrival, and stated that he had no other orders but that the troops of every arm should march for Ghent the moment they landed, without halting a single day in Ostend.

"Strange to say neither I nor the colonel recollected there was such a person in Ostend as an assistant-quarter-master-general, who should be referred to on such an occasion. Yet this was the case; and that officer, instead of attending to the debarkation of the troops, or making himself acquainted with the arrivals, kept out of sight altogether. Baffled at all points, I was returning to the sands when I met Major Drummond on the Quai Impérial, and related my story. His advice was to march to Ghystelle (a village about six miles from Ostend), and after putting up there for the night, to return and disembark my guns, &c., in the morning. While speaking, however, some one (I forget who) came up with the agreeable information that Ghystelle was already fully occupied by the 16th Dragoons. He, however, gave me directions for some large sheds about a mile off, where his own horses had passed the preceding night.

"This was some consolation: so riding off immediately to reconnoitre the place and the road to it, I returned to the beach just as it got dark; and a most miserable scene of confusion I there found. Our saddles, harness, baggage, &c., were still strewed about the sand, and these the flood, which was now making, threatened soon to submerge. *Pour surcroit de malheur*, the rain came down in torrents, and a storm, which had been brewing up the whole afternoon, now burst over us most furiously. The lightning was quite tremendous, whilst a hurricane, howling horribly through the rigging of the ships, was only exceeded in noise by the loud explosions and rattling of the incessant claps of thunder.

"Our people, meantime, blinded by the lightning, had borrowed some lanterns from the ship, and were busily employed searching for the numerous articles still missing." The obscurity, however, between the vivid flashes was such that we were only enabled to keep together by repeatedly calling to each other, and it was not without difficulty and great watchfulness that we escaped being caught by the tide, which flowed rapidly in over the flat sands. At length, having collected as many of our things as was possible, and saddled our horses (some two or three of which had escaped altogether), we began our march for the sheds a little after midnight, with a farrier and another dismounted man carrying lanterns at the head of our column.

"The rain continued pouring, but flashes of lightning occurred now only at intervals, and the more subdued rolling of the thunder told us that it was passing away in the distance. Our route lay through the town, to gain which we found some advanced ditch to be crossed by a very frail wooden bridge. Half the column, perhaps, might have cleared this, when, 'crack,' down it went, precipitating all who were on it at the moment into the mud below, and completely cutting off those in the rear. Here was a dilemma. Ignorant of the localities, and without a guide, how was the rear of the column to join us, or how were the people in the ditch, with their horses, to be extricated? Luckily none were hurt seriously, and the depth was not great — not more, perhaps, than six or eight feet; but that was enough to baffle all our attempts at extricating the horses. Some Belgic soldiers of a neighbouring guard, of which we were not aware, fortunately heard us, and came to our assistance; and one of them, crossing the ditch, undertook to guide the rear of our column and those below to another gate, whilst one accompanied us to the Quai Imperial, where, after waiting a while, we were at length assembled, drenched with rain and starving of cold and hunger.

"The Quai was silent and dark; the only light gleamed dimly through the wet from a miserable lamp over the door of a cafe, in which people were still moving; and the only sounds that broke the stillness of the quarter were the splashing of the rain and the clattering of our steel scabbards and horses' feet as we moved dejectedly on — winding our way through unknown avenues (for in the dark I found it impossible to recognise the narrow streets through which I had so hurriedly passed in the afternoon), occasionally illuminated by a solitary lamp, the feeble light of which, however, was somewhat increased by reflection on the wet pavement. After following for some time this devious course, I began to fear I had missed the road, when again we stumbled upon a Belgic guard, by whose direction and guidance we at length reached the outer barrier. Here we again came to a standstill, the officer in charge refusing to let us out. Some altercation ensued; I forget the particulars, but it ended in his opening the gate.

"Once clear of the town, we hoped soon to reach our lodging; but had scarcely advanced a hundred yards ere we found that result was more distant than we had fancied, and that patience was still requisite. The rain had rendered the fat soil so slippery that our horses could scarcely keep their legs, and the road running along the narrow summit of a dyke, with ditches on each side, rendered precaution and slow movement imperative. Every moment the fall of some horse impeded the column; our lanterns went out; and after wandering a considerable time, we at length ascertained, by knocking up the people at a house by the wayside, that we had overshot our mark, and it was not until two in the morning that we succeeded in finding the sheds. These were immensely long buildings attached to some saw-mills, for what use I know not, unless to store planks, &c., for they were now empty; but they were admirably adapted to our purpose, since we could range all our horses along one side, while the men occupied the other, in one of them. A quantity of hay, and some straw, left by our predecessors, was a valuable acquisition to man and beast under such circumstances. All our enjoyments are the effect of contrast. It would be considered miserable enough to be obliged to pass the night under such equivocal shelter as these sheds afforded, and that, too, in wet clothes; yet did we now, after twelve hours of harassing work and exposure to the weather, look upon them as palaces, and having cared for our poor beasts as far as circumstances would permit, proceeded to prepare for that repose so necessary and so longed for.

"Our road back to the town, now we had daylight, appeared very short, and having dried considerably, was not so slippery as last night. The gates were not yet opened when we arrived; a crowd of workmen of different kinds had already assembled and were waiting for admission, as were we, for a few minutes. At last they opened, and we proceeded to the harbour in search of our ship. The quais, beach, &c., were thronged as on the day before, and we added to the bustle in disembarking our guns and carriages, &c. This was completed by eleven o'clock, and we were ready to march forward; but the commissariat detained us waiting the issue of our rations until 3 P.M. — four mortal hours, considering our eagerness to get on and explore this new country, and the bore of being confined to one spot, since it was impossible to wander about the town, seeing that we could not calculate the moment when these gentry might find it convenient to supply us. Of our horses two were still missing, as were some saddle-bags and a number of smaller articles; and this is not to be wondered at when the scandalous manner in which they were thrown overboard, the badness of the weather, the darkness of the night, together with the ebbing and flowing of the tide, are taken into consideration.

"The appearance, too, of the troop was vexatious in the extreme. Our noble horses, yesterday morning so sleek and spirited, now stood with drooping heads and rough staring coats, plainly indicating the mischief they had sustained in being taken from a hot hold, plunged into cold water, and then exposed for more than seven hours on an open beach to such a tempest of wind and rain as that we experienced last night. Here was a practical illustration of the folly of grooming and pampering military horses, destined as they are to such exposures and privations. As for our men, they looked jaded, their clothes all soiled with mud and wet, the sabres rusty, and the bearskins of their helmets flattened down by the rain. Still, however, they displayed the same spirit and alacrity as that which has always been a characteristic of the horse-artillery, more particularly of G troop."

The tedium of waiting for so many hours on Ostend beach was relieved by a naval incident of an exciting quality:

"A loud cry of dismay suddenly pervaded the crowd, and all simultaneously rushed to the ramparts. I followed this movement. The morning, though somewhat overcast, had been fine, and the wind moderate; but as the day advanced, and the flood-tide set in, the south-westerly breeze had gradually increased to a gale. On reaching the rampart, I immediately observed that the flat shore to the northward, as far as the eye could reach, was covered with a sheet of white foam from the tremendous surf breaking on it; whilst the spray, rising in clouds and borne along before the blast, involved the whole neighbourhood in a thick salt mist. Nothing could be more savage and wild than the appearance of the coast.

"In the offing, numerous vessels under small sail were running for the harbour. One small brig had missed, and before assistance could be given, had been whirled round the *jetée*, and cast broadside on amongst the breakers. Her situation was truly awful. The surf broke over her in a frightful manner, sending its spray higher than her masts, and causing her to roll from side to side until her yards dipped in the water, and induced a belief every moment that she must roll over. Every now and then a huge wave, larger than its predecessor, would raise her bodily, and then, rapidly receding, suddenly let her fall again on the ground with a concussion that made the masts bend and vibrate like fishing-rods, and seemed to threaten instant annihilation. Of her sails, some were torn to rags, and others, flying loose, flapped and fluttered with a noise that was audible from the rampart, despite the roaring of the surf. The people on board appeared in great agitation, and kept shouting to those on shore for assistance, which they were unable to give.

"Intense anxiety pervaded the assembled multitude as the shattered vessel alternately rose to view or was buried in a sea of foam. Numbers ran down to the sands opposite to her; and from them she could not have been twenty yards distant, yet could they not afford the despairing crew the slightest aid. Whilst thus attending in breathless expectation the horrid catastrophe, the return of our quarter-master with the rations summoned us unwillingly from the rampart to commence our march. We afterwards learnt that a boat from the harbour had succeeded in saving the crew (she had no troops on board); but the unfortunate pilot who thus gallantly risked his own life for them was killed by the boat rising suddenly under the vessel's counter as he stood in the bow, winch dashed his brains out."

Chapter Twenty-One – On March to the Field

Mercer's description of his march across the Low Countries is full of keen observation, and rich in pictures of peasant life. At Ghent the troop halted for seven days. Here the much-wandering Louis XVIII held his Court, and Mercer gives an entertaining account of the scenes he witnessed:

"During the seven days we remained in Ghent our time was so occupied by duties that there was little leisure to look about us. Amongst other duties, it fell to our lot to furnish a guard of honour to Louis XVIII, then residing in Ghent, his own troops having been sent to Alost to make room for the British, which were continually passing through. Our subalterns were very well pleased with this arrangement, for the duty was nothing. They found an excellent table, and passed their time very agreeably with the young men of the *gardes du corps*, some of whom were always in attendance. Many of these were mere boys, and the anteroom of his most Christian Majesty frequently exhibited bolstering matches and other amusements, savouring strongly of the boarding-school. However, they were good-natured, and always most attentive to the comforts of the officer on guard. The royal stud was in the barrack stables, and consisted principally of grey horses, eighteen or twenty of which had been purchased in England at a sale of 'cast horses' from the Scots Greys.

"We frequently met French officers of all ranks, and formed acquaintance with many gentlemanly, well-informed men. At the Lion d'Or and Hotel de Flandre we found there was a *table d'hôte* every night at eight o'clock, and, by way of passing the evening, usually resorted to one or the other for supper. Here we were sure of meeting many Frenchmen, and as the same people were generally constant attendants, we became intimate, and discussed the merits of our national troops respectively over our wine or *ponche*. It was the first time most of them had had an opportunity of inspecting British troops closely, though many had often met them in the field; and they were very curious in their inquiries into the organisation, government, and equipment of our army.

Although allowing all due credit to the bravery displayed by our troops in the Peninsula, and the talents of our general (the Duke), yet were they unanimous in their belief that neither would avail in the approaching conflict, and that we must succumb before their idol and his grand army, for though these gentlemen had deserted Napoleon to follow the fortunes of Louis XVIII, it was evident they still revered the former.

"Their admiration of our troops, particularly of the cavalry, was very great, but they expressed astonishment at seeing so few decorations. It was in vain we asserted that medals were rarely given in the British army, and then only to commanding officers, &c. They shook their heads, appeared incredulous, and asked, 'Where are the troops that fought in Spain?' There might have been something more than mere curiosity in all this; there might have been an anxiety to ascertain whether their countrymen were about to cope with veterans or young soldiers. It might have been thrown out as a lure to provoke information relative to the present employment of those veteran bands. Moreover, I shrewdly suspected many of the gentlemen were actually spies.

"Amongst others who had followed Louis XVIII was Marmont. I think it was the day after our arrival, passing over the open space near the Place d'Armes by the river, I saw a French general officer exercising a horse in the *manège*, and learnt with astonishment that this was Marmont; for the man in question had two good arms, whereas for years past I had, in common with most people in England, looked upon it as a fact that he had left one at Salamanca. French deserters, both officers and privates, were daily coming in; it was said they deserted by hundreds."

On April 24 the troop received orders to resume its march, its next quarters being at Thermonde, or, as it ought to have been spelt, Dendermonde. From Dendermonde, on May 1, the troop was ordered to march to Strytem. Mercer had neither map, nor directions, nor guides, and his account of the incidents of the march, and the fashion in which (as though he were exploring some absolutely unknown land) he had to "discover" Strytem is amusing:

"May 1 — I still slept, when at five o'clock in the morning our sergeant-major aroused me to read a note brought by an orderly hussar. It was most laconic — *la voici*: 'Captain Mercer's troop of horse artillery will march to Strytem without delay. Signed,' &c., &c.

"Where is Strytem? and for what this sudden move? These were questions to which I could get no answer. The hussar knew nothing, and the people about me less. One thing was positive, and that was that we must be under weigh [sic] instanter, and pick out Strytem as best we might. The sergeant-major, therefore, was despatched to give the alert; and having given the hussar a receipt in full for his important despatch, I proceeded to clothe my person for the journey, having hitherto been *en chemise*. As the trumpeter was lodged in a house close by with my own grooms, the 'boot and saddle' quickly reverberated through the village, and set its whole population in movement.

"To my questions respecting Strytem, Monsieur could give no satisfactory answers. 'It lay in a very fine country somewhere in the neighbourhood of Brussels, and we had better take the road to that city in the first instance, and trust for further information to the peasantry as we went along.' These people are singularly ignorant in this respect, having no knowledge, generally speaking, of any place more than two or three miles from home. Monsieur, however, invited me to follow him to his study — a small room all in a litter — over the gateway, and there, after some hunting amongst books, old clothes, &c., &c., he rummaged out the mutilated fragment of an old but very excellent map, which he insisted on my putting into my sabretache, which I did, and still keep for his sake.

"'Prepare to mount!' 'Mount!' The trumpets sound a march, and waving a last adieu to the group at the gate of my late home, I turn my back on it for ever perhaps. The men were in high spirits, and horses fat as pigs and sleek as moles — thanks to rest, good stabling, and abundance of *tref.* Most of the peasants on whom many of our men had been billeted accompanied them to the parade, and it was interesting to witness the kindness with which they shook hands at parting, and the complacency with which, patting the horses on the neck, they scanned them all over, as if proud of their good condition.

"Passing through Lebbeke, we found the three brigades of 9-pounders also getting on march, and the whole village astir. The officers told us their orders were to march direct to Brussels, and they were fully persuaded the French army had advanced.

"At Assche we found a battery of Belgian horse artillery in quarters. Their men, lounging about in undress, or without their jackets, without any appearance of a move, induced us to believe our own was, after all, only another change of quarters — and we were right. The people here knew Strytem, which they said was only a few miles distant, to the south-ward of the road we were on. Accordingly I despatched an officer to precede us, and make the necessary arrangements for our reception; at the same time, quitting the *chaussée*, we plunged into a villainous cross-road, all up and down, and every bottom occupied by a stream crossed by bridges of loose planks, which to us were rather annoying, from their apparent insecurity, as well as from the boggy state of the ground for some yards at either end of them.

"The road became worse than ever deep, tenacious mud, sadly broken up. After marching a short distance we passed a wheelwright's shop; then came to a broader space, where stood a small mean-looking church, a miserable cabaret, a forge, two very large farm establishments, with a few wretched-looking cottages this our guide gave us to understand was Strytem."

At Strytem, where the troop halted for some time, Mercer had an opportunity of seeing something of the cavalry corps which the Due de Berri was forming in the Bourbon interest. The Due de Berri, according to Mercer, was a very ill-mannered brute. Says Mercer:

"One day I had a good opportunity of seeing this curious corps and its savage leader. The former presented a most grotesque appearance-cuirassiers, hussars, grenadiers *à cheval*, and chasseurs, dragoons and lancers, officers and privates, with a few of the new *gardes du corps*, were indiscriminately mingled in the ranks. One file were colonels, the next privates, and so on, and all wearing their proper uniforms and mounted on their proper horses, so that these were of all sizes and colours. There might have been about two hundred men, divided into two or three squadrons, the commanders of which were generals. The Prince, as I have said, was drill-master. A more intemperate, brutal, and (in his situation) impolitic one, can scarcely be conceived. The slightest fault (frequently occasioned by his own blunders) was visited by showers of low-life abuse — using on all occasions the most odious language.

"One unfortunate squadron officer (a general!) offended him, and was immediately charged with such violence that I expected a catastrophe. Reining up his horse, however, close to the unhappy man, his vociferation and villainous abuse were those of a perfect madman;

shaking his sabre at him, and even at one time thrusting the pommel of it into his face, and, as far as I could see, pushing it against his nose! Such a scene! Yet all the others sat mute as mice, and witnessed all this humiliation of their comrade, and the degradation of him for whom they had forsaken Napoleon. Just at this moment one of our troop-dogs ran barking at the heels of the Prince's horse. Boiling with rage before, he now boiled over in earnest, and, stooping, made a furious cut at the dog, which, eluding the weapon, continued his annoyance. The Duke, quitting the unfortunate *chef d'escadron*, now turned seriously at the dog, but he, accustomed to horses, kept circling about, yapping and snapping, and always out of reach; and it was not until he had tired himself with the fruitless pursuit that, foaming with rage, he returned to his doomed squadrons, who had sat quietly looking on at this exhibition."

As the early days of June passed, and Napoleon was preparing for his daring leap on the allied forces, the general strain grew more tense. French spies were busy all through the English and Prussian posts. Mercer describes a visit paid by a particularly daring spy to his own post:

"It was on the evening of the 15th June, and about sunset or a little later, that an officer of hussars rode into the village of Yseringen, Leathes being at the time at dinner with me at our chateau. He was dressed as our hussars usually were when riding about the country — blue frock, scarlet waistcoat laced with gold, pantaloons, and forage-cap of the 7th Hussars. He was mounted on a smart pony, with plain saddle and bridle; was without a sword or sash, and carried a small whip — in short, his costume and *monture* were correct in every particular. Moreover, he aped to the very life that 'devil-may-care' nonchalant air so frequently characterising our young men of fashion. Seeing some of our gunners standing at the door of a house, he desired them to go for their officer, as he wished to see him. They called the sergeant, who told him that the officer was not in the village.

"In an authoritative tone he then demanded how many men and horses were quartered there, whose troop they belonged to, where the remainder of the troop was quartered, and of what it consisted? When all these questions were answered, he told the sergeant that he had been sent by Lord Uxbridge to order accommodation to be provided for two hundred horses, and that ours must consequently be put up as close as possible. The sergeant replied that there was not room in the village for a single additional horse. 'Oh, we'll soon see that,' said he, pointing to one of the men who stood by, 'do you go and tell the maire to come instantly to me.' The maire came and confirmed the sergeant's statement, upon which our friend, flying into a passion, commenced in excellent French to abuse the poor functionary like a pickpocket, threatening to send a whole regiment into the village; and then, after a little further conversation with the sergeant, he mounted his pony and rode off just as Leathes returned to the village.

"Upon reporting the circumstances to the officer, the sergeant stated that he thought this man had appeared anxious to avoid him, having ridden off rather in a hurry when he appeared, which together with a slight foreign accent, then for the first time excited a suspicion of his being a spy, winch had not occurred to the sergeant before, as he knew there were several foreign officers in our hussars, and that the 10th was actually then commanded by one — Colonel Quentin. The suspicion was afterwards confirmed, for upon inquiry, I found that no officer had been sent by Lord Uxbridge on any such mission. Our friend deserved to escape, for he was a bold and clever fellow."

Chapter Twenty-Two – Quatre Bras

Napoleon's plan for what was to prove the last campaign in his own wonderful career was daring and subtle. He had to face two armies, each almost equal in strength to his own; and though the forces of Blücher and of Wellington were scattered over a very wide front, yet their outposts touched each other where the great road from Charleroi ran northwards to Brussels. Napoleon, with equal audacity and genius, resolved to smite at the point of junction betwixt the two armies, and overthrow each in turn. The risks of this strategy were immense, for if his enemies succeeded in concentrating and fighting in concert, he would be overwhelmed and destroyed as actually happened at Waterloo. Napoleon, however, calculated to win by the swiftness and suddenness of his stroke, destroying Blücher before Wellington could concentrate for his help, and then, in turn, overwhelming Wellington. By what a narrow interval that great plan failed of success is not always realised.

Both Blücher and Wellington were off their guard. On June 15, at the very moment when Napoleon's columns were crossing the Belgian frontier, Wellington was writing a leisurely despatch to the Czar explaining his intention to take the offensive at the end of the month. Blücher, only a few days before, as Houssaye records, had written to his wife, "We shall soon enter France. We might remain here another year, for Bonaparte will never attack us." Yet with miraculous energy and skill, Napoleon, in ten days, had gathered a host of 124,000 men, over distances ranging from 30 to 200 miles, and held them, almost unsuspected, within cannon-shot of the allied outposts. On June 15, while the stars in the eastern summer sky were growing faint in the coming dawn, the French columns were crossing at three separate points the Belgian frontier, and the great campaign had begun.

Its history is compressed into three furious days. On the 16th Napoleon defeated Blücher at Ligny, while Wellington, with obstinate courage and fine skill, aided by many blunders on his enemy's part, and much good luck on his own, succeeded in holding Quatre Bras against Ney. On the 17th Wellington fell back before the combined armies of Napoleon and

Ney to Waterloo. On the 18th the great battle, which sealed the fate of Napoleon and gave a long peace to Europe, was fought. Napoleon's strategy had fatally broken down. He aimed to separate the English and the Prussian armies while keeping his own concentrated. The exact opposite happened. Blüchers bold westward march from Wavre to Waterloo united the allied forces, while Napoleon's force was fatally divided — Grouchy, with 30,000 troops, being left "in the air" far to the east. Napoleon, in a word, suffered the exact strategic disaster he sought to inflict on his opponents.

We take up the thread of the adventures of Mercer and Battery G as active operations begin. It offers a curious picture of the distraction and confusion of a great campaign:

"June 16 — I was sound asleep when my servant, bustling into the room, awoke me *en sursaut*. He brought a note, which an orderly hussar had left and ridden off immediately. The note had nothing official in its appearance, and might have been an invitation to dinner; out the unceremonious manner in which the hussar had gone off without his receipt looked curious. My despatch was totally deficient in date, so that time and place were left to conjecture; its contents pithy — they were as follows, viz.

"'Captain Mercer's troop will proceed with the utmost diligence to Enghien, where he will meet Major M'Donald, who will point out the ground on which it is to bivouac to-night.

'Signed, D.A.Q.M.-Gen.'

"That we were to move forward, then, was certain. It was rather sudden, to be sure, and all the whys and wherefores were left to conjecture; but the suddenness of it, and the importance of arriving quickly at the appointed place, rather alarmed me, for upon reflection I remembered that I had been guilty of two or three imprudences.

"First, all my officers were absent; secondly, all my country waggons were absent; thirdly, a whole division (one-third of my troop) was absent at Yseringen. 'Send the sergeant-major here,' was the first order, as I drew on my stockings. 'Send for Mr. Coates' (my commissariat officer), the second, as I got one leg into my overalls. 'William, make haste and get breakfast,' the third, as I buttoned them up. The sergeant-major soon came, and received his orders to turn out instanter, with the three days' provisions and forage in the haversacks and on the horses; also to send an express for the first division. He withdrew, and immediately the fine martial clang of 'boot and saddle' resounded through the village and courts of the chateau, making the woods ring again, and even the frogs stop to listen.

"The commissary soon made his appearance. 'What! are we off, sir?' 'Yes, without delay; and you must collect your waggons as quickly as possible.' 'I fear, Captain Mercer, that will take some time, for St. Cyr's are gone to Ninove.' My folly here stared me full in the face. Mr. Coates said he would do his utmost to collect them; and as he was a most active, intelligent, and indefatigable fellow, I communicated to him my orders and determination not to wait, desiring him to follow us as soon as he possibly could. My first enumerated care was speedily removed, for I learned that the officers had just arrived and were preparing for the march, having known of it at Brussels ere we did. The two divisions in Strytem were ready to turn out in a few minutes after the 'boot and saddle' had resounded, but, as I feared, the first kept us waiting until near seven o'clock before it made its appearance. At length the first division arrived, and the animating and soul-stirring notes of the 'turn-out' again awoke the echoes of the hills and woods. Up jumped my old dog Bal, and away to parade and increase the bustle by jumping at the horses' noses and barking, as parade formed. Away went the officers to inspect their divisions, and Milward is leading my impatient charger, Cossac, up and down the court.

"We had cleared the village and marched some miles well enough, being within the range of my daily rides; but, this limit passed, I was immediately sensible of another error — that of having started without a guide; for the roads became so numerous, intricate, and bad, often resembling only woodmen's tracks, that I was sorely puzzled, spite of the map I carried in my sabretache, to pick out my way. But a graver error still I had now to reproach myself with, and one that might have been attended with fatal consequences. Eager to get on, and delayed by the badness of the roads, I left all my ammunition waggons behind, under charge of old Hall, my quarter-master-sergeant, to follow us, and then pushed on with the guns alone, thus foolishly enough dividing my troop into three columns — viz., the guns, ammunition waggons, and the column of provision waggons under the commissary. For this piece of folly I paid dearly in the anxiety I suffered throughout this eventful day, which at times was excessive.

"Rid of all encumbrances, we trotted merrily on whenever the road permitted, and, arriving at Castre (an old Roman legionary station), found there the 23rd Light Dragoons just turning out, having also received orders to march upon Enghien. A Captain Dance, with whom I rode a short distance, told me he had been at the ball at Brussels last night, and that, when he left the room, the report was that Blücher had been attacked in the morning, but that he had repulsed the enemy with great slaughter, was following up the blow, and that our advance was to support him. The road for the last few miles had been upon a more elevated country, not so wooded — a sort of plateau, consequently hard and dry; but immediately on passing Castre, we came to a piece which appeared almost impassable for about a hundred yards a perfect black bog, across which a corduroy road had been made, but not kept in repair, consequently the logs, having decayed, left immense gaps.

"The 23rd floundered through this with difficulty, and left us behind. How we got through with our 9-pounders, the horses slipping up to the shoulders between the logs every minute, I know not; but through we did get, and without accident, but it took time to do so. About noon, after threading our way through more mud and many watery lanes, doubtful if we were in the right direction, we came out upon a more open and dry country, close to a park, which upon inquiry proved to be that of Enghien. To the same point various columns of cavalry were converging, and under the park wall we found Sir Ormsby Vandeleur's brigade of light dragoons dismounted, and feeding their horses. Here we also dismounted to await the arrival of Major M'Donald; and as I looked upon the day's march as finished, deferred feeding until our bivouac should be established — another folly, for an officer in campaign should never lose an opportunity of feeding, watering, or resting his horses, &c. Having waited a good half-hour, and no Major M'Donald appearing, I began to look about for some one who could give me information, but no staff-officer was to be seen, and no one else knew anything about the matter. Corps after corps arrived and passed on, generally without even halting, yet all professing ignorance of their destination. Pleasant situation this!

"Sir Ormsby's dragoons were by this time bridling up their horses and rolling up their nosebags, evidently with the intention of moving off. Seeing this, I sought out the general, whom I found seated against a bank that, instead of a hedge, bordered the road. Whether naturally a savage, or that he feared committing himself, I know not, but Sir Ormsby cut my queries short with an asperity totally uncalled for. 'I know nothing about you, sir! I know nothing at all about you!' and starting abruptly from his seat, my friend mounted his horse, and (I suppose by instinct) took the road towards Steenkerke, followed by his brigade, leaving me and mine alone in the road, more disagreeably situated than ever. I now began to reflect very seriously on the 'to stay' or 'not to stay.' In the former case, I bade fair to have the ground all to myself, for although everybody I spoke to denied having any orders, yet all kept moving in one and the same direction. In the latter case, my orders in writing certainly were to stay; but circumstances might have occurred since to change this, and the new order might not have reached me. Moreover, it was better to get into a scrape for fighting than keeping out of the way, so I made up my mind to move forward too.

"Accordingly I had already mounted my people when Sir H. Vivian's brigade of hussars, followed by Major Bull's troop of our horse artillery, passed. Bull, I found, was, like myself, without orders, but he thought it best to stick close to the cavalry, and advised me to do the same, which I did, following him and them on the road to Steenkerke. The country about this place appeared more bare and forbidding than any I had yet seen in the Pays Baa Just as we moved off, the column of Household troops made its appearance, advancing from Ninove, and taking the same direction.

"It was now that the recollection of my absent waggons began to torment me, and I actually feared never to see them again. However, there was no help for it now, and I continued onward. A few miles farther we crossed the Senne by an old stone bridge, and about four in the afternoon arrived at Braine le Comte, almost ravenous with hunger, and roasted alive by the burning sun, under which we had been marching all day.

"We found several regiments drawn up in close columns, dismounted and feeding. It was somewhere between Enghien and Braine le Comte that we met an aide-de-camp (I believe one of the Duke's) posting away as fast as his poor tired beast could get along, and dressed in his embroidered suit, white pantaloons, &c., &c., having evidently mounted as he left the ball-room. This, I remember, struck us at the time as rather odd, but we had no idea of the real state of our affairs.

"We had formed up, and were feeding also, but the nosebags were scarcely put on the poor horse's heads than the cavalry corps, mounting again, moved off, one after the other, and we were constrained to follow ere the animals had half finished. Here, as before, I could obtain no intelligence respecting our march, the direction and meaning of which all I spoke to professed a profound ignorance. Whilst halting, Hitchins, slipping into the town, brought us out a couple of bottles of wine, the which we passed round from one to the other without any scruple about sucking it all out of one muzzle.

"A little hamlet (Long Tour, I think) lay at the foot of the hills, the straggling street of which we found so crowded with baggage waggons of some Hanoverian or other foreign corps that for a long while we were unable to pass. The cavalry, therefore, left us behind, for they broke into the adjoining fields until they had cleared the impediment. Although annoyed at being thus hindered, I could not but admire the lightness, and even elegance, of the little waggons, with their neat white tilts, and as neat and pretty *jungfrauen* who were snugly seated under them. We found the ascent of the hills more difficult than we expected, the road, which went up in a zigzag (indeed, it could not have been otherwise), little better than a woodman's track, much cut up, and exceedingly steep — so much so, that we found it necessary to double-horse all our carriages by taking only half up at once."

Now, at last, the sullen guns from Quatre Bras began to make themselves audible. Mercer's gunners were chiefly recruits; they had never yet heard the deep, vibrating sounds that tell of the shock of mighty hosts. That far-off call of angry guns stirred their blood and quickened their march; but the troop reached Quatre Bras only when the battle ended. Mercer's narrative, however, gives a striking picture of how a great battle affects everything within sound of its guns:

"At length the whole of our carriages were on the summit, but we were now quite alone, all the cavalry having gone on; and thus we continued our march on an elevated plateau, still covered with forest, thicker and more gloomy than ever. At length we had crossed the forest, and found ourselves on the verge of a declivity which stretched away less abruptly than the one we had ascended, consequently presenting a more extensive slope, down which our road continued. A most extensive view lay before us; and now, for the first time, as emerging from the woods, we became sensible of a dull, sullen sound that filled the air, somewhat resembling that of a distant water-mill, or still more distant thunder. On clearing the wood it became more distinct, and its character was no longer questionable — heavy firing of cannon and musketry, which could now be distinguished from each other plainly. We could also hear the musketry in volleys and independent firing. The extensive view below us was bounded towards the horizon by a dark line of wood, above which, in the direction of the cannonade, volumes of grey smoke arose, leaving no doubt of what was going on. The object of our march was now evident, and we commenced descending the long slope with an animation we had not felt before.

"It was here that Major M'Donald overtook us, and without adverting to the bivouac at Enghien, of which probably he had never heard, gave me orders to attach myself to the Household Brigade, under Lord Edward Somerset, but no instructions where or when. I took care not to tell him they were in the rear, lest he might order us to halt for them, which would have been a sore punishment to people excited as we now were by the increasing roar of the battle evidently going on, and hoped that by marching faster they might soon overtake us. Just at this moment a cabriolet, driving at a smart pace, passed us. In it was seated an officer of the Guards, coat open and snuff-box in hand. I could not but admire the perfect nonchalance with which my man was thus hurrying forward to join in a bloody combat much, perhaps, in the same manner, though certainly not in the same costume, as he might drive to Epsom or Ascot Heath. The descent terminated in a picturesque hollow, with a broad pool, dark and calm, and beyond it an old mill, perfectly in keeping with the scene. The opportunity of watering, our poor brutes was too good to be missed, and I accordingly ordered a halt for that purpose. Whilst so employed, an aide-de-camp, descending from a singular knoll above us, on which I had noticed a group of officers looking out with their glasses in the direction of the battle, came to summon me to Sir Hussey Vivian, who was one of them.

"On ascending the knoll Sir Hussey called to me in a hurried manner to make haste. 'Who do you belong to?' said he. I told him, and also that the brigade was yet in the rear. 'Well,' he replied, 'never mind; there is something serious going on, to judge from that heavy firing, and artillery must be wanted; therefore bring up your guns as fast as you can, and join my hussars; can you keep up?' 'I hope so, sir.' 'Well, come along without delay; we must move smartly.' In a few minutes our people, guns and all, were on the hill. The hussars, mounted, set off at a brisk trot, and we followed. Alas! thought I, where are my ammunition waggons? The hussars, to lighten their horses, untied the nets containing their hay, and the mouths of their corn-bags, which, falling from them as they trotted on, the road was soon covered with hay and oats. We did not follow their example, and although dragging with us impounders preserved our forage and also our place in the column.

"By-and-by a large town appeared in front of us, and the increasing intensity of the cannonade and volumes of smoke about the trees led us to suppose the battle near at hand, and on the hill just beyond the town. This town was Nivelle.

"Beyond the town the ground rose, also in shadowy obscurity, crowned with sombre woods, over which ascended the greyish-blue smoke of the battle, now apparently so near that we fancied we could hear the shouts of the combatants — a fancy strengthened by crowds of people on the heights, whom we mistook for troops — inhabitants of Nivelle, as we soon discovered, seeking to get a sight of the fearful tragedy then enacting. Before entering the town we halted for a moment, lighted our slow matches, put shot into our leathern cartouches, loaded the guns with powder, and stuck priming wires into the vents to prevent the cartridges slipping forward, and, thus prepared for immediate action, again moved on.

"On entering the town what a scene presented itself! All was confusion, agitation, and movement. The danger was impending; explosion after explosion, startling from their vicinity, and clattering peals of musketry, like those lengthened thunder-claps which announce to us so awfully the immediate neighbourhood of the electric cloud. The whole population of Nivelle was in the streets, doors and windows all wide open, whilst the inmates of the houses, male and female, stood huddled together in little groups like frightened sheep, or were hurrying along with the distracted air of people uncertain where they are going or what they are doing. In a sort of square which we traversed a few soldiers, with the air of citizens, probably a municipal guard, were drawn up in line, looking anxiously about them at the numerous bleeding figures which we now began to meet.

"Some were staggering along unaided, the blood falling from them in large drops as they went. One man we met was wounded in the head; pale and ghastly, with affrighted looks and uncertain step, he evidently knew little of where he was or what passed about him, though still he staggered forward, the blood streaming down his face on to the greatcoat which he wore rolled over his left shoulder. An anxious crowd was collecting round him as we passed on. Then came others supported between two comrades, their faces deadly pale and knees yielding at every step. At every step, in short, we met numbers, more or less wounded, hurrying along in search of that assistance which many would never live to receive, and others receive too late. Priests were running to and fro, hastening to assist at the last moments of a dying man; all were in haste — all wore that abstracted air so inseparable from those engaged in an absorbing pursuit. Many would run up, and, patting our horses' necks, would call down benedictions on us, and bid us hasten to the fight ere it were yet too late, or uttering trembling and not loud shouts of 'Vivent les Anglais!'

"A few there were who stood apart, with gloomy, discontented looks, eyeing their fellow-citizens with evident contempt and us with scowls, not unmixed with derision, as they marked our dusty and jaded appearance. Through all this crowd we held our way, and soon began to ascend the hill beyond the town, where we entered a fine *chaussée* bordered by elms, expecting every moment to enter on the field of action, the roar of which appeared quite close to us. It was, however, yet distant.

"The road was covered with soldiers, many of them wounded, but also many apparently untouched. The numbers thus leaving the field appeared extraordinary. Many of the wounded had six, eight, ten, and even more attendants. When questioned about the battle, and why they left it, the answer was invariable: 'Monsieur, tout est perdu! les Anglais sont abimés, en déroute, abimés, tous, tous, tous!' and then, nothing abashed, these fellows would resume their hurried route. My countrymen will rejoice to learn that amongst this dastardly crew not one Briton appeared.

Whether they were of Nassau or Belgians I know not; they were one or the other — I think the latter.

"One redcoat we did meet — not a fugitive though, for he was severely wounded. This man was a private of the 92nd (Gordon Highlanders), a short, rough, hardy-looking fellow, with the national high cheekbones, and a complexion that spoke of many a bivouac. He came limping along, evidently with difficulty and suffering. I stopped him to ask news of the battle, telling him what I had heard from the others, 'Na, na, sir, it's aw a damned lee; they war fechtin' yat an' I laft 'em; but it's a bludy business, and thar's na saying fat may be the end on't. Oor ragiment was nigh clean swapt aff, and oor colonel kilt just as I cam' awa'. Upon inquiring about his own wound, we found that a musket ball had lodged in his knee, or near it; accordingly Hitchins, dismounting, seated him on the parapet of a little bridge we happened to be on, extracted the ball in a few minutes, and, binding up the wound, sent him hobbling along towards Nivelle, not having extracted a single exclamation from the poor man, who gratefully thanked him as he resumed his way.

"A little farther on, and as it began to grow dusk, we traversed the village of Hautain le Val, where a very different scene presented itself. Here, in a large cabaret by the roadside, we saw through the open windows the rooms filled with soldiers, cavalry and infantry; some standing about in earnest conversation, others seated around tables, smoking, carousing, and thumping the board with clenched fists, as they related with loud voices — what? — most likely their own gallant exploits. About the door their poor horses, tied to a rail, showed by their drooping heads, shifting legs, and the sweat drying and fuming on their soiled coats, that their exertions at least had been of no trivial nature.

"The firing began to grow slacker, and even intermitting, as we entered on the field of Quatre Bras — our horses stumbling from time to time over corpses of the slain, which they were too tired to step over. The shot and shell which flew over our line of march from time to time (some of the latter bursting beyond us) were sufficient to enable us to say we had been in the battle of Quatre Bras, for such was the name of the place where we now arrived, just too late to be useful. In all directions the busy hum of human voices was heard; the wood along the skirts of which we marched re-echoed clearly and loudly the tones of the bugle, which ever and anon were overpowered by the sullen roar of cannon, or the sharper rattle of musketry; dark crowds of men moved in the increasing obscurity of evening, and the whole scene seemed alive with them. What a moment of excitement and anxiety as we proceeded amongst all this tumult, and amidst the dead and dying, ignorant as yet how the affair had terminated! Arrived at a mass of buildings, where four roads met (*les quatre bras*), Major M'Donald again came up with orders for us to bivouac on an adjoining field, where, accordingly, we established ourselves amongst the remains of a wheat crop.

"June 17 — A popping fire of musketry, apparently close at hand, aroused me again to consciousness of my situation. At first I could not imagine where I was. I looked straight up, and the stars were twinkling over me in a clear sky. I put out a hand from beneath my cloak, and felt clods of damp earth and stalks of straw. The rattle of musketry increased, and then the consciousness of my situation came gradually over me. Although somewhat chilly, I was still drowsy, and regardless of what might be going on, had turned on my side and began to doze again, when one of my neighbours started up with the exclamation, 'I wonder what all that firing means!' This in an instant dispelled all desire to sleep; and up I got too, mechanically repeating his words, and rubbing my eyes as I began to peer about.

"One of the first, and certainly the most gratifying, sights that met my inquiring gaze, was Quartermaster Hall, who had arrived during the night with all his charge safe and sound. He had neither seen nor heard, however, of Mr. Coates and his train of country waggons, for whom I began now to entertain serious apprehensions. From whatever the musketry might proceed, we could see nothing not even the flashes; but the increasing light allowed me to distinguish numberless dark forms on the ground all around me, people slumbering still, regardless of the firing that had aroused me. At a little distance numerous white discs, which were continually in motion, changing place and disappearing, to be succeeded by others, puzzled me exceedingly, and I could not even form a conjecture as to what they might be. Watching them attentively, I was still more surprised when some of these white objects ascended from the ground and suddenly disappeared; but the mystery was soon explained by the increasing light, which gave to my view a corps of Nassau troops lying on the ground, having white tops to their shakos.

"Daylight now gradually unfolded to us our situation. We were on a plateau which had been covered with corn, now almost everywhere trodden down. Four roads, as already mentioned, met a little to the right of our front, and just at that point stood a farmhouse, which, with its outbuildings, yard, &c., was enclosed by a very high wall. This was the farm of Quatre Bras. Beyond it, looking obliquely to the right, the wood (in which the battle still lingered when we arrived last night) stretched away some distance along the roads to Nivelle and Charleroi, which last we understood lay in front."

Chapter Twenty-Three – The Retreat to Waterloo

Mercer's battery formed part of the British rear-guard in the retreat from Quatre Bras to Waterloo, and his gunners had some very breathless and exciting experiences on the road, with the thunder rolling over their heads and the French cavalry charging furiously on their rear. Mercer tells the story with great vividness and spirit:

"On the Charleroi road and in the plain was a small village (Frasnes), with its church, just beyond which the road ascended the heights, on the open part of which, between the road and the wood towards the left, was the bivouac of the French army opposed to us. Its advanced posts were in the valley near Frasnes, and ours opposite to them — our main body occupying the ground between Quatre Bras and the wood on the left. A smart skirmish was going on amongst the hedges, &c., already mentioned, and this was the firing we had heard all the morning. Our infantry were lying about, cleaning their arms, cooking, or amusing themselves, totally regardless of the skirmish. This, however, from our position, was a very interesting sight to me, for the slope of the ground enabled me to see distinctly all the manoeuvres of both parties, as on a plan. After much tiring from the edge of the wood, opposite which our riflemen occupied all the hedges, I saw the French chasseurs suddenly make a rush forward in all directions, whilst the fire of our people became thicker and faster than ever. Many of the former scampered across the open fields until they reached the nearest hedges, whilst others ran crouching under cover of those perpendicular to their front, and the whole succeeded in establishing themselves — thus forcing back and gaining ground on our men.

"The fire then again became sharper than ever — sometimes the French were driven back; and this alternation I watched with great interest until summoned to Major M'Donald, who brought us orders for the day. From him I first learned the result of the action of yesterday — the retreat of the Prussians, and that we were to do so too. His directions to me were that I should follow some corps of infantry, or something of the sort; for what followed caused me to forget it all: 'Major Ramsay's troop,' he said, 'will remain in the rear with the cavalry to cover the retreat; but I will not conceal from you that it falls to your turn to do this, if you choose it.' The major looked rather conscience-stricken as he made this avowal, so, to relieve him, I begged he would give the devil his due and me mine. Accordingly all the others marched off, and as nothing was likely to take place immediately, we amused ourselves by looking on at what was doing.

"Just at this moment an amazing outcry arose amongst the infantry at the farm, who were running towards us in a confused mass, shouting and bellowing, jostling and pushing each other. I made sure the enemy's cavalry had made a dash amongst them, especially as the fire of the skirmishers became thicker and apparently nearer, when the thing was explained by a large pig, squealing as if already stuck, bursting from the throng by which he was beset in all directions. Some struck at him with axes, others with the butts of their muskets, others stabbed at him with bayonets. The chase would have been amusing had it not been so brutal; and I have seldom experienced greater horror than I did on this occasion, when the poor brute, staggering from the repeated blows he received, was at last brought to the ground by at least half-a-dozen bayonets plunged into him at once.

"All this time our retreat was going on very quietly. The corps at Quatre Bras had retired early in the morning, and been replaced by others from the left, and this continued constantly — every corps halting for a time on the ground near Quatre Bras until another from the left arrived, these moving off on the great road to Brussels, ceding the ground to the new-comers.

"At first every one, exulting in the success of yesterday — they having repulsed the enemy with a handful of men, as it were, unsupported by cavalry and with very little artillery anticipated, now our army was united nothing less than an immediate attack on the French position. We were sadly knocked down, then, when the certainty of our retreat became known. It was in vain we were told the retreat was only a manoeuvre of concentration; the most gloomy anticipations pervaded every breast. About this time Sir Alexander Dickson paid me a visit, having just arrived from New Orleans, where he commanded the artillery, to be our deputy-quartermaster-general. He only stayed a few minutes.

"As the infantry corps on the plateau became fewer, the fire of the skirmishers amongst the hedges gradually relaxed, and at length ceased — the Rifles, &c., being drawn, and following the line of retreat. At last, about noon, I found myself left with my troop, quite alone, on the brow of the position, just by the farm of Quatre Bras the only troops in sight being a small picket of hussars, near the village of Frasnes, in the plain below; a few more in our rear, but at some little distance, amongst the houses; and a brigade of hussars far away to the left (about two miles), close to the wood in that quarter. Thus solitary, as it were, I had ample leisure to contemplate the scene of desolation around me, so strangely at variance with the otherwise smiling landscape. Everywhere mementoes of yesterday's bloody struggle met the eye — the corn trampled down, and the ground, particularly in the plain, plentifully besprinkled with bodies of the slain. Just in front of the farm of Quatre Bras there was a fearful scene of slaughter — Highlanders and cuirassiers lying thickly strewn about; the latter appeared to have charged up the Charleroi road, on which, and immediately bordering it, they lay most numerously.

"In communicating to me the orders of our retreat, Major M'Donald had reiterated that to join Lord Edward Somerset's brigade without delay, but still he could not tell me where this brigade was to be found. Meantime Sir Ormsby Vandeleur's brigade of light dragoons having formed up in front of the houses, and supposing from this that all the cavalry must be nigh, as one step towards finding Lord Edward I crossed the road to the right of these dragoons, and rode towards the part where, as before stated, the light was intercepted by trees and bushes. On passing through these I had an uninterrupted view of the country for miles, but not a soldier or living being was to be seen in that direction. As I pushed on through the thickets my horse, suddenly coming to a stand, began to snort, and showed unequivocal symptoms of fear. I drove him on, however, but started myself when I saw, lying under the bush, the body of a. man stripped naked. This victim of war was a youth of fair form, skin delicately white, and face but little darker; an embryo moustache decorated the upper lip, and his countenance, even in death, was beautiful. That he was French I conjectured, but neither on himself nor his horse was there a particle of clothing that could indicate to what nation he belonged. If French, how came he here to die alone so far in the rear of our lines?

"I know not why, but the *rencontre* with this solitary corpse had a wonderful effect on my spirits — far different from what I felt when gazing on the heaps that encumbered the field beyond. Seldom have I experienced such despondency — such heart-sinking as when standing over this handsome form thus despoiled, neglected, and about to become a prey to wolves and carrion crows — the darling of some fond mother, the adored of some fair maid. His horse, stripped like himself, lay by — they had met their fate at once. Returning to my troop, I found Sir Augustus Frazer, who had come to order my ammunition waggons to the rear that the retreat might be as little encumbered as possible, and to tell me that what ammunition was used during the day would be supplied by my sending for it to Langeveldt, on the road to Brussels, where that to Wavre branches from it.

"Thus divested of our ammunition, it was evident that our retreat must be a rapid one, since with only fifty rounds a gun (the number in the limbers), it could not be expected that we could occupy any position longer than a few minutes. In the end, this measure nearly led to very disagreeable results, as will be seen anon."

Lord Uxbridge — afterwards the Marquis of Anglesey — was a very fine cavalry leader, a sort of English Murat, with all the dash, activity, and resource of that famous soldier. But he had too much fire in his temper for cool generalship. The tumult and shock of battle had the effect of champagne upon him. It kindled in his brain a sort of intoxication. So he took risks a cooler-headed soldier would have avoided. Uxbridge's fiery and audacious daring is vividly reflected in Mercer's account of how he covered the retreat to Waterloo:

"It was now about one o'clock. My battery stood in position on the brow of the declivity, with its right near the wall of the farm, all alone, the only troops in sight being, as before mentioned, the picket and a few scattered hussars in the direction of Frasnes, Sir O. Vandeleur's light dragoons two or three hundred yards in our rear, and Sir H. Vivian's hussars far away to the left. Still the French array made no demonstration of an advance. This inactivity was unaccountable. Lord Uxbridge and an aide-de-camp came to the front of my battery, and dismounting, seated himself on the ground; so did I and the aide-de-camp. His lordship with his glass was watching the French position; and we were all three wondering at their want of observation and inactivity, which had not only permitted our infantry to retire unmolested, but also still retained them in their bivouac. 'It will not be long now before they are on us,' said the aide-de-camp, 'for they always dine before they move; and those smokes seem to indicate that they are cooking now.'

"He was right; for not long afterwards another aide-de-camp, scouring along the valley, came to report that a heavy column of cavalry was advancing through the opening between the woods to the left from the direction of Gembloux. At the same moment we saw them distinctly; and Lord Uxbridge having reconnoitred them a moment through his glass, started up, exclaiming, in a joyful tone, 'By the Lord, they are Prussians!' jumped on his horse, and, followed by the two aides, dashed off like a whirlwind to meet them. For a moment I stood looking after them as they swept down the slope, and could not help wondering how the Prussians came there. I was, however, not left long in my perplexity, for, turning my eyes towards the French position, I saw their whole army descending from it in three or four dark masses, whilst their advanced cavalry picket was already skirmishing with and driving back our hussars. The truth instantly flashed on my mind, and I became exceedingly uneasy for the safety of Lord Uxbridge and his companions, now far advanced on their way down the valley, and likely to be irretrievably cut off.

"My situation now appeared somewhat awkward; left without orders and entirely alone on the brow of our position — the hussar pickets galloping in and hurrying past as fast as they could — the whole French army advancing, and already at no great distance. In this dilemma, I determined to retire across the little dip that separated me from Sir O. Vandeleur, and take up a position in front of his squadrons, whence, after giving a round to the French, advance as soon as they stood on our present ground, I thought I could retire in sufficient time through his intervals to leave the ground clear for him to charge. This movement was immediately executed; but the guns were scarcely unlimbered ere Sir Ormsby came furiously up, exclaiming, 'What are you doing here, sir? You encumber my front, and we shall not be able to charge. Take your guns away, sir; instantly, I say — take them away!' It was in vain that I endeavoured to explain my intentions, and that our fire would allow his charge to be made with more effect. 'No, no; take them out of my way, sir!' was all the answer I could get; and accordingly, I was preparing to obey, when up came Lord Uxbridge, and the scene changed in a twinkling. 'Captain Mercer, are you loaded?' 'Yes, my lord.' 'Then give them a round as they rise the hill, and retire as quickly as possible.' 'Light dragoons, threes right; at a trot, march!' and then some orders to Sir Ormsby, of whom I saw no more that day. "'They are just coming up the hill,' said Lord Uxbridge. 'Let them get well up before you fire. Do you think you can retire quick enough afterwards?' 'I am sure of it, my lord.' 'Very well, then, keep a good lookout, and point your guns well.'

"I had often longed to see Napoleon, that mighty man of war — that astonishing genius who had filled the world with his renown. Now I saw him, and there was a degree of sublimity in the interview rarely equalled. The sky had become overcast since the morning, and at this moment presented a most extraordinary appearance. Large isolated masses of thunder-cloud, of the deepest, almost inky black, their lower edges hard and strongly defined, lagging down, as if momentarily about to burst, hung suspended over us, involving our position and everything on it in deep and gloomy obscurity; whilst the distant hill lately occupied by the French army still lay bathed in brilliant sunshine. Lord Uxbridge was yet speaking when a single horseman,[6] immediately followed by several others, mounted the plateau I had left at a gallop, their dark figures thrown forward in strong relief from the illuminated distance, making them appear much nearer to us than they really were.

"For an instant they pulled up and regarded us, when several squadrons coming rapidly on the plateau, Lord Uxbridge cried out, 'Fire! — fire!' and, giving them a general discharge, we quickly limbered up to retire, as they dashed forward supported by some horse artillery guns, which opened upon us ere we could complete the manoeuvre, but without much effect, for the only one touched was the servant of Major Whinyates, who was wounded in the leg by the splinter of a howitzer shell.

"It was now for the first time that I discovered the major and his rocket-troop, who, annoyed at my having the rear, had disobeyed the order to retreat, and remained somewhere in the neighbourhood until this moment, hoping to share whatever might be going on. The first gun that

[6] That this was Napoleon we have the authority of General Gourgaud, who states that, irritated at the delay of Marshal Ney, he put himself at the head of the chasseurs (I think), and dashed forward in the hope of yet being able to catch our rear-guard.

was fired seemed to burst the clouds overhead, for its report was instantly followed by an awful clap of thunder, and lightning that almost blinded us, whilst the rain came down as if a waterspout had broken over us. The sublimity of the scene was inconceivable. Flash succeeded flash, and the peals of thunder were long and tremendous; whilst, as if in mockery of the elements, the French guns still sent forth their feebler glare and now scarcely audible reports — their cavalry dashing on at a headlong pace, adding their shouts to the uproar. We galloped for our lives through the storm, striving to gain the enclosures about the houses of the hamlets, Lord Uxbridge urging us on, crying, 'Make haste! — make haste! for God's sake, gallop, or you will be taken!' We did make haste, and succeeded in getting amongst the houses and gardens, but with the French advance close on our heels. Here, however, observing the *chaussée* full of hussars, they pulled up. Had they continued their charge we were gone, for these hussars were scattered about the road in the utmost confusion, some in little squads, others singly, and, moreover, so crowded together that we had no room whatever to act with any effect — either they or us.

"Meantime the enemy's detachments began to envelop the gardens, which Lord Uxbridge observing, called to me, 'Here, follow me with two of your guns,' and immediately himself led the way into one of the narrow lanes between the gardens. What he intended doing, God knows, but I obeyed. The lane was very little broader than our carriages — there was not room for a horse to have passed them! The distance from the *chaussée* to the end of the lane, where it debouched on the open fields, could scarcely have been above one or two hundred yards at most. His lordship and I were in front, the guns and mounted detachments following. What he meant to do I was at a loss to conceive; we could hardly come to action in the lane; to enter on the open was certain destruction. Thus we had arrived at about fifty yards from its termination when a body of chasseurs or hussars appeared there as if waiting for us. These we might have seen from the first, for nothing but a few elder bushes intercepted the view from the *chaussée*.

"The whole transaction appears to me so wild and confused that at times I can hardly believe it to have been more than a confused dream — yet true it was — the general-in-chief of the cavalry exposing himself amongst the skirmishers of his rear-guard, and literally doing the duty of a cornet! 'By God! we are all prisoners' (or some such words), exclaimed Lord Uxbridge, dashing his horse at one of the garden-banks, which he cleared, and away he went, leaving us to get out of the scrape as best we could. There was no time for hesitation — one manoeuvre alone could extricate us if allowed time, and it I ordered. 'Reverse by unlimbering' was the order. To do this the gun was to be unlimbered, then turned round, and one wheel run up the bank, which just left space for the limber to pass it. The gun is then limbered up again and ready to move to the rear. The execution, however, was not easy, for the very reversing of the limber itself in so narrow a lane, with a team of eight horses, was sufficiently difficult, and required first-rate driving.

"Nothing could exceed the coolness and activity of our men; the thing was done quickly and well, and we returned to the *chaussée* without let or hindrance. How we were permitted to do so, I am at a loss to imagine; for although I gave the order to reverse, I certainly never expected to have seen it executed. Meantime my own situation was anything but a pleasant one, as I sat with my back to the gentlemen at the end of the lane, whose interference I momentarily expected, casting an eye from time to time over my shoulder to ascertain whether they still kept their position. There they sat motionless, and although thankful for their inactivity, I could not but wonder at their stupidity. It seemed, however, all of a piece that day — all blunder and confusion; and this last I found pretty considerable on regaining the *chaussée*. His lordship we found collecting the scattered hussars together into a squadron for our rescue, for which purpose it was he had so unceremoniously left us. Heavy as the rain was and thick the weather, yet the French could not but have seen the confusion we were in, as they had closed up to the entrance of the enclosure; and yet they did not at once take advantage of it.

"Things could not remain long in this state. A heavy column of cavalry approached us by the chaussée, whilst another skirting the enclosures, appeared pushing forward to cut us off. Retreat now became imperative. The order was given, and away we went, helter-skelter — guns, gun-detachments, and hussars all mixed *péle-méle*, going like mad, and covering each other with mud, to be washed off by the ram, which, before sufficiently heavy, now came down again as it had done at first, in splashes instead of drops, soaking us anew to the skin, and, what was worse, extinguishing every slow match in the brigade. The obscurity caused by the splashing of the rain was such, that at one period I could not distinguish objects more than a few yards distant. Of course we lost sight of our pursuers altogether, and the shouts and halloos, and even laughter, they had at first sent forth were either silenced or drowned in the uproar of the elements and the noise of our too rapid retreat; for in addition to everything else the crashing and rattling of the thunder were most awful, and the glare of the lightning blinding. In this state we gained the bridge of Genappe at the moment when the thunder-cloud, having passed over, left us in comparative fine weather, although still raining heavily.

"For the last mile or so we had neither seen nor heard anything of our lively French friends, and now silently wound our way up the deserted street, nothing disturbing its death-like stillness save the iron sound of horses' feet, the rumbling of the carriages, and the splashing of water as it fell from the eaves — all this was stillness compared with the hurly-burly and din from which we had just emerged.

"On gaining the high ground beyond the town, we suddenly came in sight of the main body of our cavalry drawn up across the *chaussée* in two lines, and extending away far to the right and left of it. It would have been an imposing spectacle at any time, but just now appeared to me magnificent, and I hailed it with complacency, for here I thought our fox-chase must end. 'Those superb Life Guards and Blues will soon teach our pursuers a little modesty.' Such fellows! — surely nothing can withstand them. Scarcely had these thoughts passed through my mind ere an order from his lordship recalled us to the rear. The enemy's horse artillery, having taken up a position in the meadows near the bridge, were annoying our dragoons as they debouched from the town. The ground was heavy from the rain, and very steep, so that it was only by great exertion that we succeeded at last in getting our guns into the adjoining field.

"The moment we appeared the French battery bestowed on us its undivided attention, which we quickly acknowledged by an uncommonly well-directed fire of spherical case. Whilst so employed, Major M'Donald came up and put me through a regular catechism as to length of fuse, whether out of bag A or B, &c., &c. Although much vexed at such a schooling just now, yet the major appeared so seriously in earnest that I could not but be amused; however, to convince him that we knew what we were about, I directed his attention to our excellent practice, so superior to that of our antagonist, who was sending all his shot far over our heads. The French seemed pretty well convinced of this too, for after standing a few rounds they quitted the field, and left us again without occupation. The major vanishing at the same time, I sent my guns, &c., to the rear, and set off to join Lord Uxbridge, who was still fighting in the street. Our ammunition was expended the waggons having been taken away by Sir Augustus Frazer at Quatre Bras.

"On regaining my troop I found Major M'Donald and the rockets with it. They were in position on a gentle elevation, on which likewise were formed the lines of cavalry stretching across the *chaussée*. Immediately on our left, encased in the hollow road, the Blues were formed in close column of half-squadrons, and it was not long ere Lord Uxbridge, with those he had retained at Ge-nappe, came sweeping over the hill and joined us. They were closely followed by the French light cavalry, who, descending into the hollow, commenced a sharp skirmish with our advance-posts. Soon squadron after squadron appeared on the hill we had passed, and took up their positions, forming a long line parallel to ours, whilst a battery of horse artillery, forming across the *chaussée*, just on the brow of the declivity, opened its fire on us, though without much effect. To this we responded, though very slowly, having no more ammunition than what remained in our limbers.

"In order to amuse the enemy and our own cavalry, as well as to prevent the former noticing the slackness of our fire, I proposed to Major M'Donald making use of the rockets, which had hitherto done nothing. There was a little hesitation about this, and one of the officers (Strangways) whispered me, 'No, no — it's too far!' This I immediately told the Major, proposing as a remedy that they should go closer. Still there was demur; but at last my proposition was agreed to, and down they marched into the thick of the skirmishers in the bottom. Of course, having proposed the measure myself, I could do no less than accompany them.

"Whilst they prepared their machinery, I had time to notice what was going on to the right and left of us. Two double lines of skirmishers extended all along the bottom — the foremost of each line were within a few yards of each other constantly in motion, riding backwards and forwards, firing their carbines or pistols, and then reloading, still on the move. This fire seemed to me more dangerous for those on the hills above than for us below; for all, both French and English, generally stuck out their carbines or pistols as they continued to move backwards and forwards, and discharged them without taking any particular aim, and mostly in the air. I did not see a man fall on either side. The thing appeared quite ridiculous, and but for hearing the bullets whizzing overhead, one might have fancied it no more than a sham-fight.

"Meanwhile the rocketeers had placed a little iron triangle in the road with a rocket lying on it. The order to fire is given, portfire applied; the fidgety missile begins to sputter out sparks and wriggle its tail for a second or so, and then darts forth straight up the *chaussée*. A gun stands right in its way, between the wheels of which the shell in the head of the rocket bursts; the gunners fall right and left; and those of the other guns, taking to their heels, the battery is deserted in an instant. Strange; but so it was. I saw them run, and for some minutes afterwards I saw the guns standing mute and unmanned, whilst our rocketeers kept shooting off rockets, none of which ever followed the course of the first; most of them, on arriving about the middle of the ascent, took a vertical direction, whilst some actually turned back upon ourselves; and one of these, following me like a squib until its shell exploded, actually put me in more danger than all the fire of the enemy throughout the day. Meanwhile the French artillerymen, seeing how the land lay, returned to their guns and opened a fire of case-shot on us, but without effect, for we retreated to our ridge without the loss of a man, or even any wounded, though the range could not have been above 200 yards.

"As we had overtaken the rear of our infantry, it became necessary to make a stand here to enable them to gain ground. Major M'Donald therefore sent me in pursuit of my ammunition waggons, since all in our limbers was expended. Having before sent for these, we calculated that they could not now be very far off. In going to the rear, I passed along the top of the bank, under which, as I have said, the Blues were encased in the hollow road. Shot and shells were flying pretty thickly about just then, and sometimes striking the top of the bank would send down a shower of mud and clods upon them.

"The ammunition waggons I found coming up, and was returning with them when I met my whole troop again retiring by the road, whilst the cavalry did so by alternate regiments across the fields. The ground offering no feature for another stand, we continued thus along the road. The infantry had made so little progress that we again overtook the rear of their column, composed of Brunswickers — some of those same boys I used to see practising at Schapdale in my rides to Brussels. These poor lads were pushing on at a great rate. As soon as their rear divisions heard the sound of our horses' feet, without once looking behind them, they began to crowd and press on those in front, until at last, hearing us close up to them, and finding it impossible to push forward in the road, many of them broke off into the fields; and such was their panic that, in order to run lighter, away went arms and knapsacks in all directions, and a general race ensued, the whole corps being in the most horrid confusion. It was to no purpose that I exerted my little stock of German to make them understand we were their English friends. A frightened glance and away, was all the effect of my interference, which drove many of them off."

The retreat came to an end here. The rear-guard, without knowing it, had reached the low ridge running east and west across the Brussels road, where Wellington had resolved to make his final stand, and where the greatest battle in modern history was on the morrow to be fought:

"We did not long remain idle, for the guns were scarcely loaded ere the rear of our cavalry came crowding upon the infantry corps we had passed, and which were then only crossing the valley, the French advance skirmishing with these, whilst their squadrons occupied the heights. We waited a little until some of their larger masses were assembled, and then opened our fire with a range across the valley of about 1200 yards. The echo of our first gun had not ceased when, to my astonishment, a heavy cannonade, commencing in a most startling manner from behind our hedge, roiled along the rising ground, on part of which we were posted. The truth now flashed on me; we had rejoined the army, and it is impossible to describe the pleasing sense of security I felt at having now the support of something more staunch than cavalry.

"The French now brought up battery after battery, and a tremendous cannonading was kept up by both sides for some time. The effect was grand and exciting. Our position was a happy one, for all their shot which grazed short came and struck in the perpendicular bank of our gravel-pit, and only one struck amongst us, breaking the traversing handspike at one of the guns, but injuring neither man nor horse. Our fire was principally directed against their masses as we could see them, which was not always the case from the smoke that, for want of wind, hung over them; then against their smaller parties that had advanced into the valley to skirmish with the rear-guard of our cavalry.

"Here, for the second and last time, I saw Napoleon, though infinitely more distant than in the morning. Some of my noncommissioned officers pointed their guns at the numerous cortège accompanying him as they stood near the road by Belle Alliance; and one, pointed by old Quartermaster Hall, fell in the midst of them. At the moment we saw some little confusion amongst the group, but it did not hinder them from continuing the reconnaissance.

"Whilst we were thus engaged, a man of no very prepossessing appearance came rambling amongst our guns, and entered into conversation with me on the occurrences of the day. He was dressed in a shabby old drab greatcoat and a rusty round hat. I took him at the time for some amateur from Brussels (of whom we had heard there were several hovering about), and thinking many of his questions rather impertinent, was somewhat short in answering him, and he soon left us. How great was my astonishment on learning soon after that this was Sir Thomas Picton! The enemy, finding us obstinate in maintaining our position, soon slackened, and then ceased firing altogether; and we were immediately ordered to do the same, and establish ourselves in bivouac for the night.

"Thoroughly wet — cloaks, blankets, and all — comfort was out of the question, so we prepared to make the best of it. Our first care was, of course, the horses, and these we had ample means of providing for, since, in addition to what corn we had left, one of our men had picked up and brought forward on an ammunition waggon a large sackful, which he found in the road near Genappe. Thus they, at least, had plenty to eat, and having been so well drenched all day, were not much in need of water. For ourselves we had nothing — absolutely nothing! — and looked forward to rest alone to restore our exhausted strength. Rather a bore going supperless to bed after such a day, yet was there no help for it.

"Our gunners, &c., soon stowed themselves away beneath the carriages, using the painted covers as additional shelter against the rain, which now set in again as heavy as ever. We set up a small tent, into which (after vain attempts at procuring food or lodgings in the farm or its out buildings, all of which were crammed to suffocation with officers and soldiers of all arms and nations) we crept, and rolling ourselves in our wet blankets, huddled close together, in hope, wet as we were, and wet as the ground was, of keeping each other warm. I know not how my bedfellows got on, as we all lay for a long while perfectly still and silent — the old Peninsular hands disdaining to complain before their Johnny Newcome comrades, and these fearing to do so lest they should provoke such remarks, as 'Lord have mercy on your poor tender carcass! what would such as you have done in the Pyrenees?' or 'Oho, my boy! this is but child's play to what we saw in Spain.' So all who did not sleep (I believe the majority) pretended to do so, and bore their suffering with admirable heroism.

"For my part, I once or twice, from sheer fatigue, got into something like a doze; yet it would not do. There was no possibility of sleeping, for, besides being already so wet, the tent proved no shelter, the water pouring through the canvas in streams; so up I got, and to my infinite joy, found that some of the men had managed to make a couple of fires, round which they were sitting smoking their short pipes in something like comfort. The hint was a good one, and at that moment my second captain joining me, we borrowed from them a few sticks, and choosing the best spot under the hedge, proceeded to make a fire for ourselves. In a short time we succeeded in raising a cheerful blaze, which materially bettered our situation. My companion had an umbrella (which, by the way, had afforded some merriment to our people on the march); this we planted against the sloping bank of the hedge, and seating ourselves under it, he on one side of the stick, I on the other, we lighted cigars and became — comfortable. Dear weed! what comfort, what consolation dost thou not impart to the wretched! — with thee a hovel becomes a palace. What a stock of patience is there not enveloped in one of thy brown leaves!

"And thus we sat enjoying ourselves, puffing forth into the damp night air streams of fragrant smoke, being able now deliberately to converse on what had been and probably would be. All this time a most infernal clatter of musketry was going on, which, but for the many quiet dark figures seated round the innumerable fires all along the position, might have been construed into a night attack. But as these gentlemen were

279

between us and the enemy we felt assured of timely warning, and ere long learned that all this proceeded as before from the infantry discharging and cleaning their pieces.

"Whilst so employed, a rustling in the hedge behind attracted our attention, and in a few minutes a poor fellow belonging to some Hanoverian regiment, wet through like everybody else, and shivering with cold, made his appearance, and modestly begged permission to remain a short time and warm himself by our fire. He had somehow or other wandered from his colours, and had passed the greater part of the night searching for them, but in vain. At first he appeared quite exhausted, but the warmth reinvigorating him, he pulled out his pipe and began to smoke. Having finished his modicum and carefully disposed of the ashes, he rose from his wet seat to renew his search, hoping to find his corps before daylight, he said, lest it should be engaged. Many thanks he offered for our hospitality; but what was our surprise when, after fumbling in his haversack for some time, he pulled out a poor half-starved chicken, presented it to us, and marched off. This was a Godsend, in good truth, to people famished as we were; so calling for a camp-kettle, our prize was on the fire in a twinkling.

"Our comrades in the tent did not sleep so soundly but that they heard what was going on, and the kettle was hardly on the lire ere my gentlemen were assembled round it, a wet and shivering group, but all eager to partake of our good fortune — and so eager that after various betrayals of impatience, the miserable chicken was at last snatched from the kettle ere it was half-boiled, pulled to pieces and speedily devoured. I got a leg for my share, but it was not one mouthful, and this was the only food I tasted since the night before."

Chapter Twenty-Four – Waterloo

Mercer's account of Waterloo has much less of literary art and skill in it than other parts of his book. He plunges the reader, without warning and without explanation, into the roar of the great fight. His description of the ground and of the position of the army is thrust, as a sort of parenthesis, into the middle of the story of the actual struggle. Mercer's troop was stationed till long past noon in reserve on the British right. The battle to Mercer was nothing but an incessant and deep-voiced roar of guns, a vision of drifting smoke, in which would appear at times dim figures of charging horsemen, or outlines of infantry squares, edged with steel and flame, and out of which flowed tiny processions of wounded, trickling backwards over the ridge in front. About three o'clock, however, the troop was suddenly brought up to the battleline, at a point where it was in imminent peril of giving way. From that moment Mercer was in the smoky, tormented, thunder-shaken vortex of the great fight, and his description of it is graphic and impressive in the highest degree.

This is how the morning of Waterloo dawned for Mercer and his gunners:

"June 18 — Memorable day! Some time before daybreak the bombardier who had been despatched to Langeveldt returned with a supply of ammunition.

"With the providence of an old soldier, he had picked up and brought on a considerable quantity of beef, biscuit, and oatmeal, of which there was abundance scattered about everywhere. Casks of rum, &c., there were, and having broached one of these, he and his drivers, every one, filled his canteen — a most considerate act, and one for which the whole troop was sincerely thankful. Nor must I omit to remark that, amidst such temptations, his men had behaved with the most perfect regularity, and returned to us quite sober! The rum was divided on the spot; and surely if ardent spirits are ever beneficial, it must be to men situated as ours were; it therefore came most providentially. The oatmeal was converted speedily into stirabout, and afforded our people a hearty meal, after which all hands set to work to prepare the beef, make soup, &c.

Unfortunately, we preferred waiting for this, and passed the stirabout, by which piece of folly we were doomed to a very protracted fast, as will be seen.

"Whilst our soup was cooking, it being now broad daylight, I mounted my horse to reconnoitre our situation. During the night another troop (I think Major Ramsay's) had established itself in our orchard, and just outside the hedge I found Major Bean's, which had also arrived during the night, direct from England. Ascending from the farm towards the ground we had left yesterday evening, the face of the slope, as far as I could see, to the right and left, was covered with troops *en bivouac* — here, I think, principally cavalry. Of these some were cleaning their arms, some cooking, some sitting round fires smoking, and a few, generally officers, walking about or standing in groups conversing. Many of the latter eagerly inquired where I was going, and appeared very anxious for intelligence, all expecting nothing less than to recommence our retreat. I continued on to the position we had occupied last, and thence clearly saw the French army on the opposite hill, where everything appeared perfectly quiet people moving about individually, and no formation whatever. Their advanced-posts and vedettes in the valley, just beyond La Haye Sainte, were also quiet.

"Having satisfied my curiosity I returned the way I came, communicating my observations to the many eager inquirers I met with. Various were the speculations in consequence. Some thought the French were afraid to attack us, others that they would do so soon, others that the Duke would not wait for it, others that he would, as he certainly would not allow them to go to Brussels; and so they went on speculating, whilst I returned to my people. Here, finding the mess not yet ready, and nothing to be done, I strolled into the garden of the farm, where several Life Guardsmen were very busy digging potatoes — a fortunate discovery, which I determined to profit by. Therefore, calling up some of my men, to work we went without loss of time."

It is amusing to notice that Mercer was so busy digging potatoes that he quite failed to observe that the battle had actually commenced! His senses were buried in the potato-hillocks! So the regiments fell into line, the batteries moved off to their assigned places, the French guns began to speak, and Waterloo had begun; and though Mercer stood on the very edge of the field, he took no notice of the rise of the curtain on the great tragedy. He says:

"Whilst thus employed I noticed a very heavy firing going on in front, but this did not make us quit our work. Shortly after, to my great astonishment, I observed that all the bivouacs on the hillside were deserted, and that even Ramsay's troop had left the orchard without my being aware of it, and my own was left quite alone, not a soul being visible from where I stood in any direction, the ground they had quitted presenting one unbroken muddy solitude. The firing became heavier and heavier. Alarmed at being thus left alone, when it was evident something serious was going on, I hastened back and ordered the horses to be put to immediately.

"Away went our mess untasted. One of the servants was desired to hang the kettle with its contents under an ammunition waggon. The stupid fellow hung the kettle as desired, but first emptied it. Without orders, and all alone, the battle (for now there was no mistaking it) going on at the other side of the hill, I remained for a few minutes undecided what to do. It appeared to me we had been forgotten. All, except only ourselves, were evidently engaged, and labouring under this delusion, I thought we had better get into the affair at once. As soon, therefore, as the troop was ready I led them up the hill on the high-road, hoping to meet some one who could give me directions what to do."

The tragedy of the battle soon made itself visible, in very dramatic shape, to Mercer:

"We had not proceeded a hundred yards, when an artillery officer came furiously galloping down towards us. It was Major M'Lloyd, in a dreadful state of agitation — such, indeed, that he could hardly answer my questions. I learned, however, that the battle was very serious and bloody. Their first attack had been on that part of our position where his battery stood; but now the principal efforts were making against our right. All this was told in so hurried and anxious a manner, that one could hardly understand him. 'But where are you going?' he added. I told him my plan. 'Have you no orders?' 'None whatever; I have not seen a soul.' 'Then, for God's sake, come and assist me, or I shall be ruined. My brigade is cut to pieces, ammunition expended, and, unless reinforced, we shall be destroyed.'

He was dreadfully agitated, and when I took his hand and promised to be with him directly, seemed transported with joy; so, bidding me make haste, he darted up the hill again, and went to receive that death-stroke which, ere long, was to terminate his earthly career. I trust before that termination he heard the reason why I never fulfilled that promise; for weeks elapsed ere he died, no doubt — otherwise he must have set me down for a base poltroon. My destiny led me elsewhere. My tutelary spirit was at hand: the eternal Major M'Donald made his appearance, and, giving me a sharp reprimand for having quitted my bivouac, desired me instantly to return to the foot of the hill, and there wait for orders.

"Sulkily and slowly we descended, and forming in line on the ground opposite the farm of Mont St. Jean, with our left to the road, I dismounted the men that they might be a little less liable to be hit by shot and shells which, coming over the hill, were continually plunging into the muddy soil all around us. This was a peculiarly dismal situation — without honour or glory, to be knocked on the head in such a solitude, for not a living being was in sight.

"It was while thus standing idle that a fine, tall, upright old gentleman, in plain clothes, followed by two young ones, came across our front at a gallop from the Brussels road, and continued on towards where we supposed the right of our army to be. I certainly stared at seeing three unarmed civilians pressing forward into so hot a fight. These were the Duke of Richmond and his two sons. How long we had been in this position, I know not, when at length we were relieved from it by our adjutant (Lieutenant Bell), who brought orders for our removal to the right of the second line. Moving, therefore, to our right, along the hollow, we soon began a very gentle ascent, and at the same time became aware of several corps of infantry, which had not been very far from us, but remained invisible, as they were all lying down. Although in this move we may be said to have been always under a heavy fire, from the number of missiles flying over us, yet were we still so fortunate as to arrive in our new position without losing man or horse."

Now Mercer at last got a glimpse of the whole landscape of the great fight. But even when looking at Waterloo, and to an accompaniment of flying lead, Mercer has an eye for the picturesque, not to say the pastoral:

"In point of seeing, our situation was much improved; but for danger and inactivity, it was much worse, since we were now fired directly at, and positively ordered not to return the compliment — the object in bringing us here being to watch a most formidable-looking line of lancers drawn up opposite to us, and threatening the right flank of our army.

"To the right we looked over a fine open country, covered with crops and interspersed with thickets or small woods. There all was peaceful and smiling, not a living soul being in sight. To our left, the main ridge terminated rather abruptly just over Hougoumont, the back of it towards us being broken ground, with a few old trees on it just where the Nivelle road descended between high banks into the ravine. Thus we were formed *en potence* with the first line, from which we (my battery) were separated by some hundred yards. In our rear the 14th Regiment of infantry (in square, I think) lay on the ground. In our front were some light dragoons of the German Legion, who from time to time detached small parties across the ravine. These pushed cautiously up the slope towards the line of lancers to reconnoitre.

"The corn, down to the edge of the ravine nearer the Nivelle road and beyond it, was full of French riflemen; and these were warmly attacked by others from our side of the ravine, whom we saw crossing and gradually working their way up through the high corn, the French as gradually retiring. On the right of the lancers, two or three batteries kept up a continued fire at our position; but their shot, which could have been only 4-pounders, fell short-many not even reaching across the ravine. Some, however, did reach their destination; and we were particularly plagued by their howitzer shells with long fuses, which were continually falling about us, and lay spitting and spluttering several seconds before they exploded, to the no small annoyance of man and horse. Still, however, nobody was hurt; but a round-shot, striking the ammunition boxes on the body of one of our waggons, penetrated through both and lodged in the back of the rear one, with nearly half its surface to be seen from without — a singular circumstance! In addition to this front fire, we were exposed to another on our left flank the shot that passed over the main ridge terminating their career with us.

"Having little to occupy us here, we had ample leisure to observe what was passing there. We could see some corps at the end near us in squares — dark masses, having guns between them, relieved from a background of grey smoke, which seemed to fill the valley beyond, and rose high in the air above the hill. Every now and then torrents of French cavalry of all arms came sweeping over the ridge, as if carrying all before them. But, after their passage, the squares were still to be seen in the same places; and these gentry, who we feared would next fall on us, would evaporate, nobody could well say how. The firing still increased in intensity, so that we were at a loss to conjecture what all this could mean.

"About this time, being impatient of standing idle, and annoyed by the batteries on the Nivelle road, I ventured to commit a folly, for which I should have paid dearly, had our Duke chanced to be in our part of the field. I ventured to disobey orders, and open a slow deliberate fire at the battery, thinking with my 9-pounders soon to silence his 4-pounders. My astonishment was great, however, when our very first gun was responded to by at least half-a-dozen gentlemen of very superior calibre, whose presence I had not even suspected, and whose superiority we immediately recognised by their rushing noise and long reach, for they flew far beyond us. I instantly saw my folly, and ceased firing, and they did the same — the 4-pounders alone continuing the cannonade as before. But this was not all. The first man of my troop touched was by one of these confounded long shots. I shall never forget the scream the poor lad gave when struck. It was one of the last they fired, and shattered his left arm to pieces as he stood between the waggons. That scream went to my very soul, for I accused myself as having caused his misfortune. I was, however, obliged to conceal my emotion from the men, who had turned to look at him; so, bidding them 'stand to their front,' I continued my walk up and down, whilst Hitchins ran to his assistance.

"Amidst such stirring scenes, emotions of this kind are but of short duration; what occurred immediately afterwards completely banished Gunner Hunt from my recollection. As a counterbalance to this tragical event, our firing produced one so comic as to excite all our risibility. Two or three officers had lounged up to our guns to see the effect. One of them was a medico, and he (a shower having just come on) carried an umbrella overhead. No sooner did the heavy answers begin to arrive amongst us, than these gentlemen, fancying they should be safer with their own corps, although only a few yards in the rear, scampered off in double-quick, doctor and all, he still carrying his umbrella aloft. Scarcely, however, had he made two paces, when a shot, as he thought, passing rather too close, down he dropped on his hands and knees — or, I should rather say, hand and knees, for the one was employed in holding the silken cover most pertinaciously over him — and away he scrambled like a great baboon, his head turned fearfully over his shoulder, as if watching the coming shot, whilst our fellows made the field resound with their shouts and laughter."

At this point Mercer indulges in some reflections which illustrate, in a striking fashion, the confusion of a great battle, and the difficulty with which even those who are actors in it can describe what took place. It is not merely that a battle-field, by its area, and the fashion in which the all-obscuring smoke drifts over it, evades clear vision and description. The actors in the fight are themselves in such a mood of excitement, and are so passionately preoccupied by their own part in the combat and the scenes immediately about them, that no brain remains sufficiently cool and detached to take in the battle-field as a whole:

"I think I have already mentioned that it was not until some days afterwards that I was able to resume my regular journal, consequently that everything relative to these three days is written from memory. In trying to recollect scenes of this nature, some little confusion is inevitable; and here I confess myself somewhat puzzled to account for certain facts of which I am positive. For instance, I remember perfectly Captain Bolton's brigade of 9-pounders being stationed to the left of us, somewhat in advance, and facing as we did, consequently not far from the Nivelle road. Bolton came and conversed with me some time, and was called hastily away by his battery commencing a heavy fire. Query — Who, and what was he firing at? That he was himself under a heavy fire there is equally no doubt, for whilst we were not losing a man, we saw many, both of his men and horses, fall, and but a few minutes after leaving me, he was killed himself — this is a puzzle. I have no recollection of any troops attempting to cross the ravine, and yet his fire was in that direction, and I think must have been toward the Nivelle road.

"A distressing circumstance connected with this (shall I confess it?) made even more impression on my spirits than the misfortune of Gunner Hunt. Bolton's people had not been long engaged when we saw the men of the gun next to us unharness one of the horses and chase it away, wounded, I supposed; yet the beast stood and moved with firmness, going from one carriage to the other, whence I noticed he was always eagerly driven away. At last two or three gunners drove him before them to a considerable distance, and then returned to their guns. I took little notice of this at the time and was surprised by an exclamation of horror from some of my people in the rear. A sickening sensation came over me, mixed with a deep feeling of pity, when within a few paces of me stood the poor horse in question, side by side with the leaders of one of our ammunition waggons, against which he pressed his panting sides, as though eager to identify himself as of their society — the driver, with horror depicted on every feature, endeavouring by words and gestures (for the kind-hearted lad could not strike) to drive from him so hideous a spectacle.

"A cannon-shot had completely carried away the lower part of the animal's head, immediately below the eyes, till he lived, and seemed fully conscious of all around, whilst his full, clear eye seemed to implore us not to chase him from his companions. I ordered the farrier (Price) to put him out of misery, which, in a few minutes he reported having accomplished, by running his sabre into the animal's heart. Even he evinced feeling on this occasion.

"Meantime the roar of cannon and musketry in the main position never slackened; it was intense, as was the smoke arising from it. Amidst this, from time to time, was to be seen still more dense columns of smoke rising straight into the air like a great pillar, then spreading out a mushroom head. These arose from the explosions of ammunition waggons, which were continually taking place, although the noise which filled the whole atmosphere was too overpowering to allow them to be heard."

By this time the great French cavalry charges were in full course. Some 10,000 of the finest cavalry in the world were being flung on the stubborn British squares, which, as the French horsemen swept round them, seemed swallowed up in a tossing sea of helmets and gleaming swords and heads of galloping horses. The spray, so to speak, of that fierce human sea, was flung on the spot where Mercer and his gunners stood:

"Amongst the multitudes of French cavalry continually pouring over the front ridge, one corps came sweeping down the slope entire, and was directing its course straight for us, when suddenly a regiment of light dragoons (I believe of the German Legion) came up from the ravine at a brisk trot on their flank. The French had barely time to wheel up to the left and push their horses into a gallop when the two bodies came into collision. They were at a very short distance from us, so that we saw the charge perfectly. There was no check, no hesitation on either side; both parties seemed to dash on in a most reckless manner, and we fully expected to have seen a horrid crash — no such thing! Each, as if by mutual consent, opened their files on coming near, and passed rapidly through each other, cutting and pointing, much in the same manner one might pass the fingers of the right hand through those of the left. We saw but few fall. The two corps reformed afterwards, and in a twinkling both disappeared, I know not how or where.

"It might have been about two o'clock when Colonel Gould, R.A., came to me — perhaps a little later. Be that as it may, we were conversing on the subject of our situation, which appeared to him rather desperate. He remarked that in the event of a retreat there was but one road, which no doubt would be instantly choked up, and asked my opinion. My answer was, 'It does indeed look very bad; but I trust in the Duke, who, I am sure, will get us out of it somehow or other.' Meantime gloomy reflections arose in my mind, for though I did not choose to betray myself (as we spoke before the men), yet I could not help thinking that our affairs were rather desperate, and that some unfortunate catastrophe was at hand. In this case I made up my mind to spike my guns and retreat over the fields, draught-horses and all, in the best manner I could, steering well from the high-road and general line of retreat.

"We were still talking on this subject when suddenly a dark mass of cavalry appeared for an instant on the main ridge, and then came sweeping down the slope in swarms, reminding me of an enormous surf bursting over the prostrate hull of a stranded vessel, and then running, hissing and foaming up the beach. The hollow space became in a twinkling covered with horsemen, crossing, turning, and riding about in all directions, apparently without any object. Sometimes they came pretty near us, then would retire a little. There were lancers amongst them, hussars, and dragoons — it was a complete *melee*. On the main ridge no squares were to be seen; the only objects were a few guns standing in a confused manner, with muzzles in the air, and not one artilleryman. After caracoling about for a few minutes, the crowd began to separate and draw together in small bodies, which continually increased; and now we really apprehended being overwhelmed, as the first line had apparently been. For a moment an awful silence pervaded that part of the position to which we anxiously turned our eyes. 'I fear all is over,' said Colonel Gould, who still remained with me. The thing seemed but too likely, and this time I could not withhold my assent to his remark, for it did indeed appear so.

"Meantime the 14th, springing from the earth, had formed their square, whilst we, throwing back the guns of our right and left divisions, stood waiting in momentary expectation of being enveloped and attacked. Still they lingered in the hollow, when suddenly loud and repeated shouts (not English hurrahs) drew our attention to the other side. There we saw two dense columns of infantry pushing forward at a quick pace towards us, crossing the fields, as if they had come from Merke Braine. Every one both of the 14th and ourselves pronounced them French, yet still we delayed opening fire on them. Shouting, yelling, singing, on they came right for us; and being now not above 800 or 1000 yards distant, it seemed folly allowing them to come nearer unmolested. The commanding officer of the 14th to end our doubts rode forwards and endeavoured to ascertain who they were, but soon returned assuring us they were French. The order was already given to fire, when luckily Colonel Gould recognised them as Belgians. Meantime, whilst my attention was occupied by these people, the cavalry had all vanished, nobody could say how or where.

"We breathed again. Such was the agitated state in which we were kept in our second position. A third act was about to commence of a much more stirring and active nature."

Now came, and in a dramatic fashion, the summons which brought troop G into the very front of the fight; and from this point Mercer's story is clear, sustained, and vivid:

"It might have been, as nearly as I can recollect, about 3 P.M. when Sir Augustus Frazer galloped up, crying out, 'Left limber up, and as fast as you can.' The words were scarcely uttered when my gallant troop stood as desired in column of sub-divisions, left in front, pointing towards the main ridge. 'At a gallop, march!' and away we flew, as steadily and compactly as if at a review.

"I rode with Frazer, whose face was as black as a chimneysweep's from the smoke, and the jacket-sleeve of his right arm torn open by a musket-ball or case-shot, which had merely grazed his flesh. As we went along he told me that the enemy had assembled an enormous mass of heavy cavalry in front of the point to which he was leading us (about one-third of the distance between Hougoumont and the Charleroi road), and that in all probability we should immediately be charged on gaining our position. 'The Duke's orders, however, are positive,' he added, 'that in the event of their persevering and charging home, you do not expose your men, but retire with them into the adjacent squares of infantry.' As he spoke we were ascending the reverse slope of the main position. We breathed a new atmosphere — the air was suffocatingly hot, resembling that issuing from an oven. We were enveloped in thick smoke, and, *malgré* the incessant roar of cannon and musketry, could distinctly hear around us a mysterious humming noise, like that which one hears of a summer's evening proceeding from myriads of black beetles; cannon-shot, too, ploughed the ground in all directions, and so thick was the nail of balls and bullets that it seemed dangerous to extend the arm lest it should be torn off.

"In spite of the serious situation in which we were, I could not help being somewhat amused at the astonishment expressed by our kind-hearted surgeon (Hitchins), who heard for the first time this sort of music. He was close to me as we ascended the slope, and hearing this infernal carillon about his ears, began staring round in the wildest and most comic manner imaginable, twisting himself from side to side, exclaiming, 'My God, Mercer, what is that? What is all this noise? How curious! — how very curious!' And then when a cannon-shot rushed hissing past, 'There! — there! What is it all!' It was with great difficulty that I persuaded him to retire; for a time he insisted on remaining near me, and it was only by pointing out how important it was to us, in case of being wounded, that he should keep himself safe to be able to assist us, that I prevailed on him to withdraw. Amidst this storm we gained the summit of the ridge, strange to say, without a casualty; and Sir Augustus, pointing out our position between two squares of Brunswick infantry, left us with injunctions to remember the Duke's order, and to economise our ammunition.

"The Brunswickers were falling fast — the shot every moment making great gaps in their squares, which the officers and sergeants were actively employed in filling up by pushing their men together, and sometimes thumping them ere they could make them move. These were the very boys whom I had but yesterday seen throwing away their arms, and fleeing, panic-stricken, from the very sound of our horses' feet. Today they fled not bodily, to be sure, but spiritually, for their senses seemed to have left them. There they stood, with recovered arms, like so many logs, or rather like the very wooden figures which I had seen them practising at in their cantonments. Every moment I feared they would again throw down their arms and flee; but their officers and sergeants behaved nobly, not only keeping them together, but managing to keep their squares close in spite of the carnage made amongst them. To have sought refuge amongst men in such a state were madness — the very moment our men ran from their guns, I was convinced, would be the signal for their disbanding. We had better, then, fall at our posts than in such a situation.

"Our coming up seemed to re-animate them, and all their eyes were directed to us indeed, it was providential, for, had we not arrived as we did, I scarcely think there is a doubt of what would have been their fate. That the Duke was ignorant of their danger I have from Captain Baynes, our brigade-major, who told me that after Sir Augustus Frazer had been sent for us, his Grace exhibited considerable anxiety for our coming up; and that when he saw us crossing the fields at a gallop, and in so compact a body, he actually cried out, 'Ah! that's the way I like to see horse artillery move.'"

Then follows perhaps the most spirited description of a duel betwixt guns and horsemen from the gunner's point of view to be found in English literature:

"Our first gun had scarcely gained the interval between their squares, when I saw through the smoke the leading squadrons of the advancing column coming on at a brisk trot, and already not more than one hundred yards distant, if so much, for I don't think we could have seen so far. I immediately ordered the line to be formed for action — case-shot! and the leading gun was unlimbered and commenced firing almost as soon as the word was given; for activity and intelligence our men were unrivalled.

"The very first round, I saw, brought down several men and horses. They continued, however, to advance. I glanced at the Brunswickers, and that glance told me it would not do; they had opened a fire from their front faces, but both squares appeared too unsteady, and I resolved to say nothing about the Duke's order, and take our chance — a resolve that was strengthened by the effect of the remaining guns as they rapidly succeeded in coming to action, making terrible slaughter, and in an instant covering the ground with men and horses. Still they persevered in approaching us (the first round had brought them to a walk), though slowly, and it did seem they would ride over us. We were a little below the level of the ground on which they moved, having in front of us a bank of about a foot and a half or two feet high, along the top of which ran a narrow road — and this gave more effect to our case-shot, all of which almost must have taken effect, for the carnage was frightful. The following extract, from a related account of a conscript, translated from the French and published by Murray, is so true and exact as to need no comment: 'Through the smoke I saw the English gunners abandon their pieces, all but six guns stationed under the road, and almost immediately our cuirassiers were upon the squares, whose fire was drawn in zigzags Now, I thought, those gunners would be cut to pieces; but no, the devils kept firing with grape, which mowed them down like grass.'

"I suppose this state of things occupied but a few seconds, when I observed symptoms of hesitation, and in a twinkling, at the instant I thought it was all over with us, they turned to either flank and filed away rapidly to the rear. Retreat of the mass, however, was not so easy. Many facing about and trying to force their way through the body of the column, that part next to us became a complete mob, into which we kept a steady fire of case-shot from our six pieces. The effect is hardly conceivable, and to paint this scene of slaughter and confusion impossible. Every discharge was followed by the fall of numbers, whilst the survivors struggled with each other, and I actually saw them using the pommels of their swords to fight their way out of the *mêlée*. Some, rendered desperate at finding themselves thus pent up at the muzzles of our guns, as it were, and others carried away by their horses, maddened with wounds, dashed through our intervals — few thinking of using their swords, but pushing furiously onward, intent only on saving themselves. At last the rear of the column, wheeling about, opened a passage, and the whole swept away at a much more rapid pace than they had advanced, nor stopped until the swell of the ground covered them from our fire. We then ceased firing; but as they were still not far off, for we saw the tops of their caps, having reloaded, we stood ready to receive them should they renew the attack.

"One of, if not the first man who fell on our side was wounded by his own gun. Gunner Butterworth was one of the greatest pickles in the troop, but at the same time a most daring, active soldier; he was No. 7 (the man who sponged, &c.) at his gun. He had just finished ramming down the shot, and was stepping back outside the wheel when his foot stuck in the miry soil, pulling him forward at the moment the gun was fired. As a man naturally does when falling, he threw out both his arms before him, and they were blown off at the elbows. He raised himself a little on his two stumps, and looked up most piteously in my face. To assist him was impossible — the safety of all, everything, depended upon not slackening our fire, and I was obliged to turn from him. The state of anxious activity in which we were kept all day, and the numbers who fell almost immediately afterwards, caused me to lose sight of poor Butterworth; and I afterwards learned that he had succeeded in rising, and was gone to the rear; but on inquiring for him next day, some of my people who had been sent to Waterloo told me that they saw his body lying by the roadside near the farm of Mont St. Jean — bled to death. The retreat of the cavalry was succeeded by a shower of shot and shells, which must have annihilated us had not the little bank covered and threw most of them over us. Still some reached us and knocked down men and horses.

"At the first charge the French column was composed of grenadiers *à cheval*[7] and cuirassiers, the former in front. I forget whether they had or had not changed this disposition, but think, from the number of cuirasses we found afterwards, that the cuirassiers led the second attack. Be this as it may, their column reassembled. They prepared for a second attempt, sending up a cloud of skirmishers, who galled us terribly by a fire of carbines and pistols at scarcely forty yards from our front."

---

[7] These grenadiers *à cheval* were very fine troops, clothed in blue uniforms without facings, cuffs or collars. Broad buff belts, and huge muff caps, made them appear gigantic fellows.

Betwixt the cavalry rushes came little intervals of waiting, while the broken squadrons re-formed in the valley below, and the breathless gunners on the ridge renewed their ammunition. These pauses gave the French skirmishers — who had crept close up to the guns — their chance, and which were more trying to the British gunners than even the wild onfall of the horsemen:

"We were obliged to stand with port-fires lighted, so that it was not without a little difficulty that I succeeded in restraining the people from firing, for they grew impatient under such fatal results. Seeing some exertion beyond words necessary for this purpose, I leaped my horse up the little bank, and began a promenade (by no means agreeable) up and down our front, without even drawing my sword, though these fellows were within speaking distance of me. This quieted my men; but the tall blue gentlemen, seeing me thus dare them, immediately made a target of me, and commenced a very deliberate practice, to show us what very bad shots they were, and verify the old artillery proverb, 'The nearer the target, the safer you are.' One fellow certainly made me flinch, but it was a miss; so I shook my finger at him and called him *coquin*, &c. The rogue grinned as he reloaded, and again took aim. I certainly felt rather foolish at that moment, but was ashamed after such bravado to let him see it, and therefore continued my promenade. As if to prolong my torment, he was a terrible time about it. To me it seemed an age. Whenever I turned, the muzzle of his infernal carbine still followed me. At length bang it went, and whiz came the ball close to the back of my neck, and at the same instant down dropped the leading driver of one of my guns (Miller), into whose forehead the cursed missile had penetrated.

"The column now once more mounted the plateau, and these popping gentry wheeled off right and left to clear the ground for their charge. The spectacle was imposing, and if ever the word sublime was appropriately applied, it might surely be to it. On they came in compact squadrons, one behind the other, so numerous that those of the rear were still below the brow when the head of the column was but at some sixty or seventy yards from our guns. Their pace was a slow but steady trot. None of your furious galloping charges was this, but a deliberate advance at a deliberate pace, as of men resolved to carry their point. They moved in profound silence, and the only sound that could be heard from them amidst the incessant roar of battle was the low, thunder-like reverberation of the ground beneath the simultaneous tread of so many horses.

"On our part was equal deliberation. Every man stood steadily at his post, the guns ready, loaded with a round-shot first and a case over it; the tubes were in the vents; the port-fires glared and spluttered behind the wheels; and my word alone was wanting to hurl destruction on that goodly show of gallant men and noble horses. I delayed this, for experience had given me confidence. The Brunswickers partook of this feeling, and with their squares — much reduced in point of size — well closed, stood firmly with arms at the recover, and eyes fixed on us, ready to commence their fire with our first discharge. It was indeed a grand and imposing spectacle. The column was led on this time by an officer in a rich uniform, his breast covered with decorations, whose earnest gesticulations were strangely contrasted with the solemn demeanour of those to whom they were addressed. I thus allowed them to advance unmolested until the head of the column might have been about fifty or sixty yards from us, and then gave the word 'Fire!' The effect was terrible, nearly the whole leading rank fell at once; and the round-shot, penetrating the column, carried confusion throughout its extent. The ground, already encumbered with victims of the first struggle, became now almost impassable. Still, however, these devoted warriors struggled on, intent only on reaching us. The thing was impossible.

"Our guns were served with astonishing activity, whilst the running fire of the two squares was maintained with spirit. Those who pushed forward over the heap of carcasses of men and horses gained but a few paces in advance, there to fall in their turn and add to the difficulties of those succeeding them. The discharge of every gun was followed by a fall of men and horses like that of grass before the mower's scythe. When the horse alone was killed, we could see the cuirassiers divesting themselves of the encumbrance and making their escape on foot. Still, for a moment the confused mass (for all order was at an end) stood before us, vainly trying to urge their horses over the obstacles presented by their fallen comrades, in obedience to the now loud and rapid vociferations of him who had led them on and remained unhurt.

"As before, many cleared everything and rode through us; many came plunging forward only to fall, man and horse, close to the muzzles of our guns; but the majority again turned at the very moment when, from having less ground to go over, it was safer to advance than retire, and sought a passage to the rear. Of course the same confusion, struggle amongst themselves, and slaughter prevailed as before, until gradually they disappeared over the brow of the hill. We ceased firing, glad to take breath. Their retreat exposed us, as before, to a shower of shot and shells: these last, falling amongst us, with very long fuses, kept burning and hissing a long time before they burst, and were a considerable annoyance to man and horse. The bank in front, however, again stood our friend, and sent many over us innocuous."

Here is a picture of what may be called the human atmosphere of the battle in its later stages, the high-strung nerves, the weariness, the exhaustion of passion, the carelessness of close-pressing death, the fast-following alternation of deadly peril and of miraculous escape:

"Lieutenant Breton, who had already lost two horses, and had mounted a troop-horse, was conversing with me during this our leisure moment. As his horse stood at right angles to mine, the poor jaded animal dozingly rested his muzzle on my thigh; whilst I, the better to hear amidst the infernal din, leant forward, resting my arm between his ears. In this attitude a cannon-shot smashed the horse's head to atoms. The headless trunk sank to the ground — Breton looking pale as death, expecting, as he afterwards told me, that I was cut in two. What was passing to the right and left of us I know no more about than the man in the moon — not even what corps were beyond the Brunswickers. The smoke confined our vision to a very small compass, so that my battle was restricted to the two squares and my own battery; and, as long 'as we maintained our ground, I thought it a matter of course that others did so too.

"It was just after this accident that our worthy commanding officer of artillery, Sir George Adam Wood, made his appearance through the smoke a little way from our left flank. As I said, we were doing nothing, for the cavalry were under the brow reforming for a third attack, and we were being pelted by their artillery. 'D—n it, Mercer,' said the old man, blinking as a man does when facing a gale of wind, 'you have hot work of it here.' 'Yes, sir, pretty hot;' and I was proceeding with an account of the two charges we had already discomfited, and the prospect of a third, when, glancing that way, I perceived their leading squadron already on the plateau. 'There they are again,' I exclaimed; and, darting from Sir

George *sans cérémonie*, was just in time to meet them with the same destruction as before. This time, indeed, it was child's play. They could not even approach us in any decent order, and we fired most deliberately; it was folly having attempted the thing.

"I was sitting on my horse near the right of my battery as they turned and began to retire once more. Intoxicated with success, I was singing out, 'Beautiful! — beautiful!' and my right arm was flourishing about, when some one from behind, seizing it, said quietly, 'Take care, or you'll strike the Duke;' and in effect our noble chief, with a serious air, and apparently much fatigued, passed close by me to the front, without seeming to take the slightest notice of the remnant of the French cavalry still lingering on the ground. This obliged us to cease firing; and at the same moment I — perceiving a line of infantry ascending from the rear, slowly, with ported arms, and uttering a sort of feeble, suppressed hurrah, ankle-deep in a thick, tenacious mud, and threading their way amongst or stepping over the numerous corpses covering the ground, out of breath from their exertions, and hardly preserving a line, broken everywhere into large gaps the breadth of several files — could not but meditate on the probable results of the last charge had I, in obedience to the Duke's order, retired my men into the squares and allowed the daring and formidable squadrons a passage to our rear, where they must have gone thundering down on this disjointed line. The summit gained, the line was amended, files closed in, and the whole, including our Brunswickers, advanced down the slope towards the plain.

"Although the infantry lost several men as they passed us, yet on the whole the cannonade began to slacken on both sides (why, I know not), and, the smoke clearing away a little, I had now, for the first time, a good view of the field. On the ridge opposite to us dark masses of troops were stationary, or moving down into the intervening plain. Our own advancing infantry were hid from view by the ground. We therefore re-commenced firing at the enemy's masses, and the cannonade, spreading, soon became general again along the line."

Mercer, so far, had been fighting sabres with 12-pounders, and all the advantage had been on his side. He had inflicted enormous damage on the enemy, and suffered little himself. But now the enemy's guns began to speak, and Mercer's battery was smitten by a cruel and continuous flank fire, which practically destroyed it:

"Whilst thus occupied with our front, we suddenly became sensible of a most destructive flanking fire from a battery which had come, the Lord knows how, and established itself on a knoll somewhat higher than the ground we stood on, and only about 400 or 500 yards a little in advance of our left flank. The rapidity and precision of this fire were quite appalling. Every shot almost took effect, and I certainly expected we should all be annihilated. Our horses and limbers being a little retired down the slope, had hitherto been somewhat under cover from the direct fire in front; but this plunged right amongst them, knocking them down by pairs, and creating horrible confusion. The drivers could hardly extricate themselves from one dead horse ere another fell, or perhaps themselves. The saddle-bags, in many instances, were torn from the horses' backs, and their contents scattered over the field. One shell I saw explode under the two finest wheel-horses in the troop — down they dropped. In some instances the horses of a gun or ammunition waggon remained, and all their drivers were killed.[8]

"The whole livelong day had cost us nothing like this. Our gunners, too the few left fit for duty of them were so exhausted that they were unable to run the guns up after firing, consequently at every round they retreated nearer to the limbers; and as we had pointed our two left guns towards the people who were annoying us so terribly, they soon came altogether in a confused heap, the trails crossing each other, and the whole dangerously near the limbers and ammunition waggons, some of which were totally unhorsed, and others in sad confusion from the loss of their drivers and horses, many of them lying dead in their harness attached to their carriages. I sighed for my poor troop it was already but a wreck

"I had dismounted, and was assisting at one of the guns to encourage my poor exhausted men, when through the smoke a black speck caught my eye, and I instantly knew what it was. The conviction that one never sees a shot coming towards you unless directly in its line flashed across my mind, together with the certainty that my doom was sealed. I had barely time to exclaim 'Here it is, then!' — much in that gasping sort of way one does when going into very cold water, takes away the breath — 'whush' it went past my face, striking the point of my pelisse collar,

---

[8] "The field was so much covered with blood, that it appeared as if it had been flooded with it," &c. Simpson's *Paris after Waterloo*, &c., p. 21.

which was lying open, and smash into a horse close behind me. I breathed freely again.

"Under such a fire, one may be said to have had a thousand narrow escapes; and, in good truth, I frequently experienced that displacement of air against my face, caused by the passing of shot close to me; but the two above recorded, and a third, which I shall mention, were remarkable ones, and made me feel in full force the goodness of Him who protected me among so many dangers. Whilst in position on the right of the second line, I had reproved some of my men for lying down when shells fell near them until they burst. Now my turn came. A shell, with a long fuse, came slop into the mud at my feet, and there lay fizzing and flaring to my infinite discomfiture. After what I had said on the subject, I felt that I must act up to my own words, and, accordingly, there I stood, endeavouring to look quite composed until the cursed thing burst — and, strange to say, without injuring me, though so near. The effect on my men was good."

But was it really a French battery which was wrecking Mercer's guns? Or, in the mad inevitable distraction of a great battle were the Allied gunners destroying each other? Mercer's story leaves this point in a state of very disquieting doubt:

"We had scarcely fired many rounds at the enfilading battery, when a tall man in the black Brunswick uniform came galloping up to me from the rear, exclaiming, 'Ah! mine Gott! — mine Gott! vat is it you doos, sare? Dat is your friends de Proosiens; an you kills dem! Ah! mine Gott! — mine Gott; vil you no stop, sare? vil you no stop? Ah! mine Gott! — mine Gott! Vat for is dis? De Inglish kills dere friends de Proosiens! Vere is de Dook von Vellington? Vere is de Dock von Vellington? Ah! mine Gott! — mine Gott!' &c., &c., and so he went on raving like one demented. I observed that if these were our friends the Prussians, they were treating us very uncivilly; and that it was not without sufficient provocation we had turned our guns on them, pointing out to him at the same time the bloody proofs of my assertion.

"Apparently not noticing what I said, he continued his lamentations, and, 'Vil you no stop, sare, I say?' Wherefore, thinking he might be right, to pacify him I ordered the whole to cease firing, desiring him to remark the consequences. Psieu, psieu, psieu, came the shots of our 'friends,' one after another; and our friend himself had a narrow escape from one of them. 'Now, sir,' I said, 'you will be convinced; and we will continue our firing, whilst you can ride round the way you came, and tell them they kill their friends the English; the moment their fire ceases, so shall mine.' Still he lingered, exclaiming, 'Oh, dis is terreeble to see de Proosien and de Inglish kill von anoder!'

"At last, darting off, I saw no more of him. The fire continued on both sides, mine becoming slacker and slacker, for we were reduced to the last extremity, and must have been annihilated but for the opportune arrival of a battery of Belgic artillery a little on our left, which, taking the others in flank nearly at point blank, soon silenced and drove them off. We were so reduced that all our strength was barely sufficient to load and fire three guns out of our six.

"These Belgians were all beastly drunk, and, when they first came up, not at all particular as to which way they fired; and it was only by keeping an eye on them that they were prevented treating us, and even one another. The wretches had probably already done mischief elsewhere — who knows?"

Chapter Twenty-Five – After the Fight

Mercer could hardly tell when and how Waterloo began, and he can almost as little tell when and how it ended! So wild is the confusion, so overwhelming the excitement of a great battle for the actors in it:

"My recollections of the later part of this day are rather confused; I was fatigued and almost deaf. I recollect clearly, however, that we had ceased firing, the plain below being covered with masses of troops, which we could not distinguish from each other. Captain Walcot of the Horse Artillery, had come to us, and we were all looking out anxiously at the movements below and on the opposite ridge, when he suddenly shouted out, 'Victory! — victory! they fly! — they fly!' and sure enough we saw some of the masses dissolving, as it were, and those composing, them streaming away in confused crowds over the field, whilst the already desultory fire of their artillery ceased altogether.

"I shall never forget this joyful moment! — this moment of exultation! On looking round, I found we were left almost alone. Cavalry and infantry had all moved forward, and only a few guns here and there were to be seen on the position. A little to our right were the remains of Major M'Donald's troop under Lieutenant Sandi-lands, which had suffered much, but nothing like us. We were congratulating ourselves on the happy results of the day when an aide-de-camp rode up, crying, 'Forward, sir! forward! It is of the utmost importance that this movement should be supported by artillery!' at the same time waving his hat much in the manner of a huntsman laying on his dogs. I smiled at his energy, and, pointing to the remains of my poor troop, quietly asked, 'How, sir?' A glance was sufficient to show him the impossibility, and away he went.

'Our situation was indeed terrible. Of 200 fine horses with which we had entered the battle, upwards of 140 lay dead, dying, or severely wounded. Of the men, scarcely two-thirds of those necessary for four guns remained, and these so completely exhausted as to be totally incapable of further exertion. Lieutenant Breton had three horses killed under him; Lieutenant Hincks was wounded in the breast by a spent ball;

Lieutenant Leathes on the hip by a splinter; and although untouched myself, my horse had no less than eight wounds, one of which, a graze on the fetlock joint, lamed him for ever. Our guns and carriages were, as before mentioned, altogether in a confused heap, intermingled with dead and wounded horses, which it had not been possible to disengage from them.

"My poor men, such at least as were untouched, fairly worn out, their clothes, faces, &c., blackened by the smoke and spattered over with mud and blood, had seated themselves on the trails of the carriages, or had thrown themselves on the wet and polluted soil, too fatigued to think of anything but gaining a little rest. Such was our situation when called upon to advance. It was impossible, and we remained where we were. For myself, I was also excessively tired, hoarse to making speech painful, and deaf from the infernal uproar of the last eleven hours. Moreover, I was devoured by a burning thirst, not a drop of liquid having passed my lips since the evening of the 16th; but although, with the exception of the chicken's leg last night, I may be said to have eaten nothing for two whole days, yet did I not feel the least desire for food."

When the battle was over, Mercer's artistic sensibilities — his eye for landscape, his sense of sky-effects and of natural beauty — awoke. He was perhaps the only man in Wellington's army who could study cloud-effects in the night-sky, which looked down on the slain of Waterloo, or contemplate, with botanical discrimination and approval, the plants in the garden at Hougoumont the next morning:

"The evening had become fine, and but for an occasional groan or lament from some poor sufferer, and the repeated piteous neighing of wounded horses, tranquillity might be said to reign over the field. As it got dusk, a large body of Prussian artillery arrived, and formed their bivouac near us. There was not light to see more of them than that their brass guns were kept bright, and that their carriages were encumbered with baggage, and, besides, appeared but clumsy machines when compared with ours. All wore their greatcoats, which apparently they had marched in. As they looked at us rather scowlingly, and did not seem inclined to hold any communication with us, I soon returned to my own people, whom I found preparing to go supperless to bed — the two remaining officers, the non-commissioned officers, and men having all got together in a heap, with some painted covers spread under, and others drawn over them — at a distance from our guns, &c., the neighbourhood of which they said, was too horrible to think of sleeping there.

"For my part, after standing all day amongst all these horrors, I felt no squeamishness about sleeping amongst them; so pulling down the painted cover of a limber over the footboard in the manner of a tent roof, I crept under it and endeavoured to sleep. The cramped situation in which I lay, and the feverish excitement of my mind, forbade, however, my obtaining that sound and refreshing sleep so much needed; I only dozed. From one of these dozes I awoke about midnight, chilled and cramped to death from the awkward doubled-up position imposed upon me by my short and narrow bed. So up I got to look around and contemplate a battlefield by the pale moonlight.

"The night was serene and pretty clear; a few light clouds occasionally passing across the moon's disc, and throwing objects into transient obscurity, added considerably to the solemnity of the scene. Oh, it was a thrilling sensation thus to stand in the silent hour of the night and contemplate that field — all day long the theatre of noise and strife, now so calm and still — the actors prostrate on the bloody soil, their pale wan faces upturned to the moon's cold beams, which caps and breastplates, and a thousand other things, reflected back in brilliant pencils of light from as many different points! Here and there some poor wretch, sitting up amidst the countless dead, busied himself in endeavours to stanch the flowing stream with which his life was fast ebbing away. Many whom I saw so employed that night were, when morning dawned, lying stiff and tranquil as those who had departed earlier. From time to time a figure would half raise itself from the ground, and then, with a despairing groan, fall back again. Others, slowly and painfully rising, stronger, or having less deadly hurt, would stagger away with uncertain steps across the field in search of succour.

"Many of these I followed with my gaze until lost in the obscurity of distance; but many, alas! after staggering a few paces, would sink again on the ground with their entrails hanging out — and yet I gazed! Horses, too, there were to claim our pity — mild, patient, enduring. Some lay on the ground with their entrails hanging out, and yet they lived. These would occasionally attempt to rise, but like their human bedfellows, quickly falling back again, would lift their poor heads, and, turning a wistful gaze at their side, lie quietly down again, to repeat the same until strength no longer remained, and then, their eyes gently closing, one short convulsive struggle closed their sufferings. One poor animal excited painful interest — he had lost, I believe, both his hind-legs; and there he sat the long night through on his tail, looking about, as if in expectation of coming aid, sending forth, from time to time, long and protracted melancholy neighing. Although I knew that killing him at once would be mercy, I could not muster courage even to give the order. Blood enough I had seen shed during the last six-and-thirty hours, and sickened at the thought of shedding more. There, then, he still sat when we left the ground, neighing after us, as if reproaching our desertion of him in the hour of need."

After the storm of a great battle has rolled away it leaves behind a wreckage — human and animal — of a very amazing sort; and of the wreckage of Waterloo Mercer gives a grimly vivid description. The effect is that of one of Vereschagin's pictures translated into literary terms:

"June 19 — The cool air of the morning lasted not long; the rising sun soon burst in all his glory over our bloody bivouac, and all nature arose into renewed life, except the victims of ambition which lay unconscious of his presence. I had not been up many minutes when one of my sergeants came to ask if they might bury Driver Crammond. 'And why particularly Driver Crammond?' 'Because he looks frightful, sir; many of us have not had a wink of sleep for him.' Curious! I walked to the spot where he lay, and certainly a more hideous sight cannot be imagined. A cannon-shot had carried away the whole head except barely the visage, which still remained attached to the torn and bloody neck. The men said they had been prevented sleeping by seeing his eyes fixed on them all night; and thus this one dreadful object had superseded all the other horrors by which they were surrounded. He was of course immediately buried, and as immediately forgotten.

"Our first care after this was to muster the remaining force, to disentangle our carriages from each other, and from the dead and dying animals with which they were encumbered. Many sound or only slightly wounded horses, belonging to different corps of both armies, were wandering about the field. Of these we caught several in the course of the morning, and thus collected, with what remained of our own fit for work, sufficient to horse four guns, three ammunition waggons, and the forge.

Of men we had nearly enough for these at reduced numbers, so we set to work equipping ourselves without delay. Although supplies of ammunition had been sent to us during the action, yet little remained. The expenditure had been enormous. A return had been called for yesterday evening just as we were lying down to rest, but, fatigued as we all were it was impossible to give this correctly. As near as I could ascertain, we must have fired nearly 700 rounds per gun. Our harness, &c., was so cut to pieces, that but for the vast magazines around us from which we could pick and choose we should never have got off the field.

"Soon after daybreak an officer came from head-quarters to desire me to send all my superfluous carriages to Lillois, where a park was forming, and to inform me that a supply of ammunition would be found in the village of Waterloo. Accordingly the carriages were sent without delay; but this requiring all the horses, they were obliged to make a second trip for the ammunition. Whilst this was doing I had leisure to examine the ground in our immediate vicinity. Books and papers, &c., covered it in all directions. The books at first surprised me, but upon examination the thing was explained. Each French soldier, it appeared, carried a little account-book of his pay, clothing, &c., &c. The scene was now far from solitary; for numerous groups of peasants were moving about busily employed stripping the dead, and perhaps finishing those not quite so. Some of these men I met fairly staggered under the enormous load of clothes, &c., they had collected. Some had firearms, swords, &c., and many had large bunches of crosses and decorations; all seemed in high glee, and professed unbounded hatred of the French.

"I had fancied we were almost alone on the field, seeing only the remains of Major Bull's troop of horse artillery not far from us (the Prussians had gone forward about or a little before daybreak); but in wandering towards the Charleroi road I stumbled on a whole regiment of British infantry fast asleep, in columns of divisions, wrapped in their blankets, with their knapsacks for pillows. Not a man was awake. There they lay in regular ranks, with the officers and sergeants in their places, just as they would stand when awake. Not far from these, in a little hollow beneath a white thorn, lay two Irish light-infantry men sending forth such howlings and wailings and oaths and execrations as were shocking to hear. One of them had his leg shot off, the other a thigh smashed by a cannon-shot. They were certainly pitiable objects, but their vehement exclamations, &c., were so strongly contrasted with the quiet, resolute bearing of hundreds both French and English around them, that it blunted one's feelings considerably.

"I tried in vain to pacify them; so walked away amidst a volley of abuse as a hard-hearted wretch who could thus leave two poor fellows to die like dogs. What could I do? All, however, though in more modest terms, craved assistance; and every poor wretch begged most earnestly for water. Some of my men had discovered a good well of uncontaminated water at Hougoumont and filled their canteens, so I made several of them accompany me and administer to the most craving in our immediate vicinity. Nothing could exceed their gratitude, or the fervent blessings they implored on us for this momentary relief. The French were in general particularly grateful; and those who were strong enough entered into conversation with us on the events of yesterday, and the probable fate awaiting themselves. All the non-commissioned officers and privates agreed in asserting that they had been deceived by their officers and betrayed; and, to my surprise, almost all of them reviled Bonaparte as the cause of their misery.

"Many begged me to kill them at once, since they would a thousand times rather die by the hand of a soldier than be left at the mercy of those villainous Belgic peasants. Whilst we stood by them several would appear consoled and become tranquil; but the moment we attempted to leave, they invariably renewed the cry, 'Ah, Monsieur, tuez moi donc! Tuez moi, pour l'amour de Dieu!' &c., &c. It was in vain I assured them carts would be sent to pick them all up. Nothing could reconcile them to the idea of being left. They looked on us as brother soldiers, and knew we were too honourable to harm them: 'But the moment you go, those vile peasants will first insult and then cruelly murder us.' This, alas! I knew, was but too true.

"One Frenchman I found in a far different humour — an officer of lancers, and desperately wounded; a strong, square-built man, with reddish hair and speckled complexion. When I approached him he appeared suffering horribly rolling on his back, uttering loud groans. My first impulse was to raise and place him in a sitting posture; but, the moment he was touched, opening his eyes and seeing me, he became perfectly furious. Supposing he mistook my intention, I addressed him in a soothing tone, begging he would allow me to render him what little assistance was in my power. This only seemed to irritate him the more; and on my presenting him the canteen with water, he dashed it from him with such a passionate gesture and emphatic 'Non!' that I saw there was no use in teasing, and therefore reluctantly left him.

"Returning towards our position, I was forcibly struck by the immense heap of bodies of men and horses which distinguished it even at a distance; indeed, Sir Augustus Frazer told me the other day, at Nivelles, that in riding over the field, 'he could plainly distinguish the position of G troop from the opposite height by the dark mass which, even from that distance, formed a remarkable feature in the field.' These were his very words. One interesting sufferer I had nearly forgotten. He was a fine young man of the grenadiers à cheval, who had lain groaning near us all night — indeed, scarcely five paces from my bed; therefore was the first person I visited as soon as daylight came. He was a most interesting person — tall, handsome, and a perfect gentleman in manners and speech; yet his costume was that of a private soldier. We conversed with him some time, and were exceedingly pleased with his mild and amiable address. Amongst other things he told us that Marshal Ney had led the charges against us."

"I now began to feel somewhat the effects of my long fast in a most unpleasant sense of weakness and an inordinate craving for food, which there was no means of satisfying. My joy, then, may be imagined when, returning to our bivouac, I found our people returned from Lillois, and, better still, that they had brought with them a quarter of veal, which they had found in a muddy ditch, of course in appearance then filthy enough. What was this to a parcel of men who had scarcely eaten a morsel for three days? In a trice it was cut up, the mud having been scraped off with a sabre, a fire kindled and fed with lance-shafts and musket-stocks; and old Quartermaster Hall, undertaking the cooking, proceeded to fry the dirty lumps in the lid of a camp-kettle. How we enjoyed the savoury smell and, having made ourselves seats of cuirasses[9] piled upon each other, we soon had that most agreeable of animal gratifications — the

---

[9] "Here were more cuirasses than men, for the wounded (who could move), divesting themselves of its encumbrance, had made their escape, leaving their armour on the ground where they had fallen."

filling our empty stomachs. Never was a meal more perfectly military, nor more perfectly enjoyed."

By this time the artillery officer in Mercer was exhausted, the botanist and artist began to emerge, and he strolls off to visit, as a sort of country gentleman at leisure, the garden at Hougoumont! He says:

"Having despatched our meal and then the ammunition waggons to Waterloo, and leaving the people employed equipping as best they could, I set off to visit the chateau likewise; for the struggle that had taken place there yesterday rendered it an object of interest. The same scene of carnage as elsewhere characterised that part of the field over which I now bent my steps. The immediate neighbourhood of Hougoumont was more thickly strewn with corpses than most other parts of the field — the very ditches were full of them. The trees all about were most woefully cut and splintered both by cannon shot and musketry. The courts of the chateau presented a spectacle more terrible even than any I had yet seen. A large barn had been set on fire, and the conflagration had spread to the offices and even to the main building. Here numbers, both of French and English, had perished in the flames, and their blackened swollen remains lay scattered about in all directions. Amongst this heap of ruins and misery many poor devils yet remained alive, and were sitting up endeavouring to bandage their wounds. Such a scene of horror, and one so sickening, was surely never witnessed.

"Two or three German dragoons were wandering among the ruins, and many peasants. One of the former was speaking to me when two of the latter, after rifling the pockets, &c., of a dead Frenchman, seized the body by the shoulders, and raising it from the ground, dashed it down again with all their force, uttering the grossest abuse, and kicking it about the head and face — revolting spectacle! — doing this, no doubt, to court favour with us. It had a contrary effect, which they soon learned. I had scarcely uttered an exclamation of disgust, when the dragoon's sabre was flashing over the miscreants' heads, and in a moment descended on their backs and shoulders with such vigour that they roared again, and were but too happy to make their escape. I turned from such scenes and entered the garden. How shall I describe the delicious sensation I experienced!

"The garden was an ordinary one, but pretty — long straight walks of turf overshadowed by fruit-trees, and between these beds of vegetables, the whole enclosed by a tolerably high brick wall. Is it necessary to define my sensations? Is it possible that I am not understood at once? Listen, then. For the last three days I have been in a constant state of excitement — in a perfect fever. My eyes have beheld nought but war in all its horrors — my ears have been assailed by a continued roar of cannon and cracking of musketry, the shouts of multitudes and the lamentations of war's victims. Suddenly and unexpectedly I find myself in solitude, pacing a green avenue, my eyes refreshed by the cool verdure of trees and shrubs; my ears soothed by the melody of feathered songsters — yea, of sweet Philomel herself — and the pleasing hum of insects sporting in the genial sunshine. Is there nothing in this to excite emotion? Nature in repose is always lovely: here, and under such circumstances, she was delicious. Long I rambled in this garden, up one walk, down another, and thought I could dwell here contented for ever.

"Nothing recalled the presence of war except the loop-holed wall and two or three dead Guardsmen;[10] but the first caused no interruption, and these last lay so concealed amongst the exuberant vegetation of turnips and cabbages, &c., that, after coming from the field of death without, their pale and silent forms but little deteriorated my enjoyment. The leaves were green, roses and other flowers bloomed forth in all their sweetness, and the very turf when crushed by my feet smelt fresh and pleasant. There was but little of disorder visible to tell of what had been enacted here. I imagine it must have been assailed by infantry alone; and the havoc amongst the trees without made by our artillery posted on the hill above to cover the approach to it — principally, perhaps, by Bull's howitzer battery.

"I had satisfied my curiosity at Hougoumont, and was retracing my steps up the hill when my attention was called to a group of wounded Frenchmen by the calm, dignified, and soldier-like oration addressed by one of them to the rest. I cannot, like Livy, compose a fine harangue for my hero, and, of course, I could not retain the precise words, but the import of them was to exhort them to bear their sufferings with fortitude; not to repine, like women or children, at what every soldier should have

---

[10] In some accounts of the battle and visits to the field, &c., it has been stated that this garden was a scene of slaughter. Totally untrue! As I have stated in the text, I did not see above two or three altogether. There certainly might have been more concealed amongst the vegetation, but they could not have been many.

made up his mind to suffer as the fortune of war, but above all, to remember that they were surrounded by Englishmen, before whom they ought to be doubly careful not to disgrace themselves by displaying such an unsoldier-like want of fortitude.

"The speaker was sitting on the ground, with his lance stuck upright beside him — an old veteran, with a thick, bushy, grizzly beard, countenance like a lion — a lancer of the Old Guard, and no doubt had fought in many a field. One hand was flourished in the air as he spoke, the other, severed at the wrist, lay on the earth beside him; one ball (case-shot, probably) had entered his body, another had broken his leg. His suffering, after a night of exposure so mangled, must have been great; yet he betrayed it not. His bearing was that of a Roman, or perhaps of an Indian warrior, and I could fancy him concluding appropriately his speech in the words of the Mexican king, 'And I too; am I on a bed of roses?'

"In passing Bull's bivouac it was my fate to witness another very interesting scene. A wounded hussar had somehow or other found his way there from another part of the field, and exhausted by the exertion, had just fainted. Some of those collected round him cried out for water, and a young driver, who, being outside the throng, had not yet seen the sufferer, seized a canteen and ran away to fill it. Whilst he was absent the hussar so far recovered as to be able to sit up. The driver returned at this moment, and pushing aside his comrades, knelt down to enable the hussar to drink, holding the canteen to his lips, and in so doing recognised a brother whom he not seen for years. His emotion was extreme, as may be supposed."

From the narrative of the march to Paris which followed Waterloo, we take only one incident. Mercer is at Nivelles, watching the crowds and the excitement in the streets:

"Suddenly a loud shout announces something extraordinary even on this day of excitement. Every one hurries to the spot, pushing each other, jumping, shouting. 'What can it mean?' I inquired. 'Monsieur l'Officier, c'est un convoi des prisonniers que vient d'arriver,' replied my man, doffing at the same time his *bonnet de nuit* and making a most respectful salaam. I stopped to see the convoy pass. The prisoners, dressed in grey *capotes* and *bonnets de fourrage*, marched steadily on. Some *vieux moustaches* look very grave, and cast about furious glances at the noisy

311

crowd which follows them with the perseverance of a swarm of mosquitoes, *sacré*-ing and venting all kind of illiberal abuse on them and the b— of an Emperor. Many, however, younger men, laugh, joke, and return their abuse with interest, whilst the soldiers of the escort (English) march doggedly along, pushing aside the more forward of the throng, and apparently as if only marching round a relief.

"At noon arrived in the neighbourhood of Mons, where we overtook the Greys, Inniskillings, Ross's troop of horse artillery, and several other corps, both of cavalry and infantry. We had, in short, now rejoined the army. The Greys and the Inniskillings were mere wrecks — the former, I think, did not muster 200 men, and the latter, with no greater strength, presented a sad spectacle of disorganisation and bad discipline; they had lost more than half their appointments. Some had helmets, some had none; many had the skull-cap, but with the crest cut or broken off; some were on their own large horses, others on little ones they had picked up; belts there were on some; many were without, not only belts, but also canteens and haversacks. The enemy surely had not effected in a single day so complete a disorganisation, and I shrewdly suspect these rollicking Paddies of having mainly spoilt themselves. The other corps all looked remarkably well, although they, too, had partaken in the fight.

"We crossed after the Greys, and came with them on the main road to Maubeuge at the moment a Highland regiment (perhaps the 92nd), which had come through Mons, was passing. The moment the Highlanders saw the Greys an electrifying cheer burst spontaneously from the column, which was answered as heartily; and on reaching the road the two columns became blended for a few minutes — the Highlanders running to shake hands with their brave associates in the late battle. This little burst of feeling was delightful — everybody felt it; and although two or three general officers were present, none interfered to prevent or to censure this breach of discipline."

18242917R00174

Printed in Great Britain
by Amazon